Yale Studies in English, 192

RESPONSIVE READINGS

*Versions of Echo in Pastoral,
Epic, and the Jonsonian Masque*

JOSEPH LOEWENSTEIN

YALE UNIVERSITY PRESS
New Haven and London

Copyright © 1984 by Yale University. All rights reserved. This book may not be reproduced, in whole or in part, in any form (beyond that copying permitted by Sections 107 and 108 of the U.S. Copyright Law and except by reviewers for the public press), without written permission from the publishers.

Designed by Nancy Ovedovitz and set in VIP Goudy Old Style type by The Composing Room of Michigan, Inc. Printed in the United States of America by BookCrafters, Chelsea, Michigan.

Library of Congress Cataloging in Publication Data

Loewenstein, Joseph, 1952–
  Responsive readings.
  (Yale studies in English; 192)
  Includes bibliographical references and index.
  1. Jonson, Ben, 1573?–1637—Knowledge—Literature. 2. Masques. 3. Allusions in literature. 4. Imitation (in literature). 5. Classical literature—History and criticism. 6. English literature—Early modern, 1500–1700—History and criticism. I. Title. II. Series.
PR2642.M37L68   1984   822'.3   84-40198
ISBN 0–300–03156–4 (alk. paper)

The paper in this book meets the guidelines for permanence and durability of the Committee on Production Guidelines for Book Longevity of the Council on Library Resources.

10   9   8   7   6   5   4   3   2   1

To Jean and Stanley

CONTENTS

Preface	ix
Editorial Note	xi
INTRODUCTION: THE HORNS OF BACCHUS	1
1 *ALIENA VERBA*: ECHO, FAMA, AND THE LOCUS AMOENUS	10
2 *VERBIS FAVET IPSA SUIS*: THE REFLEX OF EPIC IN OVID'S *METAMORPHOSES*	33
Perpetuitas	36
The Oedipal Eye in the *Cadmeans*	41
The Schematic Voice	45
The Jurisdiction of the Past	50
3 ECHOIC PRESENCE AND THE THEATRICAL COURT: *CYNTHIA'S REVELS*	57
A True Copie: Gascoigne and the Mastery of the Revels	60
Court Marginalia I	75
Plot and Cursus in *Cynthia's Revels*	78
Cupid's Comedy	84
Yet not perplex men, unto gaze: Court Marginalia II	89
4 THE MASQUE OF MEMORY: ECHO AND AUTHORSHIP IN JONSON'S MASQUES	93
Vision and Continuity in The Masques of Blacknesse and Beautie	95
Riconosciuta Arcadia	102
The Voyce of Fame	111
The *Scene* Clos'd	118
The Pastoral Auditorium	125
5 "TRANSLATED TO THE SKIES": ECHOIC SILENCE IN *COMUS*	133
Appendix: Echo and Typology	147
Notes	149
Index	185

PREFACE

Nearly all my friends and teachers have been coerced into reading parts of this study, and they have all made valuable suggestions, which surely I have valued insufficiently. The final version, then, shows my own stubbornness triumphant over their genial intelligences. I shall list only those who have waded through, say, thirty pages or more of the MS: Leslie Brisman, Margaret Ferguson, Stephen Foley, Harris Friedberg, Tom Greene, Richard Halpern, Jon Haynes, John Hollander, Chris Kendrick, David Konstan, Naomi Lebowitz, George Lord, John Morris, Sondra Stang, Lynne Tatlock, Kate Toll, and Gordon Williams. Maryann De Julio and George Pepe caught some, and I hope all, of my philological errors. In a sense, Donald Cheney summed up their labors: the astonishing care and intellectual generosity which he brought to the penultimate version of this book was as flattering as it was instructive. But since dozens of others, at Yale, Wesleyan, and Washington universities, have been pressed into various editorial services, I have debts to institutions to discharge as well—gratitude attached to their reading rooms, offices, coffee rooms, and dining halls. In one of these coffee rooms, Howard Nemerov was kind enough to give this book its title, a title that he had himself intended to use one of these days. It was very kind of him.

I can actually be more specific about institutional debts: grants from the Graduate School of Washington University enabled me to complete a series of crucial revisions; the patient vigilance of the Faculty Committee of Yale Studies in English has saved me from scholarly embarrassment in several matters, so I am particularly grateful for its sponsorship; and the staff of the Newberry Library, particularly Lucille Wehner, got me out of a tight bibliographic spot.

With her quizzical resourcefulness, Judy Malamud abetted the initial research, making it much more interesting than it might have been. As editor, Ellen Graham mirrored Ms. Malamud's witty masteries at the other end of this enterprise. Between them sat Rita Malenczyck, who did more than type and proofread intelligently: she kept me alert to the unfailing hilarities of manuscript preparation. Francis Ingledew assisted in the preparation of the index.

The original of this study was a doctoral dissertation directed by John Hollander. When I first proposed a study of Echo and the English masque, he told me that he had already begun a study of Echo in romantic poetry, but took care to encourage my own project. Over the past few years, his encouragements—and his repeated assurances that my work was complementing his own—have been particularly cheering. He took pains that each stage of my research be as broadly instructive as possible. I hope that, as a result, I have produced an adequate supplement to his *The Figure of Echo* (Berkeley: University of California Press, 1981).

I received my introduction to Jonson from Edward Tayler, and I am very glad of it, for he managed always to remark both the urgency in Jonson's poise and the mind beneath his furies. Since then, I have had the good fortune to study Jonson with Thomas Greene; he has kindly interested himself in this book—in all its various forms—and his admonishments have been stern and invariably helpful. I have already mentioned the editorial interventions of Richard Halpern, Jonathan Haynes, and Chris Kendrick, but they must be thanked for other and less specific contributions: they have made suggestions and corrections in theoretical as well as factual matters, approving, chiding, and chuckling. This is also the occasion to join those unable to thank Margaret Ferguson for her help. Even when she had little spare time, she commented on much of this study in detail, and she did so as if commentary were her greatest pleasure; I have frequently felt that the reaction of that high-hearted mind was the most valuable product of my work.

With laughter and patience, Jane Hutchins charmed this book into existence, which is not to scant the patience and laughter of the dedicatees. She sustained; they instigated.

Washington University, 1983

EDITORIAL NOTE

I have cited Jonson from the eleven-volume edition of his works edited by C. H. Herford and Percy and Evelyn Simpson (Oxford: Clarendon, 1925–52). My references to Milton are taken from Merritt Y. Hughes's edition of the *Complete Poetry and Major Prose* (New York: Odyssey, 1957). In citing from medieval and Renaissance texts, I have modernized the script or typeface while preserving the original punctuation and orthography. There is one, possibly unnecessary, exception: I have favored the modern punctuation of possessives in referring to Jonson's plays and masques: thus I give *Cynthia's Revels*, not *Cynthias Revels*, *Pan's*, not *Pans*, *Anniversarie*.

Unless otherwise indicated, all citations from classical authors are taken from editions in the *Loeb Classical Library*. If I have occasionally adjusted the Loeb translations, my versions are obviously no more than adaptations, firmly based on the originals of the Loeb editors. Usually my renderings are more literal and less fluent than their models, the clumsy literalism having been adopted to clarify aspects of the original texts.

INTRODUCTION
THE HORNS OF BACCHUS

Critics of *The Tempest* often comment on the close association during the Renaissance of dramaturgy and thaumaturgy (the word is cognate with *theater*). According to a famous tale, "certaine Players at Exeter, acting upon the stage the tragical storie of Dr. Faustus the Conjurer; as a certain number of Devels kept everie one his circle there, and as Faustus was busie in his magicall invocations, on a sudden they were all dasht, every one harkning other in the eare, for they were all perswaded, there was one devell too many amongst them; and so after a little pause desired the people to pardon them, they could go no further with this matter,"[1] thus bringing the performance to an abrupt conclusion. The modern theater has lost this easy access to the daemonic, a loss against which only Eliot, Pinter, Guerdon, and perhaps Anouilh and Giraudoux have struggled.

At the opening of Jonson's *Cynthia's Revels*, the gods appear without any "magicall invocations," and their first exchange—

> Who goes there?
> Tis I, blind archer.
> Who, MERCURIE? [I.i.1–3]

—is hardly awesome. If "blind archer" is not quite colloquial, its slight formality is surely less otherworldly than courtly. The young actor who provides a hasty plot-summary in the induction to the play clearly thinks nothing of this opening encounter or of its holy setting:

> Here, is the court of CYNTHIA, whither hee brings CUPID (travailing on foot) resolv'd to turne page. By the way, CUPID meetes with MERCURIE (as that's a thing to be noted, take anie of our play-bookes without a CUPID, or a MERCURY in it, and burne it for an heretique in *Poetrie*). [Prologue, 44–49]

The presence of the gods hardly seems remarkable. Still, the boy's remark *is* scripted; the casual justification of mythological drama betrays the merest uncertainty about the propriety of that popular mode. Moreover, we know that Jonson held just this sort of justification in contempt, for he never allowed the conventions of contemporary artistic practice any prescriptive force over his modes and manner. *Cynthia's Revels* depends on the survival and acculturation of the pagan gods; yet if the incarnation of these gods is not exactly problematic within the play, the playwright does alert us to the curiousness of their presence.

This curiousness—it is largely a matter of tone—will serve well to introduce my theme. On stage, these gods flicker between divinity and humanity, and the effect is at once foolish and uncanny. This curiousness may do much to characterize Renaissance neoclassicism: we often note the revived interest in Greco-Roman myth, the rediscovery of the human in the divine and the divine in man, but we ought also to note the more impure forms of the rapprochement between Renaissance man and the gods. The Renaissance also saw the rediscovery of the antique demigod, of all those discomfiting creatures who live flickering between the human and the divine. They are legion: besides the Pans, Genii, Nymphs and Sileni of the landscape, there are the demigods of the Imagination—Fate, Time, Mutability, Charity, Prudence, Wisdom, and all the other personifications whose images suddenly coalesced to astonishing particularity in the pages of Renaissance iconographers. If many of these principles had long existed in the European imagination, the problem of their flickering ontology was newly acute.

What follows is primarily a study of one such flickering figure, of Echo, a nymph of sorts. Neither human nor divine, neither quite natural nor supernatural, neither instituted nor a "given," Echo is also merely echo.[2] If there is a myth and a literary history of Echo, there is also a larger cultural history of echoing. My attention focuses on the myth and the literary history, though the focus is not exclusive. That is, I shall be concentrating on the emergence of echoing as a pastoral topos, on the intrusion of Echo on the mythopoeic imagination, and finally on the marginal presence of echoing and Echo in that great kingdom of demigods, the Renaissance court theater.

The curious scene between Cupid and Mercury continues, slightly skewed, gently unbalanced. Their opening scene traffics in just the sort of witty anachronism that Jonson might have learned from almost any of the epyllia written during the preceding decades. When Cupid rails at Mercury, the syntax piles, refusing a full stop, so that only its energy preserves it from confusion; a modern vocabulary evokes the classical scene:

> What are you? any more then my uncle JOVES pandar, a lacquey, that runnes on errands for him, and can whisper a light message to a loose wench with some round volubilitie, wait mannerly at a table with a trencher, and warble upon a crowde a little, fill out *nectar,* when *Ganimed's* away, one that sweeps the *Gods* drinking roome every morning, and sets the cushions in order againe, which they threw one at anothers head overnight. [I.i.22–30]

The trivialization of divine function here hardly originated with Jonson or even with his contemporaries: most of the passage is translated from Lucian, with the diction a touch roughened. The pillow fight is Jonson's invention, but any English poet after, say, Arthur Golding might have produced such a detail. For nearly a hundred more lines nothing disturbs the pattern established here—the loose, often asyndetic style, the collocation of classical name and homely phrase, the frequent recourse to that ancient writer so beloved of Erasmus, More, and Jonson. The banter never turns away from an amused examination of what divinity may choose to do on a human stage. "S'light," laughs Cupid, "now you are on earth, wee shall have you filch spoones and candle-sticks" (71–72).

Yet repartee will sober at the name of Diana, even if the concerns of the earlier exchanges persist:

> The Huntresse, and Queene of these groves, DIANA (in regard of some black and envious slanders hourely breath'd against her, for her divine justice on ACTEON, as shee pretends) hath here in the vale of *Gargaphy*, proclaim'd a solemne revells, which (her god-head put off) shee will descend to grace, with the full and royall expence of one of her cleerest moones. [ll. 91–97]

Anaphora, a lengthening of vowels, and a slightly more adjectival style amplify this speech. The theme of divine descent grows numinous through these lines, and a phrase like "the full and royall expence of one of her cleerest moones" has a copious mystery in it. Court entertainment always involved awesome capital expenditures; the expense announced by Cupid for that public performance at Blackfriar's was an incalculable munificence.

In the opening of *Cynthia's Revels*, Jonson constructs a sequence of parentheses, preparing a dramatic enclosure more sheltered than he had devised for any previous play. None of his three earlier plays opens with the elaborate introductory sequence of this, his first mythological drama. *Cynthia's Revels* moves through an induction, in which the young actors speak *in propria persona*, to a formal prologue, and then into the encounter of Cupid and Mercury.³ Even this encounter comes to seem preparatory, simply another introduction by which Jonson "proves new wayes to come to learned eares" (Prologue, 11), for this encounter only slowly issues into the graver cadences in which Cupid announces the forthcoming revels. "I'll discover my whole project," says Cupid, and the verb involves a technical meaning, one that draws attention to the poet's interest, here, in dramatic interiority: to "discover," in the theater, is to draw open the curtains or part the shutters of an inner stage at the beginning of a play in order to reveal an emblematic tableau within.

All the arts of time are preparatory; the novelty in Jonson's procedure here lies in his demarcation of the boundaries between moments, his emphasis on the rifts in a dramatic narrative. The enrichment of the child actor's voice as the boy takes on the dignified language of the prologue, the slang divinity of Cupid and Mercury in their early exchanges, and finally, the sanctity of Cupid's announcement—all these take place in articulated stages which imitate, not the teleology of secular narrative, but the sequential divisions of ritual (indeed, the metaphor buried in "stages" is taken from that medieval religious drama which historically mediates between ritual and secular narrative). This sort of ritual encapsulation leads to a central act of reenactment, hedged round and protected from mundane temporality. The ritual paradigm will be invoked again later in the play at Act V, scenes iv through vi, as prose gives way to verse and the foolish characters withdraw, leaving first Crites and Arete, and then Crites alone, to prepare with prayer and hymn for Cynthia's descent. In Act V, the influence of the paradigm is explicit—a god is being called into human presence. Here in the first act, its influence is subtler: the ritual paradigm is invoked well before the playwright betrays a ritual purpose.

As Cupid withdraws, Mercury hints at that purpose, borrowing from the language of Luke 2:49 to maintain the mysterious tone that Cupid has created: "I am now to put in act, an especiall designement from my father JOVE" (115–16). Though it has been anticipated by the play's expository structure, this encapsulated moment is paradoxically abrupt in effect:

> Mer. Now to my charge, ECCHO, faire ECCHO, speake,
>   Tis MERCURIE, that calls thee, sorrowfull *Nymph*,
>   Salute me with they repercussive voice,
>   That I may know what caverne of the earth
>   Containes thy ayrie spirit, how, or where
>   I may direct my speech, that thou maist heare.
> Eccho. Here.
> Mer. So nigh?
> Ecc. I. [I.i.120–I.ii.3]

Jonson has constructed a ritual interior out of the play's "front matter," creating a numinous dramatic cavern appropriate to invocation. In such an environment, Mercury, divine conjurer, is susceptible to a mild version of the panic felt at the Exeter performance of *Doctor Faustus:* the proximity of the daemonic must always excite some degree of alarm.

The structural disjunctions that provide the context for Echo's abrupt appearance work to suppress the very rationale for that appearance. Mercury claims to have called up Echo at Jove's charge:

> Who (pittying the sad burthen of thy woes,
> Still growing on thee, in thy want of wordes
> To vent thy passion for NARCISSUS death)
> Commands, that now (after three thousand yeeres,
> Which have been exercis'd in JUNOES spight)
> Thou take a corporall figure, and ascend. [I.ii.5–10]

This is the only description of Jove's—or Jonson's—motive for the ritual climax that is Echo's appearance; the motive, tucked away into parentheses, is pity for an undischarged burden of grief. Echo's is a tragic situation, for, like Antigone, like Orestes and Electra, like Hamlet, she has been unable to dissolve or adjust her ties to the dead. The traditional tragic hero often suffers deferral of free action (unhindered burial); Echo suffers deferral of free speech (uninhibited mourning). Jonson indicates the unusual length of that deferral, suggesting that the play provides the first occasion at which she has been allowed "a corporall figure" since her punishment at Juno's hand. Echo's reincarnation and the emancipation of her voice involve a revival of that animate, metamorphic world which had been subdued and humanized with the withdrawal of the gods. Jonson contrives that the tragic Echo, not giddy Cupid nor light-fingered Mercury, should herald that revival, a revival that makes possible the constitution, in England, of Cynthia's court.

Cynthia's Revels is an exemplary text, then, for the study of the Renaissance recovery of classical myth. The pagan gods carry more than moral, physical, or metaphysical meanings: they have generic associations, they evoke a different phenomenology, they render the transcendent playful and the playful transcendent. To admit these more destabilizing aspects of the mythological into a consideration of Jonson's neoclassicism will inevitably require a reconception of the Jonsonian, to make him less a Dryden and more a Blake, less a Berkeley and more a Swedenborg, not exclusively a Seneca—a Hesiod and an Ovid as well.

In order to explain why Echo should have been chosen to preside over the play's ritual center, to govern that center until displaced by the descent of Cynthia herself, we need to know the history of that nymph, both before and after Juno's punishment. Echo has a place of privilege in classical and postclassical mythography, one that justifies her centrality in Jonson's fable: the myth of Echo is a myth of cultural memory. That Jonson should have transformed the mythography of Echo into a poetics will hardly surprise us. It had undergone such transformation before: Echo, being both the reflex of the fortuitous and the sign of the volitional, had become the very patron of liminality. And one of the boundaries over which she flickered is that between the "natural" tradition of myth and the "cultural" act of narrative production.

I undertake two projects in these essays. I shall be working to account for the career of Echo, but I also wish to analyze some of the mythopoeic motives in Jonson's dramaturgy. In some sense, the two projects are perpendicular to each other. Yet they intersect at the embodiment of Echo in the first act of *Cynthia's Revels*, the play in which Jonson first recommends himself as court poet and as English mythographer. In the first two essays, I treat of that pastoral milieu in which Echo developed from echo—phenomenon yielding first to simple personification and then to such fables as seek to master the uncanniness of acoustic reflection by imposing a psychic history on the phenomenon. The history of pastoral will show itself to be bound up with the career of Echo. Yet the topos of echo has an even larger import: these first essays describe the old and crucial association of echo with the continuities of literary history itself. In the 1360s, Boccaccio described Echo in the *Genealogia Deorum* as "Parnasi nympha potissime." Nearly three centuries later, in a posthumous second edition of echo-lyrics written and collected by the Dutch humanist Johann van der Does, her prestige had extended itself even further; the title page describes an "Echo, quae novem regens musis, ceu decimam comitem addidit."[4] In the Renaissance, an era of explicitly imitative poetic production, Echo had come to seem a muse of modernity: the first of van der Does's echo-poems is a "Poema Omnium operossisimum," a compliment extended to those of his contemporaries whose prestige depended on the preservation and modernization of antique modes and manners. Van der Does's book was frequently bound with another book that sums up, if somewhat crudely, all that Echo might mean to a Renaissance poet. It is Nicholas Nomexy's *Parnassus biceps* (in some editions, *Parnassus bicollis*), a commonplace book; this dictionary gathers short classical citations on a multitude of subjects, a perfect tool for the mechanical practice of *imitatio*. And to this Renaissance *Bartlett's*, Nomexy appended a glossary of useful echo-words, easily available to punning or to meaningful truncation.

My third and fourth essays address themselves to the presence of Echo on the Renaissance stage. The Renaissance developments of a secular drama, of a professional theater, and of an architecturally distinct stage space made theatrical Presence particularly uncertain: dramatic character and event had an extremely uneasy purchase on the phenomenal world of their audience. These new theatrical developments sharply separated the dramatic event from the continuities of the life of the audience just at the moment when the theatrical event became a commodity in the morally neutral economic control of that audience. In the third and fourth essays, I show some of the ways in which the furtive presence of Echo was used to figure the variously contingent presence of drama to its audience. I examine two inaugural echo-scenes—one by George Gascoigne, the other by Giambattista Guarini—as representative of many such scenes, counterpointing these examinations with a study of Jonson's theory and practice of masque-making.

In Jonson's work, the mythography of Echo would be used to figure the practice of Renaissance imitation. His respected patron, Francis Bacon, had found the representation of an ideal philosophical discourse in the myth of Echo; Jonson's Echo would eventually become a similarly idealized figure for imitative poetry, a tradition of modern making that revalues its models with free and knowing respect.[5] In *Cynthia's Revels*, however, Echo has a more intimate function, for there she represents Jonson's own tenuous purchase on the theatrical profession, on social and economic security. Restrained to such private functions, the figure of Echo does not achieve the ideality she would gain in the more stable years of Jonson's work as masque-maker for the Jacobean and Caroline court. Echo is one of the triumphs of the Jonsonian masque. She helps the poet demonstrate the coherence of his work and enables him to create a closure resistant to the extraliterary constraints of the occasion. Most important, perhaps, to the masques is Jonson's use of echoing as a display of acoustic power, a counterdisplay, in fact, to the visual displays of Inigo Jones: echo-song becomes one of the chief bulwarks in that defense of poetry built into the structure of the Jonsonian masque.

My brief concluding essay must stand as a mere introduction to echoing in Milton: the essay is a reading of Echo's silence in *Comus*. In the course of his classical studies, Milton might have read of a lost play by Euripides, the *Andromeda*, in which the bound heroine was further bound into colloquy with Echo. Euripides is one of Milton's great models—as binding is one of his great plots— and we can perhaps trace the influence of Euripides in the Lady's appeal to an echo who might reorient her, but who refuses. Such furtive influence, however, is not sufficient to account for the resonant silence of Milton's Echo. That silence is part of Milton's larger critique of pastoral voices, of the simple volubilities of nature. For Milton, genii enter into loci in pain, and the amenity of the pastoral *locus amoenus* is a pagan fiction to be surrendered, albeit with some nostalgia.

Last, a comment on method. A passage from Cartari's *Imagini degli dei antichi* will suggest the nature of Renaissance mythographic discourse; it will also enable me to say something about my own. I must cite at length, for the amplitude of Cartari's discussion is important here:

> *Diodorus Siculus* describeth Bacchus with two hornes on his head, which (sayth *Macrobius*) signifie the raies and beames of the sun, but *Diodorus* sayth, That by them rather is unshadowed and intended, that Bacchus was the first that instructed and taught men how to till their grounds, by subjugating and coupling their Oxen for the performance thereof. Some writers understand by those hornes so infixed on Bacchus, audacitie, impudencie, boldnesse, and fiercenesse, approoved by the overmuch taking of wine, which makes men hardie and adventurous, as also impudent and shamelesse, as is generally affirmed by *Philostratus, Festus Pompeius, Porphirio, Persius,* and others that have writ thereof. *Musonius* a Greeke writer sayth, That unto Bacchus were not onely hornes given, but that hee was of many Poets described and defigured in the shape and likenesse of a bull, the reason was, for that (as Poets deliver) Jove (transformed into a serpent) lay carnally with his owne daughter Proserpina, the which by him being great, brought forth Bacchus in the forme of a young bull, whereupon with the Cizenians (people inhabiting the further parts of Persia) his Image and Picture was framed to the true similitude and likenesse of a bull. But *Theopompus* and other writers say, that they gave those hornes so unto Bacchus, in that in Epirus and many places thereabouts, were buls of that hugenes and mightie bodies, that with their hornes (being answerable also in bignesse) the people there made them their great vessels to drinke in, which there was a generall cup or vessell throughout all those Countries thereabouts, and which fashion also spread itself afterwards into many other Countries round about them, among which they alwaies used and accustomed to drinke out of hornes. The Athenians afterward taking hold of that custome and manner, framed their silver vessels and bowles wherein they used to drinke, in the fashion and proportion of crooked and retorted hornes.
>
> But it is understood with some, that such hornes on Bacchus, signified certaine few haires, which from either side of the head were left growing in those daies, which likewise now at this time the Priests and holy men of Armenia (and in many places of India) doe use to weare, and observe, which doe shave all the upper part and top of their heads, and also behind in their neckes, (reserving onely two mightie long lockes, growing on either side before, towards their temples) which they used to bind with a fillet or lace very hard, and so made them to stand of themselves erect and out right. For which cause and fashion also *Moses* was said among the Hebrewes to have had hornes, and so was King *Lisimachus* with the Persians.[6]

The favored conjunction is *but*, though its force is equivocal, contributing little more than would *or*: Lynche's *but* (Cartari's *ma*) conveys a muted recognition of the uncomplementary methods or contradictions in the explanations. Macrobius gives the horns a significance to which the biography of Bacchus, the conventions of his worship, and the cultural field of his patronage are irrelevant: only his deity earns him the solar marks. With Musonius, *contra* Macrobius, the horns are the only vestiges of naturalist representation, and the human body itself is taken as a trope for deity. Diodorus ties the horns to euhemerist biography; the likes of

Philostratus link them to a moralized symbology. Theopompus's explanation depends on Bacchus's patronage of viniculture, or perhaps on his being a personification of wine, yet unlike Philostratus's, Theopompus's explanation is empty of moral reference. The last explanation links the horns to the *idea* of cult without in any way specifying Bacchic cult; it is as generalized as Macrobius's explanation, and, indeed, the two could conceivably be reconciled. Cartari does not make the effort.

Nonetheless, the heterogeneity of this portion of Cartari's handbook does not constitute a defect. I submit that this heterogeneity was instead a source of the book's tremendous popularity. The copiousness of explanatory materials is not a huckster's strategy ("well then, how about *this* one?"), though surely the hermeneutic abundance derives in part from the desperate Renaissance appetite for authority, an appetite that grew more obviously insatiable with the religious and social dislocations of the sixteenth and seventeenth centuries. But this hermeneutic *copia* made another, perhaps more powerful appeal, an appeal nearly anarchic in nature: the mythographers seem to offer a field of meaning in which *tertio dabitur*, a field in which the bonds of explanation to Necessity are relaxed. The very idea of the pagan gods was anomalous in postclassical culture, yet the mythographers were not content to alleviate the anomaly with a single explanatory gesture; rather, euhemerist, moral, and physical explanations crowd forth, creating in mythography a field in which the logical habit follows the rules of fantasy. In mythographers like Cartari, Giraldi, or Pontanus, as often in Jonson or Milton, the wealth of scholarly reference does not fix meaning; it frees it. The research in antique esoterica betrays the imaginative hunger which provided one of the primary motives of neoclassicism. In the mythographic strain of Renaissance scholarship, that appetite is indeed gargantuan.

The multivalency of the gods may stand as an extreme case of what often seems a nearly inevitable curse in cultural history. In the aftermath of composition during which I formulated this introduction, I reexamined some of the criticism with which these essays might be affiliated. Of course, they are distant relations of the texts they discuss—those encyclopedic points in a line running from Hesiod through Ovid to Boccaccio, Giraldi, Comes, Bacon, Banier, Frazer, and Graves: one cannot rigorously distinguish mythography from those products of that mythologizing impulse it claims as the field of its objective scrutiny. But these essays find more immediate methodological ancestry in the research associated with the Warburg Institute. In the work of Warburg himself, of Saxl, Kurtz, Wind, Panofsky, Gordon, Seznec, Gombrich, and—if we leave a more strictly iconographic focus—of Yates and Walker, we frequently find catalogs of imagery and allusion manifesting a most astonishing referential copia.

The central object of scrutiny, then, is often difficult to name. When he tried to describe the fundamental concern of Warburg's research, Gombrich had recourse to the casual phrase, "the life of symbols."[7] Or at least it seems casual. Yet the figure of a "life of symbols" is a defense of the idea of historical coherence, an argument that, despite the potential for semic slippage in cultural artifacts, the reference of images may always be conceived of as continuous and homogeneous, single despite manifest vicissitudes.

The biological model of historical development is a romantic construction. In the face of semic slippage, Renaissance thinkers had recourse to other constructions, other forms of defense against the historical vagrancy of antique *imagini*; the most obvious of these is the reaction formation which I refer to in my third essay as the cult of hieroglyphic meaning, an idealization of perfect signification. Like most reaction formations, it publicizes the discovery that it suppresses; in this case, it displays the discovery of *les antiquités de Rome*, stone images with sometimes cloudlike reference.[8] Another, less anxious way in which the discovery was publicized was in the genre of echo-poetry, in poems in which the identity of the iterated linguistic symbol dramatizes transformations in the symbol's reference.

Finally, Cartari's mythography suggests that many Renaissance thinkers felt rather little pressure to homogenize the reference of symbols: the horns of Bacchus provide the axis for many gyres of analogy. So Echo will function here; though I focus largely on the history of a literary symbol, my field of inquiry extends to the phenomenology of acoustic reflection itself. Of course, I recognize that in my effort to expose what seem to me to be important aspects of the acoustic imagination, I am seizing on a special case among acoustic phenomena—echo is sound at perhaps its most uncanny. Echoing points the near physicality of voice, the material ground of the word; as my first essay shows, the myths of Echo master that uncanny materiality by giving it a history. I have tried to let the materiality of voice become garrulous here.

1
ALIENA VERBA: ECHO, FAMA, AND THE LOCUS AMOENUS

> Sainct Clement Alexandrin . . . raconte ce qui se trouve dans l'histoire des Persans, à sçavoir qu'il y a trois montagnes dans une campagne rase, qui sont tellement situées qu'en s'approchant de la premiere, l'on n'entend que des voix confuses qui crient & qui chamaillent; à la seconde, le bruit & tintamarre est encore plus fort & plus violent; & à la troisiesme, l'on n'entend que chants d'allegresse & de resiuoyssance comme s'ils avoient vaincu. C'est ainsi que l'air selon la diversité des sujets forme une diversité de prodiges, que l'esprit humain admire en en recherchant les causes pour ne les plus admirer.
>
> Marin Mersenne, Harmonie Universelle[1]

The commencement of a mythographic endeavor is usually a confounded occasion, for one of the chief characteristics of myths is that they seem never to have quite *originated*. They seem, as it were, both to constitute and to represent themselves. The formulation may seem involuted; if so, Paule Demats's observations on the diction of Servius the grammarian may help me to unfold it. He writes:

> Servius n'emploi que deux verbes, *dire* et l'intraduisible *fingere*, toujours au passif, de préférence impersonnel. Toutes les nuances de l'indétermination sont ainsi exprimées. *Fictum est*, assez rare, suppose une invention ancienne, un temps, prélégendaire, un commencement de la fable, de même que sa variante exceptionelle *fabula composita est*. . . . *Fingitur* au contraire situe le récit fabuleux dans un présent abstrait, hors de la durée; c'est loin le terme le plus frequent. Avec *dicitur*, la notion de la fable s'exténue, il ne reste plus qu'une rumeur vague, sans origine et sans date.[2]

"Toujours au passif"—for Servius the story vitiates the existence of its first teller, of its origin; "invention ancienne," "recit fabuleux dans un présent abstrait," "une rumeur vague"—the story is always secondhand.[3] But Servius's *dicitur* extends the sense of fable toward the sense of fact: that which is said may be either received of the past or devised only a moment ago. With dicitur, fable gains its freedom from a distant past, yet it cannot muster a freedom from some prior telling. "Nec sinit, incipiat," writes Ovid of Echo, "sed, quod sinit, illa parata est / Exspectare sonos, ad quos sua verba remittat"; "she may *not* begin, but she is ready to do what she *may* do—to attend those sounds which she can return as her own words."[4] It is Ovid's discovery—and that of others, including Jonson, after him—that Echo's speech, always secondary, can figure forth the forms of mythological narrative. She is a genius of myth, of sorts. The suggestion of such geniality appears frequently: when Ausonius wrote his profoundly influential monologue for Echo, he gave her a genealogy that could well function as a genealogy of myth itself. "Aeris et Linguae sum filia," she says, "Daughter of the Air and of the

Tongue am I": the nymph is situated between the fact of the world and the fiction of man, a genius of myth.[5]

The gods of Olympus are patrons, but their relation to human experience is abstract, however interested. Cupid aids the lover and Mercury assists the thief, but their patronage is miscellaneously manifest; their methods are by turns dignified, ridiculous, delicate, ingenious. If the several acts of the Olympian patrons are most remarkable for their sheer variety, the historian ascribes that variety in divine action to the inclusiveness by which local cults are accommodated and transcended by national religion. Several idiosyncratic local divinities become single and complex personalities. But Echo originally had no responsibilities as a patron, and if she associated herself with particular locales, as the geographers suggest, she was more frequently merely "Arcadian," or, as in Seneca, "habitans cavis montibus" (*Troades*, 111). If she haunted a place it was her habit never to be quite *there;* she had no powers over various phenomena, being nothing more than a phenomenon herself.

Indeed personality is not always associated with the Greek ἠχώ; before the word named a *daemon*, it was used to describe all sorts of reflected sound. It could name the clear sound returning from a surface sufficiently distant that it seems a mimic repetition of a word or phrase generated near at hand, the cacophony of multiple reflections from multiple surfaces, or the resonant attenuation of an original sound caused by the proximity of the reflecting surface or surfaces. Bacon's taxonomy of acoustic reflection distinguishes between resonance ("reflexion concurrent") and repetition-by-reflection ("reflexion iterant"), a distinction depending simply on the relative distance of the reflectant surface; the Greek word, however, does not discriminate between these manifestations.[6] Yet the manifestations have different effects, for resonance manifests itself as a proof of concord, nature's assent to human discourse, while the delayed reflections which repeat—"a cry that was not ours"—deny the primary humanity of speech.[7] Through echo, an inhuman voice can arise, nature can be animated without that incarnation of the animate that subdues the daemonic to the human. When ἠχώ is manifest as articulate speech, the very humanity of the logos is challenged: in sum, while resonance does homage to human power, echo circumscribes that power.

Hence in the two earliest instances of echoing in Greek poetry—in Hesiod's *Theogony* and in the roughly contemporaneous Homeric *Hymn to Pan*—the effects of the excited sounds differ greatly. In Hesiod's poem, the Muses' song resounds upon the peaks of Olympus, and that resonance gladdens their father, Zeus. This opening is a remarkably happy contrivance in a poem celebrating divine generation; Zeus engenders the Muses, who in turn bring forth a song whose resonance excites the poet to proclaim their voice immortal.

> Come thou, let us begin with the Muses who gladden the great spirit of their father Zeus in Olympus with their songs, telling of things that are and that shall be and that were aforetime with consenting voice. Unwearying flows the sweet sound from their lips, and

the house of their father Zeus the loud-thunderer is glad at the lily-like voice of the goddesses as it spreads abroad, and the peaks of snowy Olympus resound, and the homes of the immortals. And they, uttering their immortal voice, celebrate in song first of all the reverend race of the gods from the beginning. [ll. 36–45]

Thus Hesiod displays the generosity that is to be both his style and his theme. Resonance appropriately figures Hesiod's opening itself, for that opening is a study in *amplification:* he describes the Muses' hymn to Zeus thrice in seventy-two lines.[8] Their first, nocturnal song is without resonance ("thence they arise and go abroad by night, veiled in thick mist, and utter their song"; ll. 8–10), and this dark song prefaces a sinister initiation in which the Muses challenge the shepherd-poet to reproduce their darkly parabolic hymnody: "Shepherds of the wilderness, wretched things of shame, mere bellies, we know how to speak many false things as though they were true; but we know, when we will, to utter true things" (ll. 26–28). Hesiod manages to counter this awesome vaunting, and his maneuver is as devious as the speech that provokes it: it is at this moment in the text that he endows the Muses' song with the resonance that so delights their father. The dark earth from which the Muses first arise is made to echo (*iakhe*) with their song, while the poet's repeated account of that song functions as a narrative version of that resonance (resonance transformed into repetition), an ostentatiously literary imitation. By describing the song as resonant, the poet insists that the Muses are benign, producing harmony; he simply ignores the hostility they display toward their earthly initiates. The poet subordinates his fears to the work at hand, and his portrayal of resonant song proclaims his mastery of those fears: the resonant song proves the poet's power.

Virgil takes over this Hesiodic trope, making Tityrus, Virgil's imagined self (less persona than narcissistic ideal), the supreme poet of resonance.[9] Like Hesiod, Tityrus meditates the Muse, but without effort ("patulae recubans sub tegmine fagi," reclining beneath the spreading beech; *Eclogues*, I.1); the ease with which he generates resonance attests to poetry's progress toward *otium:*

> Tu, Tityre, lentus in umbra
> formosam resonare doces Amaryllida silvas.   [I.4–5][10]

[You, Tityrus, at ease beneath the shade, teach the woods to resound with "fair Amaryllis."]

It is a poetry that rises to absolute confidence, moving from first fears ascribed to Corydon in the second eclogue (widely held to be first in order of composition)—"ibi haec incondita solus / montibus et silvis studio iactabat inani" (And there alone in fruitless passion he flings these artless strains to the hills and woods; ll. 4–5)—to a final proof of vocation—"non canimus surdis, respondent omnia silvae" (We sing to no deaf ears; the woods echo every note; X.8).[11] This response may be either resonance or echo (*resonare Amaryllida* is similarly indefinite); for Virgil, the difference between the phenomena is immaterial—his Renaissance commentators regularly cite Ovid's tale of Echo to gloss the Virgilian use of *resonare*.[12] As we shall soon see, earlier poets had taken echo as an eruption of the *Unheimlich,* so that we must take Virgil's customary pleasure in all manifestations of acoustic reflection as another index of his poetic prowess; indeed, this easy familiarity with the uncanny may provide the ground for Virgil's later reputation as *magus.*[13] In the second eclogue, Corydon's lament, word order displays the source of fear, the confrontation of the solitary with a landscape, and the verb indicates the young poet's aggressive response to the situation.[14] This is the first manifestation of what comes to be a habit of Virgilian diction, *ferre sonum ad, iacere sonum*: the doctrine of the materiality of sound, learned from Lucretius, but inherited from Democritus, dominates the vocabulary of Virgil's acoustics.[15] He frequently insists that the true poet directs and impels song, whereas the less skilled singer—the Damon of the third eclogue, for instance—merely scatters his verses: "non tu in triviis, indocte, solebas / stridenti miserum stipula disperdere carmen" (Weren't you the boor who used to stand at the cross-roads spattering away a flat-footed tune on his screeching reeds? ll. 26–27); Milton translates these lines to describe that lowest form of poetry which leaves "the hungry sheep" unfed.[16]

In the *Eclogues,* acoustic impulse seeks the confirmation of response; the landscape is rendered *docile* insofar as it resounds—"resonare doces"—and insofar as it resounds, the poet's vocation is accomplished. We may look beyond the *Eclogues* to a similar scene of vocation in the *Aeneid,* a scene in which Virgil reasserts his ascent to epic stature. At the end of the poem's first book, Iopas, bard of Dido's court, rises to sing of the wandering moon and to hymn the labors of the sun—a performance that provides a transcendent model for Aeneas's autobiography:

> Cithara crinitus Iopas
> personat aurata, docuit quem maximus Atlas.   [I.740–41]

[Long-haired Iopas, taught by mighty Atlas, made the golden lyre ring forth.]

The unusual verb for the production of resonance lightly evokes the etymology of *persona* (dramatic character conceived as that which passes, resounding, out from behind a player's mask): the verb anticipates—and I mean to suggest a Virgilian intention here—later verbal developments, both the evolution of the word *impersonation* and that meaning of *persona* which now has currency in the discourse of literary criticism. For Iopas is the epic Tityrus, a new ideal: resonance, "personation," is again the sign of achieved vocation.

Thomas Rosenmeyer distinguishes between Theocritan and Virgilian pastoral in terms of acoustic response. Theocritus's pleasance, he admits, "is filled with sound; but the sounds are not the echoes of a human voice ricocheted from the resonant surfaces of a compliant landscape [as they are in Virgil's *locus amoenus*], but the freely offered comments of the creatures who join the herdsman singer in his noon concert."[17] In the progress toward a pastoral of docile landscape, Moschus provides the middle stage: in the "Lament for Bion," the poet both describes the sonorous mourning of gods and genii—of Apollo, the Pans and dryads, of Echo herself—and encourages the Sicilian Muses and the natural constituents of the landscape (less daemonic and, perhaps, less interested) to join the dirge. In Virgil's pastorals, though Tityrus's temporary absence may provoke the forest to spontaneous mourning (*Eclogues*, I.38–39), the singer's presence subdues the natural voice. Local sounding, when spontaneous, is muffled, while more brilliant noise is always *elicited*, always under human control. Citing the *Aeneid* (VIII.215–18), Marie Desport comments that in Virgil's poetry, "Toujours, partout, le son est considéré en tant qu'*emplissant la nature*" and her remark suggests how sonorous poetry demonstrates the human sufficiency to landscape.[18] The humanity of resonance, so effortlessly asserted in the *Eclogues*, makes the poet's presence in the landscape one of ease, not of pathos.

In the second literary representation of acoustical reflection, the *Hymn to Pan*, reflection is anything but a gesture of docility, seeming rather to interrupt the joyful sound that evokes it. The nymphs dance before their god and lover, "singing by some spring of dark water, while Echo wails [*persistēnei*] about the mountain-top and the god on this side or that of the choirs, or at times sidling into the midst, plies it nimbly with his feet" (ll. 20–23). This is the first recorded personification of Echo, and her ghostly voice has the effect of wreathing through and piercing the revelry. Pan rejoices in pied settings—"on his back he wears a spotted lynx-pelt, and he delights in high-pitched songs in a soft meadow where crocuses and sweet-smelling hyacinths bloom at random in the grass" (ll. 23–26)—and Echo's mournful keening is meant to provide the kind of contrast associated with the Panic. The personification of Echo (we cannot yet speak of embodiment), her rise to nominative status, renders her alien to the voices that call her into being: engendered by Panic vitality, she answers with mourning, transforming song into dirge.

This is the first instance of echoic mourning, distant ancestor of Echo's laments in *Cynthia's Revels* and in "Adonais." Most of the loci classici of such mourning involve cries rebounding from the opposite shores at the sites of watery deaths.[19] Thus, the Argonauts, in Virgil's sixth eclogue (l. 44), and Hercules, in the *Argonautica* of Valerius Flaccus (III.596–97), cry out for drowned Hylas and hear that name returned to them; in Antoninus Liberalis's version of the tale, Hylas himself is transformed into Echo.[20] The *Hymn to Pan* contains no suggestion that Echo's is articulate speech, but the sense of response, rather than resonance, is clear, hence the possibility of personification. With the fiction of another voice, of a singer never present, comes an onslaught of mortal fear; a historian like E. R. Dodds might hear in Echo's wailing the development of a guilt-culture in which daemonic accusers enforce the development of a fearful self.[21]

But even resonance can produce the fears usually excited by echo. Despite the triumphal associations of resonance at the opening of the *Theogony*, Hesiod later endows acoustic multiplicity with a force more threatening than that attributed to Echo by the author of the anonymous *Hymn to Pan*. Hesiod's Typhoeus, hundred-headed and hundred-voiced, is capable of uttering the unspeakable (*athesphaton*):

that is, the voices of rebellious Typhoeus cannot be mastered as was the voice of the Muses. An incantatory catalog of the Typhoean voices develops toward a description of a final, resonant voice, a voice that serves as a climactic sign of power (l. 835), and this threatening resonance is also a warning voice:

> And truly a thing past help would have happened on that day, and he would have come to reign over mortals and immortals had not the father of men and gods been quick to perceive it. But he [i.e., Typhoeus] thundered hard and mightily and the earth around resounded terribly and the wide heaven above, and the sea and Ocean's streams and the nether parts of the earth. [ll. 836–41]

Here acoustic reflection has an antithetical force, for by announcing crisis it prepares for preservation: the source of echo gives itself away. I have suggested that resonance can prove a poet capable of immortal song, *carmen perpetuum*, and that the personified Echo insists on the poet's mortality, if only on his bodily mortality. But the example from the *Titanomachia* demonstrates that it would violate the inclusiveness of the single Greek term to insist on a clear division in the effects of acoustic reflection. Whenever his song is voiced abroad, a singer will likely suffer the antithetical excitements of his own display of power—excitements figured in Hesiod's narrative both as threat and as a warning-which-preserves. Thus, in the *versi echoici* of the Renaissance, a singer will often awaken the nymph with a bravura "Dic, Echo," only to find the nymph perverse and intractable. Poliziano's, the first echo-lyric in Italian, ends with a characteristic play in which the lover's affection (*amore*) returns as a momento mori, if not as a threat to his life (*Ah, muore!*). Echo herself is the unmoved beloved; the charm of song rebounds to work most strongly on the singer:

> Che fa quello achi porti amore?   Ah more.[22]
> [What does one do whose love has been taken away?   Ah, die.]

Curiously, in the early traditions of Echo, her *contingency* (which later became one of her most noteworthy characteristics) goes nearly unremarked. Only in the "Lament for Bion" does Moschus hint at her dependency—"Echo amid the rocks mourns that she is silent and can copy thy voice no more"—and even here, her inarticulate lament persists, joined to the natural resonance the poet both describes and encourages.[23] Ausonius's epigram, "De Echo dolente propter Mortem Narcissi" (Concerning Echo Mourning for Narcissus' Death), posits her very existence as contingent ("Commoritur, Narcisse, tibi resonabilis Echo," With you, Narcissus, dies resounding Echo), but the assertion is soon withdrawn: "ultima nunc etiam verba loquentis amat" (and now she loves the last words of thy speaking; ll. 1 and 4). More characteristic is the impossibly enduring Echo of Bion's pipes in Moschus's elegy: "Who will set his mouth to thy flutes? Who be so bold? Thy lips, thy breath live in them yet; those reeds shall cherish the echo of thy minstrelsy. Am I to take thy instrument to Pan?" (ll. 51–54). Echo's voice thus partakes of the immortality of Hesiod's Muses. Persistence, even in Ovid's version of the story (*Metamorphoses*, III.339–510), is one of Echo's distinguishing traits and her supposed longevity gives her particular historiographic responsibilities.

"Per Echo hominis bonam famam" ("Echo" may be taken as a man's good name), writes Arnulph of Orleans in his *Allegoriae* on Ovid's *Metamorphoses*, nearly misapprehending an old tradition that has its literary origin in Pindar's fourteenth Olympian ode, in which Echo carries the news of victory to the shades of the athlete's father and uncle in Hades.[24] Boccaccio's "per Echo . . . famam ego intelligo" more aptly represents the relation of Echo and reputation.[25]

Boccaccio proves himself a great disciple of Ovid here, for after Ovid's description of the *domus Famae* (*Met.*, XII.39–63), *fama* unmodified remains a "complex word" of the Empsonian type. For Ovid has recognized in his own master a great ambivalence to the phenomenon of reduplicating voice, an ambivalence that developed during the composition of the *Georgics* and resulted in the *Aeneid*'s divergent images of the myriad-tongued Fama and the resonant utterances of the sibyl, issuing from a hundred caves in the mountain of Cumae.[26] Ovid restores the diffused complexity of fama to a condition of tension, restoring Fama to what seems a Cumaean site:

> Fama tenet summaque domum sibi legit in arce,
> innumerosque aditus ac mille foramina tectis
> addidit et nullis inclusit limina portis;
> nocte dieque patet: tota est ex aere sonanti,
> tota fremit vocesque refert iteratque quod audit;
> nulla quies intus nullaque silentia parte.   [ll. 43–48]

> [Rumor dwells here, having chosen her house upon a high mountain-top; and she gave the house countless entrances, a thousand openings, but with no doors to close them. Night and day the house stands open. It is built all of echoing brass. The whole place resounds with confused noises, repeats all words and doubles what it hears. There is no quiet, no silence anywhere within.]

The site of Virgilian prophecy is invaded by the most debased form of Virgilian speech: Ovid's Fama yokes together glory and gossip.

Yet often enough echo seems to be associated only with the glory, with the benignity of Arnulph's "*bona fama.*" Despite the fact that Echo falls silent, perhaps perishes, in the absence of an interested speaker, later classical authors persistently invoke both resonance and Echo to figure society's lasting assent to the highest forms of human activity. Thus Cicero, in a discussion of reputation:

> Est enim gloria solida quaedam res et expressa, non adumbrata: ea est consentiens laus bonorum, incorrupta vox bene iudicantium de excellenti virtute, ea virtuti resonat tamquam imago.[27]

> [For true glory is a thing of real substance and clearly wrought, no shadowy phantom; it is the agreed approval of good men, the unbiased verdict of judges deciding honestly the question of pre-eminent merit; it gives back to virtue the echo of her voice.]

Cicero ignores both the faintness of the reflected *imago* and its inability to extend itself in time. Indeed, after Cicero, Echo is frequently used to figure the very permanence of textual memory, that immortality which subjects deeds to unending moral scrutiny—hence, for example, the simile in a poem by the thirteenth-century poet, Thibaut de Champagne, "sui com Echo, qui sert de recorder / Ce qu'autre dit."[28] The comparison may have lost its force for modern readers who live in an age of mechanical reproduction of sound. Before records could be played, they could only be read or recited, and the fact has important consequences. In antiquity, the meaning of echo was controlled by the restricted cultural analogues with which it could be grouped. Texts, both oral and written, could be conceived of as echoic, while echo had a particular textuality it has now lost. Nontextual sound recording has revolutionized cultural memory, and if the aura of bards, scrolls, and books has been depleted, the power of echo as a mnemonic figure has also declined.[29]

And so the echoic *imago*—the Latin term for reflection had not yet acquired a primarily visual force—is commemorative.[30] Indeed, in Horace, Echo is an assistant to Clio:

> Quem virum aut heroa lyra vel acri
> tibia sumis celebrare, Clio?
> quem deum? cuius recinet iocosa
> nomen imago.
>
> Aut in umbrosi Heliconis oris
> aut super Pindo gelidove in Haemo . . . ? [*Odes*, I.xii.1–6]

[What man, what hero dost thou take to herald on the lyre or clear-toned flute, O Clio? What god? Whose name shall the playful echo make resound on the shady slopes of Helicon or on Pindus' top or on cool Haemus . . . ?]

Horace charts the unavoidable fallings-away of historical portrayal as Clio's spontaneous celebration of man or god gives way to Echo's resinging of a mere name. Perhaps the *iocosa* suggests even irreverence, a literary dalliance inherent in all historiography. Some such critique is likely, for in a poem closely related to this historical paean, resonance and echo together represent a purely temporary popular acclaim.

> Vile potabis modicis Sabinum
> cantharis, Graeca quod ego ipse testa
> conditum levi, datus in theatro
>   cum tibi plausus,
>
> clare Maecenas eques, ut paterni
> fluminis ripae simul et iocosa
> redderet laudes tibi Vaticani
>   montis imago. [*Odes*, I.xx.1–8]

[Come drink with me—cheap Sabine, to be sure, and out of common tankards, yet wine that I with my own hand put up and sealed in a Grecian jar, on the day, famous Knight Maecenas, when such applause was paid thee in the Theatre that with one accord the banks of thy native stream and the sportive echo of Mount Vatican returned thy praises.]

The Sabine wine functions as a mnemonic of Maecenas's triumph, its aged vintage contrasted with the brief public resonance of that triumph; clearly the poem itself is like the vintage, its Greek form filled with a Roman draught. Yet the wine is itself a strange monument, for even as it recalls the glorious moment, the drink will inspire forgetfulness. Horace's humility in comparing his Sabine to more expensive and exotic vintages surely involves more than his characteristic renunciation of publicity and ostentation. If the poem suggests a positive ideal, that ideal would be a true fame based necessarily, if paradoxically, on privacy. Yet the ode has a stronger negative force: Horace seems convinced, here, of the impossibility of adequate memory.[31]

If Horace mildly mistrusts echo for its publicity, other mythographic poets make the echoing voice a serious threat to human privacy and to semantic stability.[32] Poets, perceiving in the inanimate voice a challenge to the humanity of language, traditionally dramatized that challenge as did Callimachus, whose praise of his beloved, Lysanias—"*kalos, kalos*" (fair, fair)—rebounds with Echo's testimony of Lysanias's inaccessibility, his alterity—"*allos*" ([he is] an Other).[33] With the overlapping of spoken word and reflected "response," the echoed word loses its opening consonant; perhaps the reflex merely marks Lysanias's infidelity ("he is another's")—most editors think so—which would make the shock only a bit less harrowing. At best, the near perfect acoustic fidelity proves the lover's infidelity—or perhaps reveals an unconscious premonition of that infidelity inhering in the speaker's praise. At worst, her voice turns intimates to Others.

Allos sums up the conventional function of this echo-device: denying the integrity of the bond between lovers, Echo also denies the integrity of the speech. A speaker can no more control his words than a lover can control the beloved, for both utterance and beloved are beyond intention. In some sense, Echo portrays the utterances that she repeats as slips of the tongue, making the semantic coherence of those utterances seem only apparent. The analyst (or the analyst-in-the-speaker) who observes the slip of the tongue finds the private context, the psychological context of speaking abruptly extended and reorganized; in Callimachus's poem, Echo acts as analyst, and her repetition, by demonstrating the semantic indeterminacy of an utterance, extends and reorganizes the public context, the narrative situation of speaking. The speaker's assumptions about Lysanias and love, about the encomium's audience, even about himself as lover and as encomiast—in short, all the speaker's notions of narrative place—are proven false: Echo's allos announces *another* scene. As analyst, Echo reveals the speaker's imperfect knowledge of his world, renders the primary utterance ironic, and so destroys that proximity of word to meaning so dear to intimate discourse.

In the lyrics that employ this echo-device (the device appears to have been quite popular in the Alexandrian period, but most of the antique echo-lyrics are lost; most of the exemplars come from the Renaissance) Echo continues to indicate the speaker's ignorance of his own situation, effecting, within the limited scope of the lyric, the speaker's *anagnorisis*. Her analytic response, then, condenses the function of complex tragic plot, but since her analysis of primary utterance is so frequently reductive (ironic, in one sense of the word), Echo is also linked to the conventions of satire: the scholiast on Euripides' *Orestes* allegorizes this ironic function of the echo-device by making Echo the mother of Iambe, the patron of satiric poetry.[34] Callimachus's lyric is not the first instance of Echo's articulate speech, and we shall see that the two prior instances situate her function at the boundary of tragedy and comedy.

Euripides' *Andromeda*, held in antiquity to be one of his most beautiful and pathetic tragedies, is now lost to us, but we know from late antique scholia that it opened with an echo-scene.[35] Andromeda, already in chains, cries out to Night to shield her from the threatening monster, Glauketes; her complaint, which replaces the conventional choral prologue, is interrupted by an answering Echo. (The Lady's address to Echo in Milton's *Mask* is a vigorous transformation of this Euripidean strategy—Euripides being one of the trinity of dramatists, of which the others are Shakespeare and Jonson, that pressed most powerfully on Milton as he composed his masque.) The similarity of the opening situations of both the *Andromeda* and *Prometheus Bound* suggests larger formal implications: in Aeschylus's play a complicated deed produces a simple plot, for anagnorisis occurs before the beginning of the play. The opening of the play reveals that Prometheus has already discovered the future consequences of his past behavior, recapitulating if not repeating the discovery. The interruption of Andromeda's invocation to Night in Euripides' play is a formal rebuke, the proper occasion either for a recapitulation of the reason for her punishment (her boast that she excelled the Nereids in beauty) or for the first revelation of that reason; that is, the opening no doubt either recapitulates anagnorisis or is itself the moment of discovery. We infer that the bound heroine must already possess her guilty knowledge, like Prometheus, or that she is soon to possess it; an echo-scene is convenient to a coming-to-knowledge, particularly when the hero or heroine must come to know the consequences of speaking incautiously.

Much of what we know about the *Andromeda* derives from the scholia on two plays by Aristophanes, the *Thesmophoriazusae* (produced one or perhaps two years after the *Andromeda*) and the *Frogs*. In the former, an assault on Euripides' *Palamede*, *Helen*, and *Andromeda*, the invocation to Echo focuses an entire body of anti-Euripidean satire. Mnesilochus, Euripides' uncle, finds himself bound in the Thesmophorion, the victim of enraged women; posturing as Andromeda, he calls upon Echo in language that parodies that of the *Andromeda*. In the earlier play, Andromeda begs for Echo's silence, but here Mnesilochus entreats her attention, calling her from the caves in which she dwells. "*Klueis*," he cries, thus rendering his address a bit problematic—indicative, interrogative, or imperative; "You hear," "Do you hear?" or "Hear!" and with an active force that can shade toward the passive, "You are reputed" or even "Be reputed!"[36] The Euripidean nymph becomes fair game for Fama. This address to Echo closely follows the long choral song to Bacchus, which ends with an evocation of the terrible and sacred resonance of the peaks of Mount Kithaeron:

> Kithaeron shudders with music a shout
> > Bursts from the stone
> The upland thickets howl in the nymphic rout.[37]

The passionate reverence of this clamor overshadows, trivializes Echo's redundant babble. One tradition reported by the scholiast held that Euripides had habitually retired to a cave to compose his tragedies, and perhaps Aristophanes is playing on that tradition when he has Mnesilochus speak of Echo as a cave-dweller. So Echo clearly represents both Euripides himself and the corpus of Euripidean work; the play at this point is built out of garbled repetitions of Euripidean texts. We have reason to believe that the actor playing Euripides would have doubled as Echo, who begins to speak a few lines after Mnesilochus's invocation—despite the invocation, Mnesilochus seems nearly as surprised by Echo's presence as is Jonson's Mercury. The significance of Aristophanes' introduction of Echo thus becomes obvious: taking a text in which Euripides' Andromeda had called for Echo's silence, Aristophanes twists that primary utterance into an invitation for Echo's intervention. The Euripidean source intends a legacy of silence, seeking both an end to the mutterings of meaningless daemons and gods and its own security from distorting and demeaning repetitions.[38] But Aristophanes revives Echo in order to counter those intentions with continuing divine chatter (as well as the inspired and impressive bacchic chorus) and the satiric technique which we have found in Callimachan Echo.

The daemons still speak in Milton's day; the Euripidean longing for silence, obstructed in Aristophanes' satire, arises again in the Nativity Ode. The rout of the pagan gods, in which the gods' persistence—even in flight—is more grandly stated than in any other Renaissance poem, begins with a declaration of silence, and not a plea for it, but that declaration issues in a continuation of daemonic murmur. We recognize the Echo of the *Hymn to Pan*, and of the *De Defectu Oraculorum*, wailing after the cessation of the oracles:

> The Oracles are dumb,
> No voice or hideous hum
> > Runs through the arched roof in words deceiving.
> . . . .
> The lonely mountains o'er
> And the resounding shore,
> > A voice of weeping heard, and loud lament.[39]

As Euripides and Milton demonstrate, as Aristophanes guarantees, the poet cannot manage to sing without a daemonic rival.

Aristophanes flaunts his own power and Euripides' weakness by giving Echo the power of independent speech. When her voice is first heard, she hails Mnesilochus-Andromeda, identifies herself as Euripides' old friend Echo, and then instructs Mnesilochus in the proper portrayal of Andromeda.[40] Aristophanes thus completes a usurpation of the Euripidean stage that began at the play's opening, when twisted citations from Euripides' *Helen* were used to recast

Euripides as Menelaus, the paradigmatic victim of usurpation. The echo that, in the *Andromeda*, rebound the captive heroine by means of a further verbal binding—a punitive restriction of her misused freedom of speech and a barrier to her colloquy with Night—now functions as a binding of the Euripidean text. Once Echo begins her characteristic repetitions (at line 1069), the witty play of the Callimachan echo-device is never employed. Echo interrupts discourse without shaping its explicit significance; barely witty and stupidly persistent, she makes Euripidean art impossible. So Fitts's translation, "How can I render a Euripidean monody if you keep on talking?" is a canny version of *nē di okhlēra g'eiserrēkas lian* (ll. 1075–76).

One of Aristophanes' contemporaries, the poet Kratinos, devised a special word for the overingenious poets of his age: the word is "euripidaristophanizer."[41] Despite differences, Kratinos perceives a link between the two playwrights. Both had constructed philosophical dramas deeply critical of the conventions of dramaturgy; in the Echo-scenes of the *Andromeda* and the *Thesmophoriazusae*, the playwrights use Echo to disrupt the patterns of traditional monody. But Aristophanes has given Echo the privileges of Fama, placing under her control a specifically literary reputation. He suggests that his invocation to Echo *is* an echo, a reevaluation of a prior text, thus figuring allusion, the *kairos* of literary history, as acoustic reflection; here for the first time, the character gives her name to the trope, as she continues to do. With Echo as vehicle and allusion as tenor, Aristophanes also authorizes a unity within the diverse senses of "reflection": the production of an imago depends upon both contemplation and the lapse in time such contemplation requires. In order to echo a text, a poet must reflect upon it, reassembling the internal structure of repeated dicta.

It would seem, then, that Aristophanes provided Callimachus with more than a model of echo as a rhetorical scheme: he provides a literary mythology for the invisible nymph. Consider the Callimachan epigram in its entirety:

> I hate the cyclic poem [*poiēma kuklikon*], nor do I take pleasure in a path which carries many to and fro. And I hate too the promiscuous lover, nor do I drink from a public well. All common acts disgust me. But, Lysanius, fair thou art, yea, very fair; but before the words are out an Echo says, "He's another's."[42]

The Alexandrian cyclic poem stands here as the paradigm of utterance debased by its susceptibility to vulgar repetition and imitation. More striking than the poet's loathing for amorous infidelity is this model of literary promiscuity. Echo's interruption implies a converse ideal, the ideal of a hysterically private, nearly solipsistic poetry, free of the influence of a public audience, free of the tyranny of the intricate form, free, in short, of anything that betrays the "slender Muse" to tradition.[43] Echo's *allos* comes as a rebuke focused on the formulaic nature of the lover's praise (*kalos, kalos*), which itself constitutes a concession to the iterative. As Aristophanes had shown, Echo is the perfect adversary for retention. Echo, as literary reputation, is a sort of *psyche*, that vitality which is only manifest when a hero breathes it forth in death.[44]

For Aristophanes and for Callimachus, Echo's presence is irresistible. Martial later attempts a resistance, attacking the Alexandrian echo-lyric as a particularly telling sign of the decline of Greek letters. He refers to the representative Alexandrian poet as a "Graecula quod recantat echo."[45] By the time of the Renaissance, only one of what had apparently been a large body of such lyrics had survived, but Martial's attack on the form preserved its memory; when Poliziano undertook a commentary on Martial's poem in his great contribution to cinquecento philology, the *Miscellaneorum Centuria Prima*, he gave the first technical definition of the echo-device and adduced the single remaining example of the echo-lyric, a poem by the Byzantine poet, Gauradas, preserved in Planudes' Greek Anthology.[46] (Poliziano claims that several such poems by Gauradas exist, but no evidence of these poems is recorded elsewhere.) He appears undaunted by Martial's censure of the form, so zealous is he to recover the lyric tradition for which Martial's poem gives evidence, and he boasts of having written several such lyrics ten years before the publication of the *Miscellaneorum* (of these, again, only one has been preserved). It is one of the pranks of literary history that the careful description of the objects of Martial's disdain revived the production of those objects.

Poliziano's echo-lyric was first published in the 1494 edition of his *Stanze per la Giostra* and *Orfeo*; the lyric is printed at the end of the *Orfeo*, prefaced by the heading, "Stanza ingeniosissima del prefato auctore fuor di materia" (an ingenious stanza by the same author on a different subject).[47] A shrewder editor seems to have supervised the later editions of this volume, for thereafter the lyric is introduced as a "Stanza ingeniosa del Poliziano in fine dell'Orfeo" (Poliziano's ingenious stanza for the end of *Orfeo*). There are several points of contact between the myths of Echo and those of Orpheus; at this stage it will suffice to notice how resonance figures in the legends of Orpheus. Nature responds to Orphean song with a submission, a docility, more complete than even that evoked by Tityrus: stones and trees not only resound; they move, weep. Tityran song hallows the pleasance and creates the scene of vocation, while the songs of Orpheus rise to narrative agency. Orphean echo impels *mythos*, or narrative (the meaning of *mythos* that developed after the scientific revolution of the fifth century B.C.), even as it transforms mythos in the Callimachan lyric; but not until comparatively late in antiquity does the phenomenon of echo acquire its own mythos.[48] Here, then, is the development to which I shall devote the remaining pages of this chapter—the process by which the personified phenomenon extended itself into narrative.

To recapitulate: the earliest literary representations of acoustic reflection produce antithetical results. I have extended my original—and to some degree, artificial—distinction between resonance and echo, by using it to distinguish between a proof of power and a daemonic circumscription of that power, the poet's claim and the auditor's prerogative, between fama as Glory and fama as Rumor. But in none of the representations discussed so far does the nymph seem to possess much of a past. Aristophanes gives Echo a history—it is merely a stage history—by presenting her as "having-appeared-before," much as Moschus, in the "Lament for Bion," records her as "having-sung-before." But the wailing Echo of the *Hymn to Pan* seems possessed of only an ominous present. The phenomenon itself, which arrests discourse and transforms a speaker's agency into pathos, is itself aggressive, but it is an aggression originally without intent. The articulation of Echo's history, the adumbration of motives for animate presence, is a reaction against that aggression.

All myths of Echo render her pathetic, are hence reactive, but we can fairly draw further conclusions from this pathos: the myths partake of the generally scientific tendencies of mythology after the archaic period. In the *Introduction to the Philosophy of Mythology*, Schelling insisted on the priority of mythos in all epistemology, and this principle became the foundation for nearly all subsequent phenomenological studies of myth.[49] Thus Seznec follows Schelling when he demonstrates how postarchaic mythography strove to explicate the implicit links between myths and the causal structure of empirical phenomena.[50] As the mythos of a simply animate nature develops toward the mythology of a psychologized nature, the scientific character of myth, its epistemological function, emerges. We can trace in the developing mythology of Echo a model instance of this reification of the scientific impulse.

Two major myths include Echo. The later one, the story of her love for the beautiful Narcissus, has attained greater currency in the modern world, but the earlier tale of Pan's love for Echo seems to have been far more popular in antiquity.[51] The association of Pan and Echo goes back at least as far as the Homeric hymns, though in the *Hymn to Pan*, their association has only the force of juxtaposition. In a fragmentary poem (*Idyll* VI), Moschus sketches a sorry chain of infatuation: Pan loves Echo, Echo loves a satyr, who in turn loves a nymph. Since Pan is both patron of pastoral poets and genius of the pleasance, the fable seems to name, and by naming master, the multiple voices that animate the locus amoenus: the thrill and threat of acoustic reflection appears refracted into a tragicomic romantic situation.[52]

Fewer characters clutter the myth in what could be called its traditional form: Pan pursues an Echo who often evades or refuses him. One of the most winning poems in the Palatine anthology includes a prayer in which the farmer, Stratomicus, dedicates a plot of fallow ground to Pan, suggesting that the spot will bring luck to the god "for Echo will be pleased with it," perhaps so pleased that she will give in to his pursuit.[53] In some accounts of this amour, Echo is less evasive: in Callimachus, Iynx is said to have been born of the union of Pan and Echo.[54]

Certainly the late antique mythographers tend to suppress Echo's refusals, figuring a perfect concord in the relationship of this god and this nymph. Macrobius began an important allegorical tradition in his exegesis of Pan's significance; for Macrobius, Pan is the sun—"non silvarum dominum, sed universae substantiae materialis dominatorem" (not master of the woods, but lord over the universe of material substance). Echo, then, becomes more than an expressive imitator; Macrobius says that she signifies celestial harmony (*harmoniam caeli*)—

in Milton's words, "Daughter of the Sphere"—making her instrumental to the solar divinity who is her paramour.[55] Macrobius's treatise inaugurates the Neoplatonic tradition in Latin mythography. Uncritical in the treatment of his sources, he argues that natural phenomenon creates fable and that mythography must penetrate both fable and phenomenon in search of a hidden philosophical core.[56] The ratio of comparison dissolves in his discussion of Pan and Echo, as he likens the nymph's invisible voice to the inaudible heavenly music. Bacon restores intellectual coherence to this interpretation; for him, Pan is simply the world, but thus conceived Pan's loves become problematic:

> Where there is plenty of everything there is no room for want. The world therefore can have no loves, nor any want (being content with itself), unless it be of *discourse*. Such is the nymph Echo, a thing not substantial but only a voice.

By discourse (*sermo*), Bacon means a perfectly mimetic philosophical discourse, "for that is the true philosophy which echoes most faithfully the voices of the world itself, and is written as it were at the world's own dictation; being nothing else than the image and reflexion thereof, to which it adds nothing of its own, but only iterates and gives it back."[57] Macrobius had taken Echo as a divine interpreter—not a respondent to human voice, but the voice of the divine nature. Bacon extends that interpretive, mediating function to make Echo the human voice raised to its most transcendent form (the Neoplatonic motive in the *Saturnalia* is here preserved: by figuring the quintessential human voice—that of the philosopher—as a disembodied philosophical discourse, Bacon's mythography enacts an aspiration to the immaterial). He achieves a rather remarkable mythographic reversal, for in the *De Sapientia Veterum* Echo no longer appears as the uncanny discursiveness *of* the world; instead, Echo figures the conformity of discourse *to* the world. Echo no longer opposes human voice, no longer mimics our voice, for her voice has become ours.

In the preface to the *De Sapientia*, Bacon anticipates the accusation that he is guilty of ingenious, applied, and inessential allegoresis. He defends himself by denying the priority of fable; the *allegoresis*, he insists, precedes the fable. This mythographic strategy empties the fabulous of its inhuman authority, and we can trace that strategy in Bacon's management of Pan and Echo, for he has exhausted her adversative power as well. Identifying Pan with the world, Bacon denies any intrinsic daemonic power in the god of fable (Christian mythographers before Bacon identify Pan both with Nature and with Christ, so that Bacon's exegesis involves a conspicuous omission). As Pan becomes a (neutralized) world, so Echo dissolves into humanity.[58]

Traditional *musica speculativa* provides Bacon with the conceptual leverage necessary to transform *harmonia caeli* into *sermo*, *harmonia* being that principle of universal organization which is the largest concern of musical philosophy. This line of exegesis endows Echo with what may seem a surprisingly generalized significance—citing Macrobius, Giraldi comments, "De Echo & in Symbolis nonnihil dictum est"—but that generality has the considerable authority of the

De Anima behind it.[59] Aristotle's analysis of echo (419b, 25–420a, 19) culminates in the observation that, just as the transmission of light always involves reflections (Aristotle takes diffusion as a necessary characteristic of the transmission of all sensory stimuli), so is echo present in all transmission of sound. This leads immediately to a description of the mechanical operation of the ear: "That is why we say that we hear with what is empty [that is, filled only with air; cf. 419b, 34] and echoes, viz. because what we hear with is a chamber which contains a bounded mass of air."[60] These are the precise terms used to describe the perfect echo chamber (419b, 25–27); that is, hearing is described as echoing.

The Aristotelian identification of hearing with echoing eventually received poetic expression; that expression, an epigram by Ausonius, became Echo's single most important independent utterance and one that Renaissance commentators would cite with remarkable regularity:

> Vane, quid adfectas faciem mihi ponere, pictor,
>   ignotemque oculis sollicitare deam?
> Aeris et Linguae sum filia, mater inanis
>   indicii, vocem quae sine mente gero.
> extremos pereunte modos a fine reducens,
>   ludificata sequor verba aliena meis.
> auribus in vestris habito penetrabilis Echo:
>   et, si vis similem pingere, pinge sonum.   [Epigram, XXXII]

> [Thou witles wight, what meanes this mad intent
> To draw my face & forme, unknowne to thee?
> What meanste thou so for to molesten mee?
> Whom never Eie behelde, nor man coulde see?

> Daughter to talking Tongue, and Ayre am I,
> My Mother is nothing when things are waide:
> I am a voyce without the bodies aide.
> When all the tale is tolde and sentence saide,

> Then I recite the latter worde afreshe
> In mocking sort and counterfayting wies:
> Within your eares my chiefest harbour lies,
> There doe I woonne, not seene with mortall eies.

> And more to tell and farther to proceede,
> I *Eccho* height of men below in grounde:
> If thou wilt draw my Counterfait in deede,
> Then must thou paint (O Painter) but a sound.][61]

The poem recapitulates the mythographic progress by which the apparently external voice of Echo is internalized. The natural semblance of an alien voice situated at a reflecting surface becomes the natural symbol of the tympanum. This transformation becomes a kind of *paideia*, leading philosophical attention from empirical phenomena *auribus in vestris*. As in Callimachus's echo-poem, the speaker who generates echo is being educated, discovering his own utterances as *verba aliena*, but here the education is far more serious. Echo no longer haunts the landscape; instead she teaches the painter that the speaking self is as haunting as any external presence, even if that external presence be invisible, for the internal interlocutor is—to use the word with its full etymological force—equally "unimaginable."

Not only does Ausonius's poem recapitulate a mythographic development, it also provides a crude account of literary history. The earliest forms of Greek lyric display a fascination with the external; the self-consciousness now associated with lyric emerged from early articulations in exhortations, pleas, dialogues—utterances for which social discourse provided the model. But Ausonius makes the externality of the respondent a delusion, and he seeks to turn the speaker's attention toward an inner interlocutor: following Plato (*Sophistes*, 263E), he makes thought a transcendent form of dialogue. This transcendentalization takes place in the very history of the lyric, beginning with Solon who internalized the dialogic form of early lyric by composing poems in dialogue with himself. Dialogic form, once separated from its merely social functions, made possible the literary imitation of the self. The relocation of an external voice, the return of Echo to her proper place of origin, becomes a fable of literary and personal achievement.

Echo's modest refusal to offer herself to the eye, her resistance to Pan's seductions, ultimately made her as much patron as personification; that is, when linked with Pan, she appears as heroine, and therefore patron, of virginity—or at least, of married chastity. In Nonnos's immense assemblage of Dionysian lore, the *Dionysica*, Echo performs just this function, if somewhat ineffectually; at one point, Echo primly answers the sounding breeze which attends on Dionysos's rape of Nicaia, transmuting the breeze's song into the marriage hymn of "Hymen, Hymenaios" (XVI.290). In Longus's pastoral romance, her characteristic denial of Pan's desires challenges the very amenity of rustic society, and she is frantically punished for that challenge:

> Pan . . . takes occasion to be angry at the maid, and to envy her because he could not come at her beauty. Therefore he sends a madness among the shepherds and goatherds, and they in a desperate fury, like so many dogs and wolves, tore her all to pieces and flung about them all over the world her yet singing limbs. [*Daphnis and Chloë*, III.23]

The tale seems to have originated with Longus, as the ingenious improvisation of his hero, Daphnis. It caps a sequence of initiations: Daphnis, having just received an introduction to adult sexuality from the aristocratic Lycaenium, seeks out his beloved Chloë hoping to share his discovery with her, but restrains himself in deference to her slightly magical virginity (this last, an initiation into continence, never before an issue in the Longan pleasance). As they embrace by the sea, Chloë notices that the songs of passing oarsmen are reflected by a nearby cave, as if the noise originated there, and she asks for an explanation of the phenomenon.[62] Though he seems familiar with physical explanations for echo, Daphnis contrives his own etiological myth, framed, perhaps as a cautionary tale to virgins, with his own repressed desires somewhat mechanically manifest as narrative violence. He handily manages the etymological habits of such tales, using the narrative to explain the relationship of limbs (*melē*) to songs (*melē*), as he works to make Chloë's discovery of echo the pretext for further initiations. Daphnis's mythological invention—note the paradox of the phrase—is also a consummate revision of Virgil, whose presence is felt throughout the romance, most obviously in the person of the old herdsman, Philetas. The poetry of the historical Philetas provided one of the chief models for Theocritan and thence for Virgilian pastoral; though Philetas functions in Longus as the human type of the pastoral poet (Pan is the divine pastoralist), his first appearance in *Daphnis and Chloë* (II.3ff.) closely identifies him with Virgil. There he tells the story of Pan's attempted rape of Syrinx, an account of the origin of the panpipes which, like the tale of Echo, predicates pastoral melody on the death of a virgin. Recalling his youthful prowess in pastoral song, Philetas recasts the first eclogue, substituting himself for Tityrus (who appears later in the book as Philetas's son)—"I praised Echo that with kindness she restored and trebled to me the dear name of Amaryllis. I broke my pipes because they could delight the kine but could not draw me Amaryllis" (II.33).[63]

Longus denies the final efficacy of Virgilian acoustics; in Daphnis's tale, Virgilian echo gives witness, not to the singer's blithe skill, but to a tragedy remembered in the landscape. To put it otherwise, Longus commemorates, not the resonant *locus amoenus* of the first eclogue, but the darker Maenalian locale of the eighth eclogue (and of the close of the *Georgics*) where a *saevus Amor* pursues its victims and song grows to frenzy:

> nunc et ovis fugiat lupus, aurea durae
> mala ferant quercus, narcisso floreat alnus,
> pinguia corticibus sudent electra myricae,
> certent et cycnis ululae, sit Tityrus Orpheus,
> Orpheus in silvis, inter delphinas Arion.
>   incipe Maenalios mecum, mea tibia, versus
> omnia vel medium fiat mare. vivite silvae:
> praeceps aërii specula de montis in undas
> deferar.   [*Eclogues*, VIII.52–60]

[Now let the wolf flee before the sheep, let rugged oaks bear golden apples, let the alder bloom with narcissus, let tamarisks distil rich amber from their bark, let owls, too, vie with swans, let Tityrus be an Orpheus—an Orpheus in the woods, an Arion among the dolphins. *Begin with me, my flute, a song of Maenalus.* Let all become mid-ocean. Farewell, ye woods. Headlong from some towering mountain crag I will plunge into the waves.]

Damon sings here, impersonating a shepherd who has been disappointed in love and whose furious song twists together revenge and self-destruction. For the shepherd intends by his own death magically to enact the death of his successful rival. "Sit Tityrus Orpheus": "Let Tityrus, the easy, the fortunate, die the death of an Orpheus, denied his beloved and cast still singing into the waves, as I myself shall be," the suicidal frenzy moaning through line 59 in the strange double caesura and the quadrisyllabic wail of *aërii*. This poetry surfaces only occasionally in the *Eclogues*, with pastoral *otium* regularly reasserting itself; in the *Georgics*, however, the furor of Damon's shepherd controls much more of the poem. Otium is rejected as ignoble in the *Georgics*, and the poem closes with the violent—one would like to say, "Maenalian"—image of bees bursting from the decaying flesh of sacrifical oxen.[64] As it had been in earlier poetry, the echo of the *Georgics* is an Orphean voice, a voice communicating between the living and the dead:

> Eurydicen vox ipsa et frigida lingua
> a miseram Eurydicen! anima fugiente vocabat
> Eurydicen tota referebant flumine ripae.   [*Georgics*, IV.525–27][65]
>
> [[Only] the voice cried "Eurydice," his voice and frigid tongue, "Ah, hapless Eurydice," cried with fleeting breath; and all the banks along the flood gave back, "Eurydice."]

The shepherd's hope is realized here: "sit Tityrus Orpheus." Tityrus, progenitor of echo, is made into a *sparagmos*, as pastoral is sacrificed to georgic. We can see the same event performed in the envoy to the *Georgics*, where Virgil claims that the *Georgics* have supplanted the *Eclogues* and suggests his wish to replace the *Georgics* in their turn. The revision of the opening line of the *Eclogues*—"Tityre, tu patulae recubans sub tegmine fagi"—in the closing line of the *Georgics*—"Tityre, te patulae cecini sub tegmine fagi"—must not be taken as nostalgia, nor as a Virgilian claim to circular, infinite canon. The *cecini* asserts the presence of Virgil, the maker (thus looking forward to the similar assertion at the opening of the *Aeneid*), as it serves to dissociate Virgil from his earlier ideal. Tityrus no longer stands as a visionary self: he becomes a construct, an objectification. He is dismembered, becomes a speaking head. The revision charts a maturation into a more perilous, Orphean poetic, one in which poetry is not the expression of ease but a laborious demonstration of the power to supplant or surpass earlier poems.

This somewhat hasty account of the shift from eclogue to georgic might be called an anatomy of Milton's Virgil; it is, in fact, the reading of Virgil implicit in Longus.[66] The complaint of Philetas in book II of *Daphnis and Chloë* is that first sign of Longus's sensitivity to the place of echo in Tityran pastoral: one might say that in Daphnis's tale of Echo, Longus makes a simple substitution—*sit Echo Orpheus*. Virgil's Orpheus, at the height of his uncanny poetic powers, but at his least efficacious, is the Georgic poet of Echo—the Georgic, dismembered version of a Tityrus. Virgil says that Orphean echo has supplanted Tityran echo, whereas Longus argues for the temporal priority of the Orphean tale: that is, the resonance of the locus amoenus is predicated on an earlier tragedy.

We may stop to consider the implications of Longus's exegesis of Virgil. Virgil never once provides a mythology of Echo; indeed, he never mentions her name—the name seems not to have been in great vogue among Latin poets before Ovid (and we have no surviving transliteration of Ἠχώ into Latin before Accius)[67]—so that Longus has done more than rearrange the order of the Virgilian corpus. Indeed his control over literary genealogy extends further, for Daphnis's tale is made prior to the georgic tale of Orpheus; Orpheus, dismembered by Maenads for having shunned the company of women, can arouse echoes because of the sympathy between his fate and that of Echo (conceived as already remembered in the landscape). Daphnis's tale provides a limiting case of the use of Echo to figure allusion, for through that tale, Longus claims *priority* to Virgil. He enforces his claim by writing in Greek, the original language of pastoral; by naming his hero Daphnis, the suffering shepherd of Theocritus's first idyll and the *model* for the crazed singer of Virgil's Maenalian eclogue; and by introducing Tityrus into the narrative as youth and novice. Had this literary event occurred in post-Miltonic literature, Harold Bloom might have guided us to call this gesture *apophrades*, the return of the dead: "the tyranny of time almost is overturned, and one can believe, for startled moments, that they [the powerful heirs] are being imitated by their ancestors."[68] But Longus is not what Bloom would call a strong poet; he shrugs off any such epithet. The improvised character of Daphnis's story is not a show of strength with respect to Virgil, rather it is a witticism that demonstrates the playful power of late mythology.[69] A playful demonstration, but analytic as well: we shall not be able to apprehend the full measure of Longus's achievement without considering the functions of etiological narratives.

Bruno Snell, providing a historical grammar for the epistemological shift from mythology to science, compared Thales's "scientific" postulate—that "the origin and nature of things is water"—with its source, Homer's statement that Ocean is the origin of the gods.[70] Both statements are analytic, though of course only Thales's statement treats of causality. Nor does Hesiod present a causal cosmogonic system in the *Theogony*, for genealogy remains the sufficient model for natural order; Homeric myth and the *Theogony* are "tautegorical," to use Schelling's term. The development of science, though it does not vitiate the tautegorical *gnosis* of myth, seizes upon the genealogical pattern in so many myths and misjudges it, for science overestimates the etiological pretensions in myth. Greek science discovered myth as a human institution, found it out as an intellectual product, a thing, by *attempting* an assault on its immediate gnosis (I use the term to mean, "the knowledge in the telling") and by making myth an imitation (the word here gathers all its Platonic associations) of knowledge. The sophistication of causal models authorizes the proliferation of "mythological," self-consciously secondary narratives.

In *The Symbolism of Evil*, Paul Ricoeur discusses how, in authentic mythic etiologies of evil, the narrative extension of myth mediates "the discordance between the fundamental reality—state of innocence, status of a creature, essential being—and the actual modality of man, as defiled, sinful, guilty. . . . It is a narration precisely because there is no deduction, no logical transition, between the fundamental reality of man and his present existence."[71] In a scientific era, the narratives of existing etiological myths are perceived as means of warding off the causal. Gnosis is banished, but myth itself becomes conceivable, "visible": as Ricoeur has it, "when we lose the myth as immediate logos, we rediscover it as myth."[72] Lucretius constantly encapsulates this history; in Lucretius, causal account regularly gives way to a record of etiological myth, closing with a Latin version of the Miltonic "thus they relate / Erring."[73]

Longus keeps the Lucretian order, but nearly elides the causal account: knowing how echo functions (*prattōmenon*), Daphnis laughs and contrives an etiology. To some degree, all etiology is defensive, an attempt to insert the ratio of human narrative into an alien Nature, and in this sense, Longus's light usurpation of literary priority is attended by an argument for the metaphysical priority of the human. Daphnis may be the first mythologist to give Echo a mortal father, thus emphasizing that the phenomenon to which she gave her name need be accepted neither as a natural condition nor as the simple product of divine fiat, independent of human history. A mythos of human priority *to* landscape again displaces the pastoral ethos of human accord *with* landscape. The tale restrains the daemonic by taking charge of the birth of the daemon.

Of course, the tale does more than circumscribe the daemonic, has more particular aims. When Ricoeur analyzes mythic etiologies of evil he speaks of narrative as mediation between essence and accidence, human ontology and human modality; a lesser etiology, like Daphnis's, also narrates the onset of the modal. Science—Ricoeur uses *history* for Snell's *science*—gives aims to late, literary "myths." In Daphnis's story, the modalities of Echo are discrete and surprising—surprising mainly because Daphnis's tale does not account for what we now take as Echo's chief characteristic, her status as Repeater. The nymphs and Muses teach Echo her imitative skills, but the detail is almost prenarrative, offered as evidence of some preparation for an adulthood which will signify the beginning of her mythological activity, her participation in a narrative event; that is, her mimic voice is one of the givens of the story, essential, not modal, to Echo's nature. Hence, Daphnis describes the voice of her limbs as a persistence: "And they imitate all things now as the maid did before [*kathaper tote*]" (III.23). Though the repetition of the mariners' songs prompts Chloë's request for explanation, Daphnis's tale attends very little to that repetition, a fact that may explain the relative indifference of medieval and early Renaissance mythographers to Daphnis's tale. Three modalities of Echo control the narrative: her eternality, her invisibility, and her ubiquity.

In Longus, as in Ovid, Echo persists between death and life; Daphnis gives her one mortal and one immortal parent. But this genealogy precedes the narrative that is central to Daphnis's etiology, so within the body of that inner narrative he gives a second explanation for the persistence of Echo's voice: the Muses themselves provide that her limbs may continue to sing as before. They ordain that her voice, indeed her identity, will survive her corporeal integrity. She endures, then, because of the continued protection of the Muses, her tutors in music; her other tutors, the nymphs (Meliae, Dryades, and Heleae), intervene on behalf of her invisibility. Whereas Ovid's Echo goes through a complicated psychogenetic self-consumption, in Longus, Echo's limbs are simply concealed by Ghea, at the instigation of the nymphs (*kharizomenē numphais ekrupse*). Finally, unlike Ovid, Longus takes pains to account for Echo's ubiquity, by making Echo a *sparagmos* on the Orphic model. As a result of Echo's scattered voice, Pan is said to be confounded, searching not so much to capture as to know (*mathein*) his imitator.

All three modalities of Echo seem to derive from a hostility between Pan, on the one hand, and the nymphs and Muses, on the other, a hostility that splits the patrons of rural song into rival groups.[74] Echo is under the patronage of the female group, educated as if she were a votaress of a cult, and bound, it seems, to a law of virginity.[75] Pan contrives an overwhelming violation of that virginity, an assault on her wholeness itself; the nymphs and Muses band together and in female accord with Ghea, conceal the shame of their now mutilated novice. They provide for her persistent song, and that persistence seems contrived particularly as a challenge to Pan. No longer accessible to physical taint, to any kind of corruption, Echo continues to sing in such a way that Pan's desire to seize the singer is replaced by a desire to know her identity; no longer mortal, she will arouse and confound that desire forever.

This recapitulation of the story in terms of its aims should serve to reveal its tautegorical function, for the rivalry of Pan and the divinities of female voice manifests an implicit rivalry taking place between gnois and knowledge, between myth and science; it is a competition for the allegiance of such uninitiates as Chloë. We have observed that Pan's desire for carnal knowledge is replaced by a desire for a less physical knowledge, and the verb *mathein* suggests the scientific character of the knowledge sought. Yet perhaps we should say that, in the tale, physical desire is not *replaced by* scientific zeal, that it is rather *revealed as* a scientific passion. Pan's only success is the distribution of Echo's limbs, and it seems fair to say that his achievement is fundamentally scientific, an analytic revenge. This analysis assaults a feminine chastity that Daphnis describes as historically original, sanctioned and defended by the divinely original Ghea. Though the female group defends itself against the loss of its primal integrity of consciousness, that immediacy and integrity of mind cannot be preserved. At best, its loss can be hidden; its *disiecta membra* can only be covered, rendered immortal, and finally, made inaccessible to further scientific interference.

It is an almost perfect story. Daphnis decides to tell a tale rather than to give an explanation, and his decision, cast as an homage to Chloë's virgin naivete, mimes the female defenses within the story; in the context of a string of initiations, the choice of etiology over explanation is exquisitely decorous. The tale cannot be a myth, can only recall mythology; the diversity of tales and the enduring possibility of fiction is all that remains of mythic gnosis, or so this tale would suggest. Yet after the telling, the tale is confirmed, "for Echo said almost the same, as if to bear witness that he did not lie" (III.23), that is, as if mythic gnosis were indeed recoverable in etiologies imitative of prescientific myth.

I can now suggest why repetition is not one of the modalities of this tale. I have already remarked on Echo's ties to Fama, her function as a figure for the nodes along a continuum of literary history; these associations depend on the very iterative habits that so violate the historical utterances she repeats. In Daphnis's tale, Echo is the site, not the source of violence. Her impotence gives evidence of Longus's shrewd discovery that late mythology, in the age of science and history, had lost its power: as fiction, the echoic imitations that produce this new mythology could divert, but had lost the power to charm. Recounting a myth differs radically from echoing, for each telling of a true myth preserves an original efficacy, performs an original function, while we have seen that Echo's speech marks—indeed, specifies—the loss of original force.[76] Echo, in Callimachus, exposes the diversity of the experiences that can authorize identical utterances; she marks time and mutability. We recall Demats's observation that the first speaker of myth disappears, that the verbs for myth-making are "toujours au passif," another way of saying that, unlike echoing, mythical telling has no psychological motive. In *Daphnis and Chloë*, Echo becomes the afterlife of myth; if her history does not treat of echoing itself, it is because the history, as history, is an echoing—a repetition of mythic *form*, though faint, and with changed timbre.

2

VERBIS FAVET IPSA SUIS: THE REFLEX OF EPIC IN OVID'S METAMORPHOSES

> The story runs that Echo answered this Memnon when it spoke, uttering a mournful note in response to its mournful lament and returning a mimicking sound in response to its expressions of joy.
>
> Callistratus, "On the Statue of Memnon"[1]

Daphnis's tale, so sophisticated an inquiry into the nostalgia of fiction for myth, is nonetheless a rather flat narrative—if not exactly a crude one—and its meaning depends nearly as much on its contexts (Daphnis's sexual initiation, his modern epistemology) as on the text itself. In this respect, it differs considerably from the other, far more influential etiology of Echo, the version on which this chapter focuses. Ovid's version succeeds by severing its ties to mythic form entirely; its subsequent appeal lies in its stylistic bravura and psychological nuance.

Pausanias records a tale of uncertain ancestry in which the beautiful boy, Narcissus, falls in love with his sister; when she dies, he seeks her semblance in a reflecting pool, knowing full well that he sees merely his own image.[2] Unlike that story, of course, Ovid's tale of Echo and Narcissus is a tale of delusion, yet it does share the fascination with the symmetrical that organizes Pausanias's wistful story. Indeed, Ovid intensifies the play of symmetries, for at the center of that episode, dialogue balances the desires of an Echo afflicted with acoustic reflection against the desire of a Narcissus afflicted with visual reflection. This balancing center challenges the tradition that gives the entire episode over to Narcissus (Boccaccio heads his redaction "De Narcisso filio Cephisi"; an English translation of the episode, one of the first English epyllia, is entitled *The Fable of Ovid treting of Narcissus*), for at the core of the episode, Narcissus' fate is in dialogue with Echo's.[3]

Such balance is frequently enacted within the very structure of the line. I shall have more to say about the implications of Ovidian rhetoric and prosody, but here it will be sufficient to remark the play of antitheses in lines like these which describe the effects of Narcissus' beauty; if Ovid ever arraigns Narcissus he does so thus:

>   poteratque puer iuvenisque videri:
> multi illum iuvenes, multae cupiere puellae;
> sed fuit in tenera tam dura superbia forma. . . .   [III.352–54]

[And he might seem either boy or man. Many youths and many maidens sought his love; but in that slender form was pride so hard. . . .]

33

All the resources of the antithetical style are here arrayed. The poised calibration of the first line and the more expansive seesaw of the next prepare for the cantilevering of the third, where *expectation* leads us to enforce what would otherwise be perceived as a precarious semantic and rhythmic balance on "in tenera tam dura superbia forma." The play of *tenera* against *dura* pits *superbia* against *forma* as it insists on their phenomenal comparability. In many respects, the line has impressive lucidity of form: word placement establishes the relationship of container to contained; the prosody possesses extreme regularity and symmetry (*DDSDDS*); and the caesura, the firmly emphatic postcaesural stress, and the diaeresis at the end of the fifth foot provide rhythmic guides to syntactic construction. The schemata of composition wield an unusual sovereignty over the semantics of this line as they force the abstraction of *superbia* to succumb to tropic dwelling in the materiality of *forma*. That it has succumbed is clear from the next line—"nulli illum iuvenes, nullae tetigere puellae" ([pride so hard] that neither youth nor maiden touched him)—which transforms abstract appetite into more particular lusts, even as it extends the antithetical scheme.

The issue of *superbia* will be crucial to my discussion, for it points to vestiges of tragedy that linger within Ovid's tale. Tragedy is not, however, the only genre to have left its traces on the episode. At precisely the moment at which Narcissan behavior alludes to the *hybris* of tragedy, the lines enact a countervailing allusion, for Ovid's lines imitate lines from Catullus's second epithalamium:

> multi illum pueri, multae optavere puellae
> idem cum tenui carptus defloruit ungui
> nulli illum pueri, nullae optavere puelles.   [*Carmina*, LXII.42–44]
>
> [many boys and many girls desire it; when the same flower fades, nipped by a sharp nail, nor boys, nor girls desire it.]

This is one of Catullus's two dialogic poems; here the maiden chorus defends virginity by praising the untouched flower in lines that probably hark further back to an epithalamium by Sappho.[4] The argument of Catullus's maidens is doomed, of course. Every strophe of their defense ends with a refrain encouraging the approach of Hymen, so their claims to vulnerability are wry and perhaps even a bit coy, though the fact of their vulnerability is not, I think, entirely deprived of its weight. At any rate, whatever complexities of tone accumulate around their defense, the metaphoric tenor here remains untouched: the flower has a nearly ideal purity, both sexual and semantic, its fear of the *tenui carptus ungui* providing a standard of shrinking withdrawal to which the maidens may or may not care to attain. Ovid's tale of Narcissus is an anti-epithalamium, for it resolves ambivalent human sexuality by restoring that original, floral sexlessness. This larger diachronic pattern—the second, or Ovid's half, of which is both a restitution and a degradation (the characteristic procedures of Ovid's response to prior literary culture as a whole)—shows us balance and symmetry, the schematic manner expanding from its original place within the verse line into the larger field of cultural history.

These, then, are my themes: balance, generic revision, the erotic and its discontents, restitution and response. My thesis is simple—that, like Longus's, Ovid's Echo voices the persistence of a past made marginal. In Ovid we find the first important historical example of that Echo who will be central to these essays, an Echo whose suffering has a mildly, cannily antiauthoritarian bias. Her *vocula* will murmur against a variety of repressive forces—chastity, discretion, science, vanity, the courts of Elizabeth and James. And perhaps *against* puts it too strongly, for the voice of Echo can bespeak conversion as well as adversion; indeed, Echo has this broad range of tones within the Ovidian episode itself.

A methodological caveat: when, in the fifth or sixth century, the pseudo-Lactantius made his prose summary of the *Metamorphoses*, the so-called *Narrationes*, he disentangled the tales from their various tellers and occasions, numbered them, and made them into units. Lactantius shattered the intellectual harmonics of Ovid's epic, but in so doing he demonstrated the internal sturdiness of its narrative constituents. In his hands, the *Metamorphoses* achieved the form—or rather, the formlessness—in which it would persist, becoming a collection of wonderful tales, an anthology. Lactantius's project is nearly invisible now, and his book seems mere superfluous clutter, more prose crowding the pages of annotated editions of Ovid. Yet the apparent redundancy of his book indicates his own overwhelming influence. By making the *Metamorphoses* into an anthology, he makes a study of Echo possible, even as he made Ovid more popular, more accessible, and perhaps, more useful than that poet's great model and rival, Virgil—more useful because he opened the *Metamorphoses* to a particularity of exegesis which would finally provide the model for nearly all postclassical analyses of secular literature.

Yet the Lactantian dissolution of the *Metamorphoses* has had concomitant ill effects, for it makes the temptation to read Ovid's tales and not Ovid's epic very strong. I have hardly been immune to that temptation. The reading of the tale of Echo and Narcissus to which this essay tends is no doubt sustained by the dislocation of narrative initiated by Lactantius, yet I aim to honor the balance (in Ovid's poem, not in Lactantius's encyclopedia) between the isolation of the tale and its densely contextual status. By its contextual status, I mean its place within that larger narrative unit which I shall call the *Cadmeans*, within the poem as a whole, and even within the epic tradition that Ovid cunningly reshapes as his cultural environs. Ovid called his poem a *carmen perpetuum* despite its almost intransigently episodic constituents; a critic as sensitive to formal concerns as Quintilian would remark an abstract compulsion in Ovid's art, a "necessitas . . . res diversimae in speciem unius colligentem."[5] This compulsion to weld together diverse subjects into a continuous whole may well be the primary motive of Ovidian art, and I intend to respect it. If there are privileged moments in the poem—the tale of Echo and Narcissus is certainly one—that privilege is always restrained, attenuated to participate in larger unities. At its fullest, the tale of Echo and Narcissus is an erotic allegory of tensions at work in the poem as a whole, tensions between the mute introversions of narrative episode and the passionate glossolalia of *perpetuitas*. Before turning to this tale, those formal tensions, the tensions in what I propose to call the poem's *taxis*, demand somewhat more careful treatment.

PERPETUITAS

A distinguished line of Ovid scholars—Fränkel, Otis, Galinsky, and Williams—have devoted major portions of their studies in Ovid's epic to articulations of its taxis.[6] Dryden earlier initiated such a critical approach, and in perhaps a more radical manner, by commenting on how perpetuitas emerges even at the level of prosody—"minding only smoothness, he wants both variety and majesty." Certainly, by avoiding the acceptable, but inhibiting, spondee, Ovid ensures dactylic velocity and abjures weight.[7] Yet in order to make sense of Dryden's observation, we must assume an extremely narrow definition of *variety*. It will have to mean something like a constantly shifting relation of speech stress to metrical ictus and a tense relation of syntax to such formal patterns as line ending and caesural placement—in short, the variety Dryden misses in Ovid will have to refer to the prosodic characteristics of the *Aeneid*. We are forced to assume so restricted a definition because of the manifest rhetorical variety of Ovidian verse; although Ovid's caesurae and line endings regularly *punctuate*, and although spoken Latin will scan his verse, this unstrained prosody is, after all, most variously decorated. A poem of patina, rather than of texture, the *Metamorphoses* cuts itself off from that oral tradition in which the impact of aural density and complexity sustains a sense of the immediacy, the insistent present of epic performance.[8]

The poised amplitude of Ovid's verse, its apparently effortless extension has suggested a trivial superficiality to even his best critics, so that at their hands he becomes an amorous fancy's child, oblivious to the ethos—we might call it the "spondaic ethos"—of the Virgilian "norm." In the *Aeneid*, the spondee has thematic and ideological force, the resistant progress of the verse being in accord with the resistant progress of the hero: like the story of Spenser's Red Crosse Knight, Aeneas's biography begins in the furrow of the *versus*. Of course, Ovid's epic has no biographical core: the transparence of the line is coordinated not only with the disappearance of the hero, but with a near dissolution of subjectivity which is the poem's favored topic. If the theme of *formas mutatas* is superficial, it is not necessarily trivial, and it reveals the astonishing psychological and technical achievement of setting aside the Virgilian ethos. Prosodic modesty provides a foil for rhetorical and narrative virtuosity.

Virgil's enjambed lines reappear as Ovid's enjambed books. The tragedy of Phaethon spans the first and second books; the tale of Achelous, the eighth and ninth; the competition for Achilles' arms, the twelfth and thirteenth. Consider the first enjambed tale. Impressive as it is, it has proven a slight critical stumbling block, for Phaethon undergoes no metamorphosis whatsoever:

Naides Hesperiae trifida fumantia flamma
corpora dant tumulo, signant quoque carmine saxum:

> HIC SITVS EST PHAETHON CVRRVS AVRIGA PATERNI
> QVEM SI NON TENVIT MAGNIS TAMEN EXCIDIT AVSIS
>
> [Met., II.325–28]
>
> [Naiads in that western land consign his body, still smoking with the flames of that forked bolt, to the tomb and carve this epitaph upon his stone: HERE PHAETHON LIES: IN PHOEBUS' CAR HE FARED, AND THOUGH HE GREATLY FAILED, MORE GREATLY DARED.]

Not a natural death, perhaps, but a natural burial (which is itself exceptional in this poem): the inscription, usurping upon the narrator's voice, marks the interruption of the narrator's thematic program ("In nova fert animus mutatas dicere formas / corpora," I intend to speak of forms changed into new bodies; Met., I.1–2). A few lines later, Phaethon's mourning sisters become poplars and his friend, Cycnus, becomes a swan, but to insist upon these as guarantees of a perpetuitas within the narrative program is to impose a new *mutata forma* on the tale of Phaethon, to make this very long tale into a mere pretext. Ovid included several nonmetamorphic tales (e.g., Pentheus, Perseus, Proserpina, Medea, Cephalus and Procris, Meleager), not all of them so easily converted into pretexts for thematic perpetuitas. But we must feel the violence even of this conversion: Phaethon's epitaph, by providing one of the few moments of real narrative arrest in the early part of the epic, cuts the story proper off from the ensuing metamorphoses, so that its own nonmetamorphic character remains emphatic. The tale is included, it seems, for the very purpose of interrupting the thematic program, interrupting it before, and *just* before, even the first book of the epic is concluded. The thematic interruption serves a correlative formal purpose, its boldly articulated conclusion emphasizing the incongruity of formal hiatus (the end of the book) and narrative boundary.[9]

After this blithe violation of the metamorphic theme, Ovid takes up the tale of Callisto, reminiscent of the tales of divine rape that had preceded the Phaethon episode—Apollo and Daphne, Jove and Io, and (embedded in the latter) Pan and Syrinx.[10] The turn to Callisto is a return to thematic unity: the language of enamorment-as-inflammation ("acceptis caluere sub ossibus ignes"; and felt the fire burn within his limbs; II.410) recalls the rhetoric of both the Apollo-Daphne episode and the catastrophe of the Phaethon tale. The Phaethon tale is now framed, marked as intrusive; an earlier order is reestablished. The pattern of recollection receives further emphasis when Callisto is transformed:

> oblita quid esset,
> ursaque conspectos in montibus horruit ursos
> pertimuitque lupos, quamvis pater esset in illis. [II.493–95]

[forgetting what she was; and though herself a bear, shuddered at sight of other bears which she saw on the mountain-slopes. She even feared the wolves, although her own father, Lycaon, ran with the pack.]

The reference to Lycaon reaches back to the beginning of the human drama of book I, well before that grandest movement of the first book, the account of the

Flood. The firm recovery of the metamorphic theme also proffers a new rigor of narrative organization:

> pertimuitque lupos, quamvis pater esset in illis.
>   Ecce Lycaoniae proles ignara parentis,
>   Arcas adest ter quinque fere natalibus actis [II.495–97]
>
> [She even feared the wolves, although her own father, Lycaon, ran with the pack. And now Arcas, Lycaon's grandson, had reached his fifteenth year, ignorant of his mother's plight.]

Here for the first time in the poem a genealogical pattern offers itself, a human version of the Hesiodic epic structure. Yet we are only being teased with such stable "referentiality" of structure, for Saturnia's flight after wreaking vengeance on Callisto provides the most tenuous thread of continuity. Saturn is borne by peacocks, whose feathers were decked with eyes at the same time that the raven turned black. A relatively loose-limbed sort of chronological articulation takes over for genealogy, but only to degenerate further into a tangle of avian metamorphoses in which the tales of Corvus, Cornix, and Nictymene lace through the tale of Coronis. Secure in our return to tales of the loves of Apollo, we are made insecure by the winding narrative pattern (Ovid's syntax is, moreover, uncharacteristically tortured in this passage). Indeed, the avian tales mask the fact that Coronis, like Phaethon, is slain, not transformed.[11]

This poem, so devoted to shapes, is thus anything but shapely. The crux of the writhing sequence just examined is the manifest diversity of its taxis, a diversity extreme even for the *Metamorphoses*. This diversity alerts the reader to the manifold strains to be suffered by perpetuitas in the ensuing books: the Phaethon narrative provides a limiting case for violations of thematic unity, the Callisto tale both indicates the limit of redundancy in the poem (it is, in effect, a composite of Apollo-Daphne and Jove-Io, as other tales will be) and measures the (also limited) usefulness of genealogy as an instrument of continuity, while the confused Coronis sequence acts as an emblem of the way in which rivalry among tales can obstruct the very continuity of any single tale. By such manifold disjunctions, all our apprehensions of form are made to appear willful acts.

If these are the wages of disjunction, the wages of continuity are similar, and we can test those effects by beginning with the death of Coronis. Issuing in still another offer of the genealogical, her death yields the birth of Aesculapius, itself something of a laboratory of literary genetics. The infant, deprived of parental nurture, is entrusted to the care of the centaur, *geminus Chiron*—*geminus* because his form is the emblem of the metamorphic, being perpetually arrested between the human and the bestial. Aesculapius is to be reared on a wisdom so serious that it seems almost out of place within this poem, but then he is not just any child: *divinae stirpis alumnus* (II.633), he is clearly also *Virgiliani alumnus*. Chiron's prophetic daughter, Ocyrhoë, easily recognizes the esteemed lineage of her father's protégé:

adspicit infantem "toto" que "salutifer orbi
cresce, puer!" dixit; "tibi se mortalia saepe
corpora debebunt, animas tibi reddere ademptas
fas erit." [II.642–45]

[she looked upon the child and cried: "O child, speed thy growth as health-bringer to the whole world. Often shall mortal bodies owe their lives to thee, and to thee shall it be counted right to restore the spirits of the departed."]

Reincarnation of the Virgilian *parvus puer*, the young Aesculapius enters this poem bringing the largest continuities in his train. Not only will this child preserve the vitality of other souls, he will also ensure a phoenix-like tradition in prophetic poetry. Moreover, his own fate at first provides a model for cultural history, the temporal career of human artifacts:

"eque deo corpus fies exsangue deusque,
qui modo corpus eras, et bis tua fata novabis." [II.647–48]

["So, from a god shalt thou become but a lifeless corpse; but from this corpse shalt thou again become a god and twice renew thy fates."]

The memory incarnated in Aesculapius proves resilient, for he reappears as a shade in the last book of the *Metamorphoses*, still capable of healing Hippolytus; he returns to substantiate that Pythagorean doctrine expounded in the famous passage that precedes his return. Even mortality does not constrain the power of this parvus puer, whose maturation is coincident with and masked by, but also implicit in, the intervening books of the poem. The continuity of prophetic poetry and the continuity of this poem become his property: the Pythagorean return of the dead reverses the progress toward stasis we expect from the poem, finally relieving the poem's disjunctions and healing its *corpus lacerum* (XV.532).

G. Karl Galinsky, in his own discussion of Ovidian perpetuitas, takes the Pythagorean episode as Ovid's "foil to his own *Metamorphoses*."[12] Pointing to the many reminiscences of the Phaethon story in Pythagoras's catalog of metamorphoses, Galinsky suggests that his speech is presented to show, by contrast, how very prosaic absolute unity of theme can be. The suggestion is extremely valuable, though the poem hardly creates any *pressure* for this sort of apologetics; the value of Galinsky's observation is that it helps us see an element of blithe play even in the Pythagorean reevaluation of the metamorphic theme. The play suggests that Ovidian reevaluation, no matter how philosophical, can never have a fully transcendental force. For the Pythagorean treatise on the (metamorphic) sublime is a formal *peri bathous*, and this will also be true of that final essay on political sublimity, the apotheosis of Caesar. In fact, the fifteenth book is filled with brilliant overinflations. Even the westering of Aesculapius, the metamorphosed parvus puer now further transformed into a divine serpent, repeats the great accounts of Aeneas's wanderings, both Virgil's and Ovid's own account, so that the mighty Virgilian allegory that unites heroic biography and literary genetics becomes a grand redundancy.

The diction of the invocation that precedes the westering episode, the poem's sole invocation to the Muses, tells us enough of Ovid's intent: "Pandite nunc, Musae" (XV.622). *Pandite* calls not so much for the sublimity of song as for the expansiveness of catalog. Catalog has a privileged place in epic, of course, but that place is, properly, in the middle. Pythagoras's directory of metamorphoses together with the gazetteer implicit in Ovid's account of the Aesculapian journey seem witlessly inclusive—it is a climax of Ovidian wit—and that garrulous inclusiveness spills over to mar the final apotheosis.

Pythagoras's speech is the first stage of an argument for the immortality conferred by writing, an argument that shapes the entire fifteenth book of the *Metamorphoses* and that will conclude with the poet's final word: "Siquid habent veri vatum praesagia, vivam" (If the predictions of prophets have any truth, I shall live; XV.879). The discourse on metempsychosis is a dead man's utterance, as much a conquest of death as that apotheosis which closes the book. The perpetuation of the Virgilian child as *deus opifer* is a similar conquest, but when "in serpente deus praenuntia sibila misit" (the god, in serpent form, gave forth a hiss; XV.670), the sibylline becomes sibilant.

Critics like Galinsky have tried to map the Ovidian misrepresentation of Virgil with considerable but not complete success; Galinsky himself certainly provides the most useful cautionary advice—"To construe Ovid's intentions as a deflation or 'undercutting' of Vergil's epic is both unduly narrow and misleading."[13] Ovid intends a literary history modeled formally on the carmen perpetuum, and this intention controls his relation to Virgil. In the *Aeneid*, the stages of the narrative envy each other—Troy, Carthage, and Italy are locked together in mutual jealousies; the tales of Ovid's epic usually repose in more affable taxis, and there is a gay fortuitousness in the transformation of text into pretext. If the *Aeneid* is to the *Metamorphoses* as the tragedy of Phaethon is to the tale of Callisto, or as nearly any tale of Ovid's poem is to the next, the first poem hardly suffers any violence from the second.

In this casual perpetuitas we may recognize the compensatory workings of a poet who felt cut off—first by his own youth, then by the deaths of his models, and finally by actual exile—from the civilized community of great poets.[14] From his first literary effort to his last, Ovid undertakes a leisurely program of accumulation, its programmatic character consistently belying the leisureliness. Note the form of his titles: with only one exception, they are plural nouns. Ovid attempts to gather up all possible amorous situations, to bring all possible fictions into narrative adjacency, so that his texts themselves may represent the ideal coherence of literate culture. This impulse to total inclusion masters the individual discontinuities of the *Metamorphoses*: Ovid leaves his tales manifestly disordered in order to prove the absolute resilience of literary form and in order to render radical deformation an apparent impossibility. Genealogical structure would seem to be under such frequent attack for two reasons. First, genealogy is regularly challenged in order to prepare for the final replacement of genealogical descent by metempsychotic continuity—a displacement of biological lineage which may well be part of the implicit critique of Augustus, who had threatened the Republican ideal of an aristocracy of the (aristocratic) virtuous with a restoration of dynastic government. Second (and probably more important), genealogy comes under fire for its extraliterary origins, which challenge the autonomy and comprehensiveness of literary taxis. Genealogy is a natural usurpation of the poet's own control over continuities. It is connectedness that Ovid wants, that arouses his urbane, but hardly dainty appetite. Hence when he takes up Echo to figure literary allusiveness, he will represent her as a wanton and a babbler.

THE OEDIPAL EYE IN THE CADMEANS

Yet Ovid does avail himself of genealogy, of Hesiodic construction, on several occasions, and not merely out of some prudential adherence to the prescription of his opening lines.[15] Ovid introduces genealogical taxis as a reaction formation against such liminal anxieties as threaten when narrative units draw to an end.[16] (It will soon be clear that Echo takes over these functions of genealogy.) Thus at the close of book II:

> pavet haec litusque ablata relictum
> respicit et dextra cornum tenet, altera dorso
> inposita est; tremulae sinuantur flamine vestes.   [II.873–75]

[She trembles with fear and looks back at the receding shore, holding fast a horn with one hand and resting the other on the creature's back. And her fluttering garments stream behind her in the wind.]

Europa's fears attend upon the end of a book, the end of the first of the four thematic units into which Brooks Otis attempts to divide the poem. It is the end of the land as well; she and the narrative are left at sea.[17] The next lines of the poem register not only wider dislocations but also the narrator's effort to restore stable continuity in the face of those dislocations:

> Iamque deus posita fallacis imagine tauri
> se confessus erat Dictaeaque rura tenebat,
> cum pater ignarus Cadmo perquirere raptam
> imperat et poenam, si non invenerit, addit
> exilium, facto pius et sceleratus eodem.
> orbe pererrato (quis enim deprendere possit
> furta Iovis?) profugus patriamque iramque parentis
> vitat Agenorides.   [III.1–8]

[And now the god, having put off the disguise of the bull, owned himself for what he was, and reached the fields of Crete. But the maiden's father, ignorant of what has happened, bids his son, Cadmus, go and search for the lost girl, and threatens exile as a punishment if he does not find her—pious and guilty by the same act. After roaming over all the world in vain (for who could search out the secret loves of Jove) Agenor's son becomes an exile shunning his father's country and his father's wrath.]

Europa, like the second book, is lost, and Cadmus thus becomes the historical type and literary antitype of both Aeneas and Ovid, going into exile on behalf of home and homeland; by this exile Ovid asserts a literary filiation that is nonetheless powerless to restore narrative location. The thin narrative enjambment here recalls that earlier transgression of the shore which completed mankind's fall from the Golden, Silver, and Brazen ages—when "men knew no shores except their own" "nullaque mortales praeter sua litora norant"; I.96):

> quaeque prius steterant in montibus altis,
> fluctibus ignotis exsultavere carinae
> communemque prius ceu lumina solis et auras
> cautus humum longo signavit limite mensor. [I.133–36]
>
> [And keels of pine which long had stood upon high mountain-sides, now leaped insolently over unknown waves. And the ground, which had hitherto been a common possession like the sunlight and the air, the careful surveyor now marked out with long-drawn boundary line.]

Like Blake's Ulro, the world of this new age is ensnared in a dialectic of boundary and transgression. This dialectic is also a *narrative* condition within the Age of Iron: Cadmus shares the quest for reunion with Ovid (for which he earns the double epithet "pius et sceleratus"). But Ovid and Cadmus are both cut off, left to their own devices. The next movement of the poem will wrestle, not with divine identity—for "deus . . . se confessus erat" (III.1–2)—but with Cadmean identity, that paradoxical coincidence of pious filiation and heinous discontinuity that establishes a rival filiation: banished from his father's house, Cadmus enters the lines of Odysseus and of Aeneas.

Thus the *Cadmeans,* an open-ended thesis informing books III and IV: its length is indeterminate precisely because it unfolds a variety of overlapping organizing plots.[18] The stories that follow the tale of Cadmus waver between several principles of organization. The *Cadmeans* continues to assert itself well into book IV when, after hearing of his unfortunate progeny, we are told of Cadmus's metamorphosis into a serpent (making for an ouroboric construction); the serpent reappears frequently in books III and IV, organizing this section of the poem by leitmotif; associated with the Cadmeans is a more generalized integrative principle which yields a *Thebaiad*; and, as we shall see, there is an even more general thematic taxis, closely bound up with the tales of Theban locale, a unity among tales which treat of verifications of the fabulous. Ovid counterpoints the taxic devices themselves in this sequence—hence, I shall use the term *Cadmeans* as a convenience, making circumscribed claims for its adequacy as a definition.[19]

The Cadmean matter has its most potent source, of course, in Sophocles' Theban plays. Thus when Ovid abruptly turns from Cadmean genealogy to consider the story of Teiresias, the tale of Oedipus appears on the horizon of our expectations. The story of Oedipus was, after all, the preeminent episode in the matter of Thebes, preeminent in a body of narratives whose central theme was recurrence.[20] So the turn to Teiresias seems only a brief departure from biological, local, or historical sequence. Yet if we expect a return from the tale of Teiresias to that of Cadmean Oedipus, this expectation is promptly thwarted. Narcissus occludes Oedipus.

Cadmean transgression is frequently informed by a visual motif—obviously so in the tales of Pentheus, Semele, Actaeon, and Narcissus, obtrusively so in the tale of Teiresias, the blinded seer. Late in the Cadmean sequence, Ovid will turn the narrative over to the Minyeides, archetypal storytellers who tell tales to alleviate the patient boredom of artisanry. Yet they have turned to their looms and to their tales out of skepticism, denying the *factum mirabile* of the new god, Bacchus, and withdrawing from the Bacchic festivity that enthralls the other women of Thebes. And Ovid attends to the visual origins of skepticism as he articulates the god's revenge, a sadistic version of cure: the Minyeides become bats—"lucemque perosae / nocte volant seroque tenent a vespere nomen" (and hating the light of day, they flit by night and from late eventide derive their name; ll. 414–15). Their offending skepticism is over.

Thus, the tales of the *Cadmeans* seem to return us to Ovidian autobiography, for like a Cadmean hero, Ovid blames his eyes:

> cur aliquid vidi? cur noxia lumina feci?
>   cur imprudenti cognita culpa mihi?
> inscius Actaeon vidit sine veste Dianam:
>   praeda fuit canibus non minus ille suis.   [*Tristia*, II.103–06]
>
> [Why did I see anything? Why did I make my eyes guilty? Why was I so thoughtless as to harbour the knowledge of a fault? Unwitting was Actaeon when he beheld Diana unclothed; none the less he became the prey of his own hounds.]

Guilt is linked to sight, not to will, in the Cadmean tragedies, be they Ovidian or Sophoclean.

An account of the substitution of Narcissus for Oedipus can begin here with the observation that the visual axis of transgression is intensified in both their tales. Just as Cadmus's crime is converted, or distilled, to its visual component, so Oedipus implicitly reinterprets incest and parricide by blinding himself; as if the offending organ were the eye, he

> struck into the ball-joints of his eyes [*kukloi*].
> He shouted that they would no longer see
> the evils he had suffered or had done,
> see in the dark those he should not have seen.   [*Oedipus the King*, 1270–73][21]

To point to the instrument of punishment, Jocasta's brooches, is to acknowledge the confluence of transgressive categories here: the several crimes *recapitulated* in this punishment are uncovering nakedness, acting without ritual circumspection ("blindly"), and spilling "one's own" blood; but the single crime *arrested* in this punishment is, simply, seeing.

The central scopophilia associated with this punishment is displaced by the recapitulated crimes which lie so much closer to the narrative surface. The displacement befits the mystery, the problems of identification, that dogs all aspects of the Oedipus story. It is frequently pointed out that the way Oedipus recognizes himself in the narratives of the other characters has been anticipated by his generalized self-recognition in the narrative of the Sphinx's riddle (the solution to the riddle is myself, a man); we might fairly say that the action of the *Tyrannos* is an ironic pursuit of the Delphic injunction, *gnothi sauton*. Self-recognition enables Oedipus to complete his crime (by solving the riddle he gains access to Jocasta's bedchamber), and the later, more particular recognitions—that the stories he hears are his biography—drive him to self-punishment. So the involution of the king's biography is imitated in the dynamics of the play's plot: the multiplicity of characters in that series of narratives presented to the king is dissolved, the variables of person falling into equations, until the variables are determinate and the agents of the action are restricted to the dramatis personae.

This biographical involution is abjured in Ovid's tale of Narcissus, but the Delphic presence persists in Teiresias' prophecy:

> de quo consultus, an esset
> tempora maturae visurus longa senectae
> fatidicus vates "si se non noverit" inquit. [III.346–48]

[When asked whether this child [i.e., Narcissus] would live to reach well-ripened age, the seer replied: "If he ne'er know himself."]

Admittedly, the prophecy affects the action in no way whatsoever. In fact, Ovid manages his tale nearly without the continuity of causality; Teiresias' prophecy, once solicited, rests static in mere adjacency to the rest of the plot, even though Narcissus' history is intended as a *temptamen* (l. 341), a proof of Teiresian skill. "Exitus illam / resque probat letique genus novitasque furoris" (But what befell proved its truth—the event, the manner of his death, the strangeness of his infatuation; III.349–50): even as the line argues for ensuing logic, the rhythm and syntax disperse the argument. The tale of Echo follows, capturing attention and alienating all expectation of "temptamina"; the plot preserves no memory of Teiresias' words.

The principle of forgetful adjacency is nearly constant throughout the tale, and the continuities of causality are left diffuse: the event may be the harsh work of Rhamnusia (406), the passive work of prophecy, or even the result of Narcissus' own later prayer, "o utinam a nostro secedere corpore possem! / votum in amante novum, vellem, quod amamus, abesset" (Oh, that I might be parted from my own body! and, strange prayer for a lover, I would that what I love were absent from me; III.467–68). Only the first of these causes would seem to indicate Narcissan criminality, and that criminality has none of the obsessive power over the tale that Oedipus's had. The cognitive density of Oedipus's dramatic present points backward to the phenomenal complexity of his past; Narcissus' textual present points only to itself, to the workings of his own experience. His death is telling— "croceum *pro* corpore florem / inveniunt foliis medium cingentibus albis" (in place of his body they find a flower, its yellow center girt with white petals;

III.509–10; emphasis mine)—for it issues in a substitution instead of the continuities of metamorphosis.

This may explain why Ovid does his most conspicuously uncomplicated imitative writing in the account of Narcissus' enamorment and death. A structure of thorough self-absorption, the narrative mirrors the antisocial self-regard of the youth. The suppression of narrative causality accompanies a devaluation of the judicial motive in the tale it occludes; the sources of Narcissan destiny remain unrelated and so thwart jurisprudence. To put it most simply—Narcissus is not quite *guilty* of narcissism, for the category of criminality is nearly impertinent to his suffering, and the guilt won't stick (we may mark the contrast with Oedipus, whose criminal agency is made to overshadow the *cause*, which is Fate); his fault, *superbia*, is a rupture, a denial that one has any relation to society or to the social concept of criminality. This superbia is distinct from Oedipal hybris, which (though it transcends the social order) is perpetually embedded in a defining theological order. Like that of Virgil, the Sophoclean ethos is also abjured.

THE SCHEMATIC VOICE

We can return now to that balanced arraignment, "sed fuit in tenera tam dura superbia forma," in which abstracted pride succumbs to the incarnation of forma. The impositions that rhetorical form effects in these poised lines can be found throughout the tale of Echo and Narcissus. Indeed, the tale itself, taken as a substitution for Sophocles' story of Oedipus, seems a similar imposition: its Narcissistic attention to a private and present suffering replaces the Oedipal probings of a social and past criminality; its emphasis on patterned juxtaposition replaces Oedipal causal involution; its superficiality replaces Oedipal (or Sophoclean) interiority. The schematism of Ovid's slight arraignment, the closure of the central setting, the motif of reflection—all these divert tragic seriousness to the rhetorical elegance of Ovidian surface. Balance is everywhere, and all.

John Brenkman has produced a valuable study of the episode in which he notices a decided centripetal drive in the narrative.[22] Consider the structure of the episode: the account of Narcissus' youth is followed by the story of how Echo lost her capacity to initiate discourse, and this sequence issues on the central tale of Echo's enamorment and Narcissus' rebuke. This central tale, really a transcription of their dialogue, is in turn followed by Echo's second transformation—the loss of her body—and finally by the story of Narcissus' own enamorment. This is chiasmus writ large, another manifestation of the schematic motives in the tale.[23]

Narcissan chiasmus often seems pointless, like the campaign of the Brave Old Duke of York Who Had Ten Thousand Men. Even the ornamental constriction of the *foliis medium cingentibus albis* makes peripety seem inconsequential: the antithetical forces of *cinctus*, a defensive fortification and an aggressive siege, make this blossom seem no consummation at all, a struggle to no end. Aimless cycle most obtrudes at the point when delusion gives way to anagnorisis, the event which, in the tragic form that stands behind the *Cadmeans*, would lead to fully conscious guilt and punishment. Teiresias' prophecy has taken hold, Narcissus has seen his image—"'et placet et video; sed quod videoque placetque, / non tamen invenio'" ("I am charmed and I see; but what I see and what charms me I cannot find"; ll. 446–47)—and chiasmus has established itself in insistent imitation of the visual reflection that has entrapped him. The image continues incapable of finally collapsing *iste* into *ego*: "'hic, qui diligitur, vellem diuturnior esset; / nunc duo concordes anima moriemur in una'" ("I would he that is loved might live longer; but as it is, we two shall die together in one breath"; ll. 471–72). *Duo concordes*: a single fate, with two subjects.[24]

Yet unlike the tragic Oedipus, Narcissus recovers his delusion:

et lacrimis turbavit aquas, obscuraque moto
reddita forma lacu est; quam cum vidisset abire,
"quo refugis? remane nec me, crudelis, amantem
desere!" clamavit; "liceat, quod tangere non est,
adspicere et misero praebere alimenta furori."   [ll. 475–79]

[His tears ruffled the water, and dimly the image came back from the troubled pool. As he saw it thus depart, he cried: "Oh, whither do you flee? Stay here, and desert not him who loves thee, cruel one! Still may it be mine to gaze on what I may not touch, and by that gaze feed my unhappy passion."]

Suddenly refracted and blurred, the image regains its status as seemingly animate Other, for so I construe the shift from third-person description ("'hic, qui diligitur'") to direct address ("'remane'").[25] The image, then, does not remain demystified; Narcissus perceives the imperfection of the visual as the departure of the object.

Here again we can discern how Ovid's narrative style has been modeled on the foibles of the Narcissan psyche. The elaborate empirical apparatus by which such gradual and continuous processes as growth, motion, and sequence are perceived suddenly collapses: the world of Narcissus is metonymic at best. Continuity and disjunction replace each other almost at random; evidence suggests to Narcissus that he himself is the cause of the image, but the cognitive continuity of induction is no sooner achieved than forgotten, abducted. The image grows abruptly obscure, and that change does duty for the kind of smoothly continuous visual shift that would signify departure, in much the same way as the collocation of Narcissus and the croceus does duty for the metamorphosis of one into the other. We have seen how Ovid makes the interruption of sequence the tool of his larger construction; here the technique serves to disable the causal presuppositions of tragic forensics. Narcissus comes to no Oedipal awareness of fault; indeed, awareness itself ("'iste ego sum'") dissolves into a desperate allegiance to delusion ("'remane!'").

Yet causality is by no means banished from this portion of the *Cadmeans*, for Echo herself is implicated in a criminal process that provides the first and only etiology of her repetitive habits. (Recall that, in Longus's later tale, ubiquity, invisibility, and immortality—not dependent repetition—are the objects of etiological attention.) Ovid has split the etiology of Echo into two parallel narratives, arrayed like swags on his chiastic decor. The first portion of her tale has unorthodox features which set it off from the other Cadmean tales of retribution, as well as highly traditional characteristics, which bind it to Virgilian epic. Her crime may possess a comic superficiality, but she incurs a grave and classic wrath:

> Iuno, quia, cum deprendere posset
> sub Iove saepe suo nymphas in monte iacentis,
> illa deam longo prudens sermone tenebat,
> dum fugerent nymphae. postquam hoc Saturnia sensit,
> "huius," ait, "linguae, qua sum delusa, potestas
> parva tibi dabitur vocisque brevissimus usus,"
> reque minas firmat. [ll. 362–68]
>
> [for often when Juno might have surprised the nymphs in company with her lord upon the mountain-sides, Echo would prudently hold the goddess in long talk until the nymphs were fled. When Saturnia realized this, she said to her: "That tongue of thine, by which I have been tricked, shall have its power curtailed and enjoy the briefest use of speech." The event confirmed her threat.]

Prudens, primarily benign, mitigates the criminality of Echo's stratagem. At the same time, it does distinguish her from such inadvertent transgressors as Cadmus, Pentheus, Teiresias, or most important, Actaeon.[26] Echo's prudentia makes her oral crime a premeditated one and one that simultaneously shares the name of virtue. Such ambiguous criminality is of course characteristic of epic error, of those willful crimes that excite the *ira Iunonis*. That ire operates briskly in Ovid: with the phrase "illa deam longo prudens sermone tenebat," we are deprived of that full narrative offered, say, when Mercury deceives Argus. With "hoc Saturnia sensit" we are given, not a discovery, but the précis of a discovery; we see the results and not the operation of ire.

The account is so sketchy that its etiological function seems inadequately performed (we find a similar inadequacy in the second etiological description of Echo, in which her invisibility is explained as the self-consumptive dessication of the lovelorn [395–99]); Juno's curse, "huius linguae potestas parva tibi dabitur vocisque brevissimus usus," is itself *brevissimus*, for it does not articulate the peculiar manifestations of the punishment, "reddere de multis ut verba novissima posset." Yet Ovid makes its precise nature evident, so that little mystery remains to hover around divine wrath. Still, some mystery persists: the effects of wrath are clear, but the diction of curse is not. Juno's use of *tibi* is slightly loaded, for it serves to reinforce the importance of certain legal concepts affecting the notion of persons and of their property in this passage, concepts that hover most obtrusively around the idea of *usus vocis*. I want to give these concepts special consideration here, for emphasis on the *property* of speech turns out to be an abiding aspect of the mythography of Echo, an aspect of which I shall have more to say in these essays.

What is this *usus* of which Echo is deprived? From the institution of *usufruc-*

tion, the profitable employment of property belonging to another, from *usucap-[t]ion*, employment that eventually creates ownership, and from *usus*, meaning both the validation of *manus*, marriage (the concept is closely related to transfer of property) by continuous cohabitation, as well as the employment (without fruits) of another's property, derives a sense of the word that had begun penetrating colloquial language as early as Plautus's day.[27] Behind all these forms is a legal notion of utility as an entelechy that challenges the boundary between object and subject. To use a property is to bring its propriety into question, to discover it as a movable and, in the cases of usucapion and marital usus, to effect a transfer of property. In the Roman system, such transfer is a small metaphysical revolution, for from the time of the Twelve Tables, Roman *dominium* virtually identifies the property with the proprietary subject; hence Roman "vindication" of property is more an epistemological matter than a criminal one.[28]

Usus is a Janus-concept at the limits of property, sometimes splitting an object's utility off from its essential status of being-owned, sometimes revising ownership. In the latter case (again, in the cases of usucapion and marital usus), utility comes to be metaphysically continuous over time with that essential being-owned of the body and, hence, with the nature of the owner.

Thus, in the final moments of the second etiology of Echo, that phase of the narrative in which her invisibility is explained, we watch a dismantling of Echo's property:

> vox tantum atque ossa supersunt:
> vox manet, ossa ferunt lapidis traxisse figuram.
> inde latet silvis nulloque in monte videtur,
> omnibus auditur: sonus est, qui vivit in illa. [ll. 398–401]

[Only her voice and her bones remain: then only voice: for they say that her bones were turned to stone. She hides in woods and is seen no more upon the mountain-sides, though she is heard by all: *sonus est, qui vivit in illa.*]

"There is a sound which lives in her" or "She is sound, which lives in her": in the first translation sound is extrinsic to Echo; in the second it is both partly and entirely constitutive of her. And then again, not totally so: the line asks us to fabricate a being in which *sonus* can persist; but *vox* as *usus* can never be quite coextensive with this *illa*.[29]

Thus this etiology of the echoic is situated on a weird frontier. Juno's curse exposes a demarcation between native and translated speech, between a speech in (*et cum*) propria persona and a speech that must always be the borrowed language of another, always held in fief. Ovid's Echo is not merely belated; her speech is doomed to be alien and inauthentic. (Doomed—that is the point: etiology describes what might have once seemed necessary as conditional, modal.) And still we are left to puzzle over what that *illa* might be who can provide the locus for this movable sound. We can begin to define that *illa* by falling back on the antithetical, schematic manner of the episode, defining *illa* with respect to Narcissus.

At first the schematism seems to provide reasonably simple oppositions: his self-deceiving visual fixation counterpoised against her self-revealing aural fixation; her self-constitution that is everywhere referred to an Other and his opposing integrity, nearly impervious to external influence. Thus, in the core dialogue between the two, the phrase "vocat illa vocantem" (l. 382) is to be weighed against the similar, but unequal, "ille fugit fugiensque . . ." (l. 390). Her behavior is directed toward another; his is simply a constant self-repetition. We may even contrast her finally thwarted desires with what might be taken as some fruition for him: he survives paradoxically— "se . . . in Stygia spectabat aqua" (he regards himself in the Stygian waters; ll. 504–05)—more self-regarding than before because, as shade, his imago is now phenomenally equivalent to his gazing subject. In the underworld, his love is finally brought into some sort of equilibrium. We even take him as original and her as derivative when the means of relation between the two are not verbal:

> ergo ubi Narcissum per devia rura vagantem
> vidit et incaluit, sequitur vestigia furtim,
> quoque magis sequitur, flamma propiore calescit,
> non aliter quam cum summis circumlita taedis
> admotas rapiunt vivacia sulphura flammas. [ll. 370–74]

[Therefore, when she saw Narcissus wandering through the fields, she was inflamed with love and followed him by stealth; and the more she followed, the more she burned by a nearer flame; as when quick-burning sulphur, smeared round the tops of torches, catches fire from another fire brought near.]

Her secondhandedness is legion; even the inflammation of love seems to have been preceded by some flame already associated with Narcissus. The repeated *sequitur* of these lines implies more than movement through space, for the opening *ergo* not only suggests this sequence as the fullest manifestation of Juno's curse, it also intensifies the specifically logical sense of the verb: her actions are *consequences*, of both Juno's curse and Narcissus' behavior. The antithetical definition of *illa* and *ille* could thus be extended here: causality is suppressed in his fate; causality everywhere intrudes upon hers.

But these lines also disrupt the defining balance, for Narcissan originality frequently remains merely a construct; he is the agent of inflammation here only within the figure of the *taedae*. In the phrase cited above—"vocat illa vocantem"—word order qualifies his precedence. Echo is answering his cry of "veni," and her ambiguous reply suggests that she may already await him. Indeed, Ovid often restricts Narcissus' presence as much as his precedence; the enamored Echo pursues, not Narcissus, but his *vestigia*. Though the narrative certainly depends on the contrast between Narcissus and his imago, his own substantiality is called into question when Ovid, roused to violate the steady detachment of narration, interjects:

> credule, quid frustra simulacra fugacia captus?
> quod petis, est nusquam; quod amas, avertere, perdes!
> ista repercussae, quam cernis, imaginis umbra est:

nil habet ista sui; tecum venitque manetque;
tecum discedet, si tu discedere possis.   [ll. 432–36]

[*Credule*, why vainly seek to clasp a fleeting image? What you seek is nowhere; turn yourself away, and the object of your love will be no more. That which you behold is but the shadow of a reflected form, and has no substance of its own [or, to use the colloquial residue of the dative construction: "there is nothing to it."] With you it comes, with you it stays, and it will go with you—if you can go.]

The key line, "ista repercussae, quam cernis, imaginis umbra est," anticipates Narcissus' Stygian end. But the phrase also plainly asserts a doubly derivative ontology of the image, and one that affiliates the episode with Platonic aesthetics and metaphysics: Narcissus loves the shade of an *image*. This makes sense of an earlier description of the stupefied Narcissus, "ut e Pario formatum marmore signum" (like a statue formed of Parian marble; l. 419). Ovid reverses the direction of the Platonic analogy: the human relation to an original ideal imitates the relation of objet d'art to its model.[30]

THE JURISDICTION OF THE PAST

As mentioned above, the entire episode is customarily given over to Narcissus. Yet the episode is perhaps more echoic than Narcissan: for example, his gaze into the Stygian pool repeats an earlier gaze, which is to say that it is, like an echo, a replication articulated in time. Our proper objection to such an assertion is that literary doubling *has* to be articulated thus, hence the designation of literature as an art of time.[31] Ovid renders this necessity thematic in his account of Narcissus' enamorment. The episode begins with simultaneous agency and pathos—"dumque sitim sedare cupit, sitis altera crevit" (and while he seeks to slake his thirst, another thirst springs up; 1.415), or the pricklier "dumque petit, petitur, pariterque accendit et ardet" (and while he seeks, is sought; equally he kindles love and burns with love; l. 426)—but the youth misrepresents that representation:

spem mihi nescio quam vultu promittis amico,
cumque ego porrexi tibi bracchia, porrigis ultro.
cum risi, adrides.   [ll. 457–59]

[Some ground for hope you offer with your friendly looks, and when I have stretched out my arms to you, you stretch out yours. When I have smiled, you smile back.]

Note the verb tenses: act and image are described here as sequential.[32] Atomistic physics may have provided Ovid with a theory of sequence in visual reflection, but it can hardly vitiate the primary experience of simultaneity; this passage is Narcissus' lie against that primary experience, and the manner of that lie has been learned from his dialogue with Echo. The reflex of both verbal and visual imago has a sluggishness both tempting and maddening. *Echoic* replication is rising to authority.

Similarly, what Brenkman has described as the "erasure" of Juno's punishment, the twist that enables Echo fully to represent her intentions to Narcissus, seems more than a mere recovery of the expressive: it reasserts her personality, her personal propriety. In "illa parata est / exspectare sonos, ad quos sua verba remittat" (she is ready to await the sounds to which she may give back her own words; ll. 377–78) and "rettulit Echo / et verbis favet ipsa suis" (Echo responds, and she helps her own words . . .; ll. 387–88), the pronouns, syntactically gratuitous, constitute an emphatic assertion of possession. We witness here a usurpation (*usu rapere*), a momentary transfer of property in which Narcissus' claims to voice are denied. Her dominion is then reasserted at his death by the echoic function of the text: as she echoes his final words and repeats the lamentations of the attendant naiades and dryades, the text becomes a riot of allusion:

> cumque suos manibus percusserat ille lacertos,
> haec quoque reddebat sonitum plangoris eundem.
> ultima vox solitam fuit haec spectantis in undam:
> "heu frustra dilecte puer!" totidemque remisit
> verba locus, dictoque vale "vale" inquit et Echo.
> ille caput viridi fessum submisit in herba,
> lumina mors clausit domini mirantia formam.   [ll. 497–503]

[And as his hands beat his shoulders she gives back the same sounds of woe. His last words as he gazed into the familiar spring were these: "Alas dear boy, vainly beloved!" and the place gave back his words. And when he said "Farewell!" "Farewell!" said Echo too. He drooped his weary head on the green grass and death sealed the eyes that marvelled at their master's beauty.]

In his remarkable edition of the *Metamorphoses*, Pontanus glosses the last line thus—"Virg. de Turno moriente in 12. *In aeternam clauduntur lumina noctem.* Propert. eleg. 13.1.2. *Quamdocunque, igitur nostros mors claudet ocellos.*"[33] Much could be said of the knotty intertextuality of this passage, and one could well begin by observing that the line cited from the *Aeneid* doesn't refer to the death of Turnus. The resonances of epic mourning are more social: "consurgunt gemitu Rutuli totusque remugit / mons circum et vocem late nemora alta remittunt" (Up spring the Rutulians all, the whole hill re-echoes round about and far and near the wooded steeps send back the sound; XII.926–29). Generically more archaic, the isolation of Narcissus' death is tempered, as in pastoral elegy, by the mourning of nymphs and not by the sympathy of comrades. The vestiges of pastoral resonance in Virgil's epic measure the distance traveled, the degree to which the *Aeneid* transfigures the *Eclogues*. Surely that is the point of the Virgilian passage from which Ovid's phrase does in fact derive:

>   Podalirius Alsum,
> pastorem primaque acie per tela ruentem,
> ense sequens nudo superimminet: ille securi
> adversi frontem mediam mentumque reducta
> disicit et sparso late rigat arma cruore.
> olli dura quies oculos et ferreus urget
> somnus, in aeternam clauduntur lumina noctem.   [XII.304–10]

[Podalirius, pursuing Alsus with naked steel, hangs over the shepherd as in foremost line he rushes amid the darts; but Alsus, swinging back his ax, severs full in front his enemy's brow and chin, and drenches his armour with widely spattered gore. Stern repose and iron slumber, and iron slumber sealed his eyes in eternal night.]

Here the shepherd triumphs and so too does the echoic mimesis of the older genres, for the lines describing Podalirius's death are formulaic, having been used to describe the death of the Trojan Orontes in book X. Ovid, then, has cited an atavistic Virgil, a Virgil *qui resonare docet carmen*.

The degree of Virgil's atavism in the passages cited can be gauged when we recall the rest of Pontanus's annotation. Virgil is engaged in an homage to Sextus Propertius, for his formula is taken from Propertius's extraordinary poem on the "funeris acta mei" (II.xiii). Propertius's poem also measures itself against the traditions of pastoral mourning: by allusion, Propertius seeks some of the perdurability that the *Lament for Adonis* had won for Bion:

> testis, qui niveum quondam percussit Adonem
>   venantem Idalio vertice durus aper;
> illis formosus iacuisse paludibus, illuc
>   diceris effusa tu, Venus, isse coma.   [II.xiii.53–56]

[Witness the cruel boar that struck snow-white Adonis as he hunted on the Idalian peak. There in the marsh, 'tis said, thou wentest, Venus, thy tresses unbound.]

Bion had devised a scene of attendant echoic mourning and a text replete with internal repetitions as an imitative coding of that cultic fact that Adonis dies to live again, a fact the poem otherwise suppresses. Propertius's allusion also codes that resurrection; *percussit* recalls both the means of death and the manner of mourning, while its frequentative form reminds us that the biography of Adonis is cyclical, "eterne in mutabilitie." But Propertius seems set on disabusing Bion's readers by relocating the Adonis story in a poem whose explicit theme is self-commemoration. Propertius knows that Bion shared that theme, and he makes Bion seem to have been inhibited by a faintly superstitious squeamishness about claiming the advantages of cult for the province of craft. Propertius's self-commemoration has proceeded without scruple.

Yet Propertius's urbanity immediately reveals its own bitterness, for the next, and final, lines of the poem attest to the anguish of the disabused: "sed frustra mutos revocabis, Cynthia, Manes: / nam mea quid poterunt ossa minuta loqui" (But in vain, Cynthia, shalt thou recall my voiceless Manes to life; for what answer shall my crumbled bones have strength to make?; ll. 57–58). *Manes* was just coming to mean "soul" in Propertius's day; its more established meaning was "ancestral spirits." So Propertius seems to humble both himself *and* that ancestral elegist recalled in the preceding lines. *Mea ossa* is the presiding figure, a debilitating figure of the poet, for no matter how long verse can survive, the bones are always silent. Against the immortality of art is pitched the radical death of the body, the silent end of Bion (the Manes) and of Propertius (mea ossa).

So there is something slightly pathetic to Virgil's homage. His source in

Propertius has already shrugged off the apparatus of allusion as a means of commemoration, and even Virgil seems powerless against that deadpan logic. Perhaps the victory of Alsus is a means of rehabilitating the ethos of pastoral elegy, so thoroughly dismantled by his fellow poet. Insofar as the semidivine agents of pastoral mourning are no longer needed in epic contexts to ensure death amidst a community, Virgil's efforts succeed. He does not cite his Propertian model verbatim, but the impulse to echo resurfaces in the repetitions within his own poem, and the repetitions, I think, betray the desperation with which Virgil contemplated a peer so fully resigned to his own end.

This regress from the Ovidian passage should show the remarkable extent of its contexts. Narcissus is mourned as Adonis had been, so that the episode takes on the ethos of pastoral elegy; the description of Narcissus' death points as well to a more recent moment when Virgilian epic elevates that ethos; that description finally points to a Propertian dismantling of the pastoral ethos—an anticontextual context. Propertius's stance seems quite Ovidian, yet Propertius is at once more private, more exclusive, and more radical in his sensibility, while Ovid subverts tradition by eclecticism. Propertius *excludes* the traditional trade-off by which the survival of poetic production (figured as voice) compensates for physical death (the compensation-for figured as conquest-of); Ovid *reproduces* the tradition by reference to Virgil. This indicates perhaps the signal feature of Ovidian writing. As always, he develops his relation to tradition by means of inclusion; here in the *Cadmeans*, the characteristic inclusion entails contradiction and competition. The death scene of Narcissus attests to an endless debate, unjuried and unresolved.

I am by no means suggesting that the episode is undiscriminating. As was noted in the first chapter, the story of Echo's love for Narcissus is of uncertain ancestry; in fact it has been argued that Ovid devised the episode himself.[34] The matter of the episode certainly accords with the schematic matter of Ovid's particular telling; with the tale of Echo joined to the tale of Narcissus, the episode becomes less a work of psychological realism (as Freud might have it) than a formalist study of replication. And Ovid has taken some pains to give the tale a certain thematic purity and isolation that secures it a genuinely distinguished place within the epic. The widely popular tale of Hylas, certainly suited to Ovid's purposes, has been excluded from the *Metamorphoses*, I suspect both because Ovid wanted no rival tales of entrapment by water and because, in at least one version of the Hylas story, Hylas is himself transformed into Echo after his disappearance.[35] Nearly suppressed in Ovid's narrative is a tale which we find preserved in Conon's *Narrations*, in which the slighted youth, Amenias, after persistent pursuit of Narcissus, prays for the latter's destruction; the cast of identifiable characters is kept restricted in Ovid in order to guard the centripetal schematism of the episode. There are other, similarly schematic versions of the story. I have already mentioned Pausanias's tale of a Narcissus who falls in love with his sister; though closer to the buried Oedipal motive in Ovid, this melancholy narrative carries none of the visual-acoustic opposition that Ovid chooses to organize the episode.

54 • THE REFLEX OF EPIC

Acknowledging the thematic centrality of the opposition, we return to the narrative center of the episode, the dialogue between Echo and Narcissus; taken in terms of the tragic model which the episode displaces, we see the dialogue as an agon.

The usurpation of Narcissus' voice during the dialogue is only temporary:

perstat et alternae deceptus imagine vocis
"huc coeamus" ait, nullique libentius umquam
responsura sono "coeamus" rettulit Echo
et verbis favet ipsa suis egressaque silva
ibat, ut iniceret sperato bracchia collo;
ille fugit fugiensque "manus conplexibus aufer!
ante" ait "emoriar, quam sit tibi copia nostri";
rettulit illa nihil nisi "sit tibi copia nostri." [ll. 385–92]

[He stands still, deceived by the answering voice, and "Here let us meet," he cries. Echo, never to answer another sound more gladly, cries: "Let us copulate"; and to help her own words she comes forth from the woods that she may throw her arms around the neck she longs to clasp. But he flees at her approach and, fleeing, says: "Hands off! embrace me not! May I die before I give you power o'er me!" "I give you power o'er me!" she says, and nothing more.]

The usurpation hardly leaves Echo victorious; indeed, her final words open themselves up to multiple construction, for this gift of person bears with it a surrender of her equal sway over the balance of the episode. The ambiguity has a lively wit to it, reminding us of the linguistic grounds for this Callimachean echo-device: like the speaker of Callimachus's echo-poem, Ovid's Echo does not know the full reference of her words. In Callimachus's epigram, the answering words project a spirit of curt irony personified as Echo but not psychologized; Ovid has extended the technique, so that his Echo's response is cathectic, conversant: "coeamus" projects a needy psyche.

The conflict here, between the delimited encounter of Narcissus' coitus and the fuller union that Echo seeks, complements the opposition of visual and acoustic that organizes the episode. With Echo's redefinition of the verb, Narcissus flees and, fleeing, seeks to restore his self-protective precedence: the "'ante' ait" of line 391 contains a pun—*anteit*—which counters Echo's desire and does so in the typically Narcissan manner of substitution and separation. Notice that Ovid, or his Alexandrian predecessor, wrote this first biography of Echo as a narrative of thwarted desire; while desire endows the personified Echo with a history, the thwarting regulates that threat to consciousness implicit in the phenomenon of echo. The alien voice is subjected to control as soon as it becomes a subject.

Personification, as the preceding chapter has suggested, is itself a means of control; what seems so striking here is how carefully Ovid restrains his power to personify. This illa, in whom sound lives or who is sound, has a meticulously circumscribed personality, being an uncertain mixture of patient desire and borrowed sound. Her patience is barely rewarded; at best, her desire for sexual union is converted into that fulfilled but confused achievement of literary historical continuity that she finally imposes at Narcissus' death.[36]

Ovid has a habit of taking the woman's part or even of writing from the woman's perspective in his erotic poetry. But I suspect that his solicitude on behalf of Echo's plight depends on more than this habit. The tale of the amorous Echo here shares that acute sense of cultural loss we find later in the tale Longus's Daphnis tells of the chaste Echo. Ovid's sense of the loss is by far the more nostalgic, and it manifests itself at the moment of Narcissus' death, the moment at which the Platonic theory of art is temporarily removed from the poem, in an almost undiscriminating incorporation of earlier poetic activity. Louise Vinge has observed that in the other antique tales of Narcissus, his vanity is often the object of pity; only in Ovid is Narcissus scorned.[37] It is Ovid's allegiance to the echoic that transforms Narcissus into *credule*.

The moment deserves a second look. Ovid speaks that "credule" in the superior voice of an ironist, and the direct address surely is directed both at Narcissus and at the sympathetic reader who may himself be deluded by the virtual image in the narrative. The vocative has much the same force as that of Narcissus' imperative, "remane"; if Narcissus deludes himself about the independent origins of the *umbra imaginis*, Ovid is similarly deluded, treating the imago, Narcissus, as a real and corrigible person, and at precisely that moment in the episode when the poet most earnestly analyzes the mechanics of delusion. He will save more careful analysis for book X, where he considers Pygmalion (ll. 243–97); here in the *Cadmeans*, the irony is more fully distributed. Narcissus, ourselves (as readers, not hearers), and Ovid (here behaving like a reader) are invoked with that "credule." Thus, Ovid continues his allegiance to Echo's doomed orality in his address to the credulous Narcissus, whose untrained eye imposes separate reality on what is merely his own imaginary extension. Yet Narcissus cannot heed the speaker's warning—he is the worst of conversationalists—for the necessary proximity of poet to his audience had been lost for five centuries, and affective poetics no longer preserved their preeminence. This is perhaps the proper occasion to reconsider the Platonic aesthetics which the scornful speaker of "credule" invokes in this assault on the affective.

Eric Havelock reminds us that the imitative art which Plato bans from the Republic is itself oral, its delusive power entailed by the ritual scene of performance.[38] Yet Plato begins his critique of that poetry by figuring it as an indiscriminate mirroring; Socrates tartly suggests that the "craftsman" (the term accrues pejorative force as book X of the *Republic* develops) is as powerful as the divine artificer, for he, too, can make all things:

> You could do it most quickly if you should choose to take a mirror and carry it everywhere. You will speedily produce the sun and all the things in the sky, and speedily the earth and yourself and the other animals and implements and plants and all the objects of which we just now spoke.

> Yes, he [i.e., Glaucon] said, the appearance of them, but not the reality and the truth.
>
> Excellent, said I [Socrates], and you come to the aid of the argument opportunely.[39]

Certainly the choice of visual reflection to figure oral mimesis must seem curious. Plato was surely ambivalent about the visible written word, for although it was his ally in the assault on mimesis, it was his besieging enemy in the defense of memory. I think this passage further suggests that the visible word was still somewhat anomalous, hence the slight awkwardness of Plato's figure. The opposition of the oral-aural and the graphic-visible certainly doesn't threaten the argument of the *Republic;* Plato's argument here seems to depend on the possibility of simple analogical play between the categories. By Ovid's time the categorical opposition had fixed itself; no better evidence than the story of Echo and Narcissus can be found for this historical shift. But Ovid has revised the critique by fixing on the visible (and, by Ovid's day, graphic) vehicle of Plato's metaphoric argument and, insofar as he is capable, by dismissing it in favor of that orality which was the true tenor of the Platonic critique. It is an echoic trick, one that we sometimes erroneously call "literalism" but sometimes more wisely describe as "taking someone at his or her word."

Two centuries or so later, Longus will not share Ovid's nostalgia; Longus's Echo is dead, an unassailable presence with circumscribed, purely oppositional power. Her oral, conservative chastity is punished, but preserved. Ovid's Echo persists as desire, an immortal desire which cannot achieve the coital unity of a culture in which storytelling is self-authenticating and uncalculated; that desire is cheated both by the skepticism of the Minyeides and the related scopophilia of Narcissus. At best, as Narcissus dies, Echo can open the *Metamorphoses* up to an uncritical allusiveness in which older sounds and other meanings pour in from myriad texts, texts that suddenly, in the hiatus of the Narcissan, attain the presence of voice and confer the largest perpetuitas upon the poem.

> Cognita res meritam vati per Achaidas urbes
> attulerat famam, nomenque erat auguris ingens. [ll. 511–12]
>
> [When the thing became known it spread the well-deserved fame of the seer throughout the cities of Greece, and great was the name of the prophet.]

Echo's sway is short-lived, converted so quickly into her parodic double, Fama.

3

ECHOIC PRESENCE AND THE THEATRICAL COURT: *CYNTHIA'S REVELS*

Perhaps the most striking novelty within Renaissance culture may be found in the concept of intellectual utility. When we speak of the Renaissance secularization of thought, or of the transformation of *scientia* into science, we indicate a new commutability, even a congruence, between Knowledge and Power. Perhaps nothing illustrates the alliance between the new utility of knowledge and the traditions of mythography quite so deftly as a plate from Athanasius Kircher's mammoth encyclopedia of *musica speculativa*, the *Musurgia Universalis* (Rome, 1650).[1] The plate appears in the midst of book 9 (*Magia Phonocamptica*) in a chapter concerning "Phonurgia Echonice"; it depicts a number of architectural constructions that could be used to produce artificial echoes with predictable acoustic characteristics. (One of the three principal illustrations shows a man standing before an array of walls spaced so that his cry of "clamore" will be returned first as "amore," then "more," "ore," and "re" before the clamor dies out.) Kircher's treatise here adapts the theoretical principles of his research to systematize some practical principles culled from Vitruvius; the ninth book of the *Musurgia* is the first great modern work in acoustic engineering. High on this particular plate, etched faintly to suggest distance, is a Pan with arms outstretched toward a mass of trees over which hovers a cloud-enshrouded female figure: there at the very top of the plate, is Echo. The pictorial allusion to pastoral is extended somewhat into the foreground of the plate, with clumps of grass dotting even the crumbling masonry of the echoing walls. The new engineering blends with the ruins of time, which have made the urban rural, weakly rural, once more—beside the illustrative constructions we find a deteriorating coliseum, a toppled obelisk, a tree, once vigorous, now sparsely leaved, its trunk broken.

The illustration suggests a great deal about the Renaissance use of myth. The nostalgic iconography, which combines the imagery of pastoral with that of ruin (prehistory thus represented as an inaccessible "green thought"), and the hovering of myth over technology together represent modernity as a breach that can be healed only by the blandishments of narrative. We would be wrong to take the faint image of Pan as a mere embellishment or even as a mere blandishment, for the engraver here provides a pictorial representation of the syncretism of Kircher's discourse; we can compare the image to Kircher's own preface to part IV of the *Musurgia*:

> Echo ludibundae naturae iocus, a Poetis imago vocis, iuxta illud Virgil. *Saxa sonant, variisque offensa resultat imago.* a Philosophis reflexa, repercussa, reciproca vox, ab Hebræis *bat col* filia vocis dicitur. [II.sig. Gg₃]

"The propagation of sound: reflections and echoes," from Athanasius Kircher, *Musurgia Universalis*, volume 2, 1650.

[Echo is a joke of playful Nature. The Poets call her *imago vocis* (as in Virgil's line, "The rocks ring out and the *imago vocis* rebounds from the shock"); the Philosophers call her reflected, repercussive, or reciprocal voice; the Hebrews call her the *bat kol*, or Daughter of the Voice.]

The mythography of Echo authorizes his discourse, which is to treat of what he calls either *Echosophia* or *Phonocamptica*, the bending of sound.[2] The same blending of practical knowledge and mythographic scientia motivates the illustrative image later in the chapter. In Kircher's major contemporary source, the *Sphaera Mundi* (Bologna, 1620) of Giuseppe Biancani (Kircher claims that Biancani is the first to have broached the subject of echometry), we find the same recourse to the mythographer's method. For Biancani, the authority of Ovid and Virgil is quite as powerful as the more practical passages on theatrical acoustics from book V of Vitruvius's *De Architectura*.[3]

Though Kircher tentatively extends the technical aspect of Biancani's work from architecture into the theory of musical composition, adapting a theory of echo to enrich contrapuntal theory, theatrical architecture maintains the importance in Kircher's echometry that it held in Biancani's. Frances Yates and Allardyce Nicoll have revealed the breadth of the Vitruvian revival that shaped the theater architecture of the High Renaissance, though little has been said of how the growth of the theater as an institution of aristocratic culture combined with this theoretical revival to generate the new researches in architectural acoustics.[4] And we should not mistake the aim of these researches, for they were not intended simply to produce acoustic environments in which sound would remain unmuddied and unmuffled. Biancani and Kircher wanted to produce articulate sound, but articulately *echoing* sound; Vitruvian architecture was not thought to have aimed at acoustic purity per se, but at effects more baroque. Thus, we should not be surprised that one of the reasons the fashionable Charles I suspended the presentation of masques in the Banqueting House at Whitehall in 1635 was its faulty acoustics, as Balthazar Gerbier explains in his *Brief Discourse Concerning the Three Chief Principles of Magnificent Building* (London, 1662):

> Neither can all great Rooms of Princely Palaces serve for this use [i.e., for the production of "Scheames"], except they be after the Moddell of such as the Italians have built, as there is a good one at *Florence*, in *Italy*, with conveyances for Smoak, and capacities for Ecchoes, which *Inigo Jones* (the late Surveyor) experimentally found at *Whitehall*, and by his built Banqueting House, so as having found his own fault, he was constrained to Build a Woodden House overthwart the Court of *WhiteHall*. [sig. D$_2$v]

Is there some condescension in Gerbier's account? It suggests that Jones has made inadequate provision for the two great constituents of Jacobean revelry—spectacular light and stupendous sound.

It should be said in Jones's defense, that the Banqueting House served quite well for many years: there are no significant objections to its design recorded before Rubens painted his famous canvases for the ceiling fifteen years after its erection in 1619. So Gerbier judges Jones a bit harshly. Charles put a stop to performances in the Banqueting House in order to safeguard the paintings, so smoke became a *grave* problem only when the interior design of the hall was wrested from Jones's control. Still, Gerbier's remarks about echo are intriguing, for they suggest that, like adequate ventilation, adequate sonorousness was something a royal patron might fairly expect an architect to provide. Jones could fail by demonstrating insufficient expertise in acoustic engineering. It seems that Palladian symmetries had distracted Jones from Vitruvian theatrical accommodations; although construction of the Banqueting House began a few months before Jones could have had the benefit of Biancani's echometry, Jones was immersed in the Vitruvian tradition and would have been aware of the importance given to resonance and echo in the *De Architectura*.[5] Antique theaters (and such ancient oracular sites as Dodona) were fitted with resonators, and a true Renaissance stage would require similar acoustic grandeur. If, by 1619, Jones was simply more interested in spectacle or was insufficiently ingenious as an acoustic designer, Gerbier could find this architectural lapse remarkable. So the burden of courtly echoing was left to Jonson.

It is curious that the story of Echo, which in Ovidian epic takes the place of the story of Oedipus, the dramatic plot par excellence, should find itself a new life in that second great period of Western dramatic activity, on the (usually Vitruvian) Renaissance stage—as if some repressed dramatic motive had forced its return. The logic of that return is complex and sometimes shadowy. And indeed it would be inaccurate to suggest that the story of Echo was exclusively dramaturgic in Renaissance literature. Echo extends, but does not forsake, her earlier domain in lyric and epic, pushing not only into drama but also into the Erasmian colloquy; she becomes the painter's model and the object of the scientist's inquiry.[6] Echo continues as an analyst of literary fama, takes on new functions as a figure for the distortions of *translatio studii*, and—in Elizabethan England—assumes an important role in the public meditations on royal sexuality. She continues as a significant interlocutor for the Renaissance pastoralist, an interlocutor at once satiric and sympathetic. But surely her most unexpected function in Renaissance discourse has to do with the new theatricalities of the age. It is primarily to this function that the following essays will address themselves.

The intensifying focus on Echo in the sixteenth century has a number of causes. Poliziano's description of the echo-lyric and his publication of the single surviving classical exemplar, Gauradas's epigram from the Planudean anthology, surely fostered interest in the form, an interest considerably nurtured by the sixteenth-century annotation of Virgil's *Eclogues* and Ovid's *Metamorphoses*, and by the vernacular publication of *Daphnis and Chloë* at mid-century. The recovery and interpretation of the Pythagorean dictum, *Anemon pneonton ton ekho proskunei*, by both Ficino and Giraldi, contributes to disentangling the mythos of Echo from exclusive association with that of Narcissus; indeed, Giraldi's *De Deis Gentium*—and, as is often the case, Cartari follows him here—treats Echo, not as an adjunct to the Narcissus tale to which Lactantian tradition had consigned her, but as part of a powerfully extra-Olympian mythography built up around the figure of Pan.[7] But I suspect that the particular cultural prestige which the Renaissance conferred upon the echoic may find its most important impulse in the recovery of the *De Architectura* and the publication of an *editio princeps* at Rome in 1486, events that are nearly as important for literary history as they are for the history of architecture. For surely the new and powerful generic affiliation of Echo with the theatrical is Vitruvian in origin.

But the echoes of Vitruvian architecture were insufficiently witty, so in the early 1580s an ingenious Giambattista Guarini—perhaps inspired by Daniel Barbaro, who included his own Gauradan echo-lyric in his annotations to his translated edition of Vitruvius—contrived a *scripted* theatrical echo, a dialogue between Silvio and Echo in that most influential of Italian plays, *Il Pastor Fido*.[8] The echo-scene became a popular dramatic device, particularly in pastoral drama, so popular, in fact, that we must take Mercury's shock, in *Cynthia's Revels*, at the proximity of Echo to the theatrical scene as approaching disingenuousness. And perhaps this popularity explains why Jones forsook traditional Vitruvian concerns in 1619; several decades of such echo-scenes may well have persuaded the designer that the provision of echoes was fundamentally the responsibility of poet and composer. From Ben Jonson's point of view, anything that could be claimed as fundamentally a linguistic device, as proper to the poet's part, was to be claimed as constitutive of the soul of the masque.

A TRUE COPIE: GASCOIGNE AND THE MASTERY OF THE REVELS

> The question then becomes: How can one reduce the great peril, the great danger with which fiction threatens our world? The answer is: One can reduce it with the author. The author allows a limitation of the cancerous and dangerous proliferation of significations within a world where one is thrifty not only with one's resources and riches, but also with one's discourses and their significations. The author is the principle of thrift in the proliferation of meaning.
>
> Michel Foucault, "What Is an Author?"[9]

That Echo's first speeches in English mark a moment of generic instability can hardly surprise us, for among her functions in antiquity is that of ironist of genre. When Queen Elizabeth visited Kenilworth for two and a half weeks during July of 1575, a consortium of England's most eminent scholar-poets provided entertainments to punctuate the public moments of her rather long residence as guest of Robert Dudley, Earl of Leicester.[10] George Gascoigne wrote three of these interludes, the first of which includes perhaps the first echo-scene in European dramatic history. In 1576 he provided Richard Jones, a printer who specialized in ballads, with a scenario of the Kenilworth entertainments which Jones published under the somewhat anomalous title, *The Princelye Pleasures, at the Courte at Kenelwoorth*. The title itself is revealing, for "pleasures" both marks the author's uncertainty about the genre of such a literary text and provides an index of how that uncertainty might be resolved: royal entertainment has its final cause (and often claims its formal and moving causes) in the monarch him- or herself.

Though the actors may "play," the significance of the event resides, more than in any other form of theatricality, in the pleasure of this focal spectator.

There is more to this title. It emphasizes the native spirit of Elizabethan entertainment, the celebration of national (princely) and local (Kenilworth Castle) genius. Court drama may be distinguished from popular drama in this period by its repeated and explicit efforts to coordinate national and classical mythologies, hence the particular allegiance to the historiographically discredited Brut legend. Thus, the Kenilworth entertainments begin with the prophecy of Sibylla, and this classicism is followed by Arthurian giants and a Hercules who is domesticated to a porter's status. The third "pleasure" involves the appearance of that most English of heroines, the Lady of the Lake (further localized: "I am the Lady of *this* pleasant Lake" [emphasis mine]).[11]

This blend of modern and classical, native and alien, strong-stress, alliterative measures and suave, quantitative meters was hardly macaronic in spirit.[12] We should need a new label—something rather like "anthological"—to indicate the kinship of the Kenilworth entertainments with such monuments of early Elizabethan culture as *The Mirror for Magistrates*, *The Adventures of Master F. J.*, or *The Shepheardes Calender*. But that kinship should not obscure the strangeness of *The Princelye Pleasures, at the Courte at Kenelwoorth*—or the neater title from its second edition in the *Whole Woorkes* of 1587, *The Princely Pleasures at Kenilworth Castle*—a strangeness that even Gascoigne felt. Stephen Orgel has rightly observed the pioneering importance of Gascoigne's devices. By publishing his texts of the Montacute masque (1572) and of the Kenilworth entertainments, Gascoigne asserts that the masque can have permanent importance as a literary text, that it is memorable as well as occasional. (Or perhaps *because* it is occasional: as we shall see, the masque enables us to explore the ahistorical power of the occasional as no other occasional form can.) Gascoigne's assertion of "the English masque-as-literature" (to use Orgel's phrase) was somewhat tentative, and the printed text at first seems to show nervous deference to the occasion.[13] Gascoigne's subtitle suggests that the actual performance is the bulwark of all the text's pretensions; he describes the work, in the 1587 edition, as "a briefe rehearsall, or rather a / true Copie of as much as was presented be- / fore her majesti[e] at Kenelworth, during / her last aboade there, As / followeth"—at which point titles stumble off into text.

In fact, the Kenilworth entertainments were in many ways more elaborate on paper than they were in actuality. Three strands of courtly devices were to have been intertwined during the course of the queen's stay—"the deliverie of the Lady of the Lake," under the general supervision of William Hunnis, Master of the Chapel; the "quest of *Zabeta*," entirely the work of Gascoigne; and a curious little drama in which a Savage Man sees and becomes enamored of the royal guest, again written by Gascoigne and performed by him as well. These three plots were themselves to have been complemented by two more rustic performances by a local troupe. Apparently only the locals realized all their plans. The weather may have interfered with the festivities—Richard Laneham, whose published *Let-*

ter . . . from a freend officer attendant in the Court provides the only source of information about the queen's progress other than Gascoigne's *Princely Pleasures*, suggests as much.[14] But more than the weather may have deterred the full realization of the devices: a mishap early in the queen's stay may well have made her leery of the exuberances of these performances.

On Monday the eleventh, the third day of the queen's visit, Gascoigne made the first of his theatrical appearances "clad like a Savage Man, all in Ivie." He concluded his performance by avowing himself awestruck at the queen's presence; Laneham's letter gives details that Gascoigne omits:

> As this Savage for the more submission brake his tree a sunder [a staff, of unspecified proportion, being one of the obligatory props of the traditional Wild Man], kest the top from him, [so that] it had almost light upon her highnes hors head: whereat he startld and the gentleman mooch dismayd. Seé the benigniteé of the Prins, az the foot men lookt well too the hors, and hee of Generositee soon callmd of him self, no hurt no hurt: quoth her highness. Which words I promis yoo wee wear all glad to heer, & took them too be the best part of the play. [sigs. B₃v-B₄]

Laneham's letter attests to the tensions of the occasion as well as to the complex sorts and various sources of its pleasures. Those pleasures derive at least in part from the perils of festival, from the dignity of an aloof but benign queen in the presence of the insignificantly maladroit. She needed her distance, needed to preserve herself as the immovable object of compliment; and a shrewd intelligence may well have guided the decision to shift enactment back toward presentation. Hunnis had planned for the queen to make a barge trip to witness a mock battle against Sir Bruce, but the battle was canceled and the queen made her passage to the Lady of the Lake's isle of captivity by means of a footbridge. The prudent revision provides for a more impressive gestural magic in lieu of the purposed war games, so that the queen could be told that

> yoor only prezens shall be matter sufficient of abandoning this uncurtess knight [Sir Bruce], and putting all his bands too flight, & also of deliverauns of the lady oout of this thralldom. [sig. C₆r-v]

The stimulus of prudence produces the richer act.[15]

Whether it were prudence or the weather that dictated the abridgement of Hunnis's device, Gascoigne clearly felt the change to have been made for the worse. He was, no doubt, particularly sensitive to such changes, since his own devices had suffered even more gravely.

Just before his nearly disastrous gesture of "submission," Gascoigne-as-Savage-Man had also taken on the role of master of ceremonies:

> On Thursday next (thinke I)
>   here will be pleasaunt Dames:
> Who bet then I may make you glee
>   with sundry gladsome games.   [p. 101]

These "games" were to have been a performance of Gascoigne's *Zabeta*, a masque of chastity which purified the popular story of the Hue and Cry after Cupid by substituting the chaste nymph, Zabeta, for the wanton boy—a cunning revision of Moschus I.[16] Gascoigne prints the script as the penultimate device of the *Princely Pleasures*, appending the following note:

> This shewe was devised and penned by M. Gascoigne, and being prepared and redy (every Actor in his garment) two or three dayes together, yet never came to execution. The cause whereof I cannot attribute to any other thing, then to lack of opportunitie and seasonable weather. [p. 120]

It is true that, on the Thursday to which Gascoigne refers, the day's entertainment, a bearbaiting, ended up being held indoors; true, too, that the queen seems to have gone hunting whenever time and weather permitted and did not do so on the Thursday in question; yet the weather did not prevent a show of fireworks in the evening.[17] Gascoigne's "the cause whereof" must seem at least a trifle disingenuous, for, in fact, there are good reasons to suppose that *Zabeta* was canceled— the script is less than five hundred lines long and could easily have been squeezed into an hour of fair weather, and the second half of the queen's stay offered more than a handful of such hours. I suspect that Gascoigne is suppressing the embarrassing facts of the case, trying to salvage self-esteem. Surely something like the same motive informs his afterword to the text of the earlier, ill-fated first performance as Savage Man: "These verses were devised, penned, and pronounced by master G[a]scoyne; and that (as I have heard credibly reported) upon a very great sudden" (p. 102).[18] We can take this as an excuse for Gascoigne's clumsy execution of his part, yet a good case can be made for the suspicion that Gascoigne had rather more to apologize for. In fact, we can begin to account for the indefinite postponement of *Zabeta* by taking a steadier look at this first device.

If it is not pure disingenuousness, then there is certainly much *sprezzatura* in the assertion that the device was hastily composed. It is not Gascoigne's finest verse, yet the Savage Man does manage a persuasive argument for the coherence of the apparently eclectic array of the Kenilworth devices. Gascoigne begins with a summary of the first day's shows, and he neatly toys with the recapitulative function of his device by arranging it as a dialogue between his Savage self and the disembodied Echo:

> What meant the woman first
>   which met hir as she came?
> Could she devine of things to come,
>   as *Sibelles* use the same?
> Eccho.   The same   [p. 98]

The echoes are seldom witty, but their rhythmic value is undeniable: here, as throughout the body of his work, Gascoigne shows an instinct for avoiding the risks inherent in poulter's measure. The hypermetrical, marginal echoes, which add so little mere *information*, arrest the trifling relentlessness of the form.[19] (Enjambment also denies the nursery-rhyme caesura after the sixth syllable:)

ECHOIC PRESENCE AND THE THEATRICAL COURT • 65

>   The same? what *Sibill?* She
>   which useth not to lye?
>   Alas what dyd that beldame there?
>   what [,] dyd she prophecie?
> *Eccho.*   Prophecie
>   O then by lyke she causde
>   the worthy Queene to knowe:
>   What happy raigne she still should hold,
>   Since heavens ordeyned so.
> *Eccho.*   So.   [p. 98]

The dialogue continues its enumeration and elucidation of the previous day's performances; but its invention, as the first English echo-scene, has a distinction to which the verse never rises. The encounter breaks off after twenty-five such exchanges, and the Savage Man begins addressing his compliments directly to the queen. The change of address produces oscillations within the speaking character between the courtly and the crude, and those oscillations render compliment stunningly complex:

> And death or drearie dole,
>   (I know) will end my dayes,
> As soon as you shall once depart,
>   or wish to go your wayes.
> But comely peerelesse Prince,
>   since my desires be great:
> Walke here sometimes in pleasant shade,
>   to fende the parching heate.   [p. 101]

How to resolve the final invitation? Perhaps the leafy orator speaks as genius loci, seeking that fruition of place that only the queen can provide; perhaps he speaks as courtier, seeking a civil conversation that will slake a civil thirst—in both of these postures he will be speaking both for Gascoigne and for Leicester. But perhaps he speaks as satyr, seeking a consummation so indecorous that it could only be taken as voiced by a character utterly opaque to the actor within. The lines exploit the full flexibility of masque-impersonation, in which character possesses what might be called an infinitely variable index of dramatic refraction, shielding, shading, or uncovering the actor himself.

In these lines, in which rhetorical control is so little in evidence, Gascoigne is in his top form. The voice, created two and a half years earlier in "Gascoignes woodmanship," a voice of crude pedagogy and imperfect self-consciousness, saves the earnest poet from accusations of *arriviste* pretension. The "since" of "since my desires be great" presses toward a logic the lines cannot sustain, *worrying* the relations of monarch's to subjects' will, of poet's aspirations to character's, of royal grace to necessitous nature, but not presuming to specify an ideal form for these relationships. The poet calculates his speaker's subservience to that privileged group which Jonson would later call the "understanders"; Gascoigne makes nearly no claims to authority here.

These are admirable, cunning lines, their pointedness restrained almost to invisibility. Such circumspection was certainly in order, for Gascoigne could afford to offend no one; his military career in the Low Countries (1572–74) had done nothing to improve his finances, so badly eroded by a decade of almost incessant litigation following on his marriage in 1561. He had returned from the wars to find his first published volume, A Hundred Sundrie Flowers, confiscated and himself accused of libel and slander. His subsequent revisions for an enlarged volume, the Posies of 1575, had apparently failed to eliminate all censure.[20] Although he was much respected as a poet and had proved himself a serviceable maker of aristocratic entertainments in 1572, when he arranged a masque for a double wedding celebration hosted by Anthony Browne, Viscount Montague, his reputation was tainted by the apparently scandalous Adventures of Master F. J., which had been the main object of attack in the collections of both 1573 and 1575. So we may well wonder at his having been chosen to participate in the Kenilworth devisings at all.

And surely Leicester could ill afford any indelicacies in his hospitality. This sumptuous reception of the queen is sometimes taken as Leicester's attempt to revive a romance between the queen and himself, a romance that had flourished in the early 1560s but had been dashed by rumors attendant on the death of Leicester's wife, Amy Robsart, in 1562. After thirteen years, the whisperings had subsided (though a less damaging scandal had arisen in 1568 with Leicester's seduction of Douglas Sheffield during the queen's progress to Belvoir Castle), and Leicester was once again the most likely match in the kingdom.[21]

Into this painfully delicate situation Gascoigne comes, barely shielded by the fictive crudeness of his speaking persona. If Leicester had already seen and sanctioned Gascoigne's text, then he would have been watching the queen's merest reactions, particularly as Gascoigne pronounced the lines cited above. Did the bumbling conclusion to Gascoigne's performance disqualify him from presenting Zabeta, or had the queen already shown signs of displeasure sufficient to foil the next production? The slightest aloofness might have done so, for the amorous heat of the Savage Man is, as it turns out, only a preparatory impulse, the first exploration of the problem of the queen's sexual mystique, a problem that the second of Gascoigne's devices was to have probed without the slack license of Savagery.

Zabeta actually begins with an evocation of erotic risk. The device opens with Diana's address to her nymphs, an exhortation to chaste wariness even within such pleasant surroundings, for "the sundry gladsome graces, / (Whiche in this soil we joyfully have seene) / Are not unlike some Court to keepe at hand" (p. 108)—nice occasion for arch laughter and grave assent. Then Diana interrupts herself; her sense of place deepens, and recognizing that the Kenilworth grounds in which she finds herself are English grounds, she remembers that it was in England, some sixteen years earlier, that the chaste Zabeta had become separated from Diana's troop and was lost "by great myshap." She urges her three attendants, Castibula, Anamale, and Nichalis, to search out the lost nymph, whereat Castibula delicately expresses her fear that Juno might well have "layde some snare, hyr fancie to entrap, / And hopeth so hyr lofty mynde to lyft, / On Hyme[n]s bed, by height of worldly hap" (p. 110). Thus begins a hue and cry after Chastity, the great original, perhaps, of Spenser's book III and of Milton's *Comus*. The search fails at first. Kenilworth has lost some of its local amenity: we can measure the new rigors of the terrain in Nichalis's speech:

> If ever *Eccho* sounded at request,
> To satisfie an uncontented mind,
> Then *Eccho* now come helpe me in my quest,
> And tel me where I might *Zabeta* finde
> Speake *Eccho*, speake, where dwels *Zabeta*, where? [p. 113]

The voice of Echo, easily evoked by the Savage Man, is suddenly uncooperative: "Alas, alas, or she, or I am deafe, / She answered not." The echoic silence anticipates that of *Comus*; the dispute on the "sage and serious doctrine of virginity" is yet to come.

Though the quest has been unsuccessful, Mercury appears to reassure Diana's troop of both Jove's sympathy and Zabeta's persistent chastity. Finally, having promised to bring Diana and her nymphs to Zabeta's presence, Mercury directs their attention to the audience—a rebuke, perhaps, to any masquing so self-absorbed that it shades off into drama—and departs. Then, as is to be expected in this form, the actors voice that "discovery" which so neatly reverses the discovery procedures of the conventional dramatic opening tableau:

> What, doe I dream? or doth my minde but muse?
> Is this my leefe, my love, and my delight?
> Or dyd this God my longing minde abuse,
> To feede my fancie with a fained sight?
> Is this *Zabeta*, is it she in deede?
> It is she sure: *Zabeta* mine all haile. [p. 117]

So far, hardly objectionable. Diana even acknowledges the attraction of the worldly responsibility in which her audience is embedded:

> And since by prudence and by pollicie,
> You winne from *Juno* so much worldly wealth,
> And since the Piller of your chastitie,
> Still standeth fast as *Mercurie* me telleth,
> I joy with you, and leave it to your choice
> What kind of life you best shall like to holde. [p. 117]

Diana completes her salutation and she and her train depart, thus concluding that praise of chaste policy which was the favorite hymn of the cult of Elizabeth. But a rift in this conventional composure opens immediately with the hasty entrance of Iris:

> Ah las I come too late,
>   that babling God is gone:
> And Dame *Diana* fled likewise,
>   here standes the Queene alone. [p. 118]

Note the lapse in Diana's dignity here. *Zabeta* is one of the first great documents in a carefully subversive tradition of what we may call—by analogy to anti-Petrarchanism—"anti-Cynthianism." Iris offers a counterauthority to the Cynthian ideology of all that has preceded her—"The Queene of heaven her selfe, / did send me to controle / That tatling traytor Mercurie" (p. 118)—and effects a powerful revision of the ethics of the masque's opening, together with a metalepsis of its fictive conventions.[22] Diana has *fled*, not departed, leaving the queen, not Zabeta, behind. The shift is pertinent: Juno retains a regal aloofness from the dramatic scene, an aloofness of which Elizabeth is now deprived. Some continuity between the Cynthian and post-Cynthian dramatic moments obtains, but Iris, in firm imperatives, makes that persistence the immediate object of ethical scrutiny:

> Call you to minde the time
>   in which you did insue,
> *Dianaes* chase, and were not yet
>   a quest of *Junos* crue.
> Remember all your life,
>   before you were a Queene:
> And then compare it with the daies
>   which you since then have seene.
> Were you not captive caught?
>   were you not kept in walles? [p. 119]

The dignity of the poulter's measure is only the least considerable of Gascoigne's effects here. Diana had become reconciled to the possibility that the choice between rural retirement and courtly engagement might be neutral with respect to the higher standard of chastity, but now Iris takes the momentum of that first demystification and presses toward a toppling of the cult of chastity itself. The first demystification aligns the ethics of the masque perfectly with Elizabeth's own mystique and policy, whereas the second destroys that alignment and adopts demystification itself as the ethics of the masque. For Iris's speech does more than challenge the complacent authority of Diana's fictive world; it challenges ethical authority itself:

> Then geve consent O Queene,
>   to *Junoes* just desire
> Who for your wealth would have you wed,
>   and for your farther hire
> Some Empresse wil you make,
>   she bad me tel you thus:
> Forgeve me (Queene) the words are hers,
>   I come not to discusse.
> I am but Messenger . . . [p. 120]

Other readers have suggested that, through *Zabeta*, Leicester renewed his suit for the queen's hand; as a suit, it is impertinent.[23] But Gascoigne's text by no means willingly takes on the function of unambiguous advocacy. Leicester may well have thought that the masque was a suit of sorts and would certainly have been justified in supposing that it would be *taken* as a suit. My own sense of *Zabeta* is that it was intended to be *about* suit, but that its social context destroyed its neutrality. Gascoigne seems to have misjudged his ability to internalize and defer the courtly context which is the masque's occasion.

This is a hazy area, for more than any other written literary form, a masque's arc of meaning is shaped by its occasion. As such, it shares the economic attributes of oral literatures in which artisan and patron confront each other without a great deal of elaboration within the literary marketplace; the masque-maker, like the minstrel, is rewarded for the creation and immediate gratification of aristocratic interest, while the function of his art is also immediately controlled by the disposition of the patron. Leicester, more accustomed than Gascoigne to the occasional organization of festival rhetoric, would have recognized that the extent of *Zabeta*'s demystifications would be imperceptible within the occasional context, that the masque would *become* a tactlessly renewed suit for the queen's hand. Even putting aside the considerable pressure of the occasion, the queen's virginity was properly a subject only for praise, not for critical debate, and certainly not for the sort of contradictory evaluation with which *Zabeta* concludes. The masque fails to master either social context or rhetorical convention.

The pattern of rival demystifications creates an ideological drama, a conflict on the intellectual plane generated from a rather flat succession of presentations. Here we have Gascoigne's signal contribution to English masquing. We see Jonson at work in similar fashion quite early in his career as courtly maker when, in the *Entertainment at Althrope* (June 1603), the grounds of Lord Spencer's country seat yield two genii loci, one classical and one native. A satyr responds to the presence of queen and prince with naive wonder, the fairy Mab, with courtly grace. She presents a jewel, he, a bow, horn, and hound. These would seem perfectly complementary—the satyr speaking to the prince, Mab to the queen—yet the two genii show considerable hostility to each other in their rival advocacy of the hardy virtues of rural retirement and the sooth elegance of court life (which latter finds expression in Mab's "soft pastoralism"). Jonson does not give us the kind of celebratory reconciliation of *vita activa* and *vita contemplativa* we might expect; there is too much animus and its expression is too petty. Where some sort of psychomachia might work out the conflict, Jonson provides for a permanence of unresolved grouchiness, thus aiming for a fiction mimetic of the muted but persistent incompatibilities of an absolutist state and a seigneural confederation. When Mab presents her gift, arguing it to be "as farre from cheape intent, / In particular to feed / Any hope that should succeed / Or our glorie by the deed" (ll. 141–44), the denial of interest rouses suspicion, and when the satyr presents his gift without any such denial, the equal grace and widely different intent of the two presentations force us to recognize how many pressures work to inhibit the *disin-*

voltura of courtly gesture and how unavoidable interest must be: that recognition becomes the goal and not the guilty secret of the Althrope entertainment. And Jonson learned the technique for enforcing such recognition from Gascoigne.

Yet as we have seen, the Kenilworth entertainments could not free themselves of occasional control and so could not achieve a truly autonomous rhetoric. The fact must have disappointed Gascoigne. The festivities had an ideal shape in his mind, and the text of *The Princely Pleasures*, so complicated in its aims, is primarily a documentation of an unachieved, ideal performance. Hence the exclusion of a thorough account of the Coventry guildsmen's plays, hence the attention to the unperformed but more elaborate version of the freeing of the Lady of the Lake, hence—though in this case there are other reasons as well—the publication of a complete text of *Zabeta* and an exclusion of Gascoigne's ineptitude as the Savage Man. We can see the development of that critical rift between the aims of a performance and the aims of its documentation; the truth of Gascoigne's "true copie" transcends mere journalism.

The final device of the Kenilworth entertainments recalls the clumsy opening performance of the Savage Man, for in that final performance Gascoigne appears "clad like unto *Sylvanus*, God of the Woods" (p. 120). In the situation of pleading that governs this entire final performance, we have more evidence that the Savage Man's offense had been calculated (or miscalculated): the unifying theme of Gascoigne's inventions for Kenilworth is the justification of speakers.[24]

Sylvanus's introductory tale, of the heavenly rejoicing at the queen's arrival at Kenilworth and the heavenly sorrow at her departure, had involved a rich system of correspondences—the mutual reflection of heavenly and earthly action, a complementarity of the divine and the mundane (and of the fictive and the real) which both Sylvanus and Elizabeth possess. This complementarity enables Sylvanus, in his ensuing speech, to assert the absolute coherence of the entertainments by finally absorbing the Savage Man's infatuation with Elizabeth into the coincident tale of Zabeta.[25]

> All [of those who have "sued unto her for grace"] she hath so rigorously repulsed, or rather (to speake playne English) so obstinatly and cruelly rejected, that I sigh to thinke of some their mishaps, I allowe and commende her justice towardes others, and yet the teares stande in mine eyes (yea and my tongue trembleth and faltereth in my mouth) when I begin [to] declare [the] distresses wherein some of them doe presently remayne. I could tell your highnesse of sundry famous and worthy persons, whome shee hath turned and converted into most monstrous shapes and proportions. [p. 124–25]

The suspended critique in *Zabeta* is taken up again in this uncanny metamorphic vision.[26] Zabeta becomes a virgin Circe, transforming her suitors into rocks, mountains, fish, fowl, and, chiefly, flora. Constancy becomes an oak, Inconstancy, a poplar; Due Desert becomes a laurel, while the most passionate of her lovers, Deep Desire, is transformed into a holly bush. Zabeta takes on the function of a pastoral demiurge, wreaking natural forms on the personifications of pastoral eros, distorting Juno's court by representing it as Diana's wood.

Deep Desire, the voice of the holly bush and, thus, a parodic *genius locus*, proceeds to make an extended plea that the queen remain, in terms predictably reminiscent of the Savage Man's first invitation to the pleasance, and that plea subsides into farewell greetings. Sylvanus intervenes with a final request that the queen amend the chaste cruelty of Zabeta "in the conversion of *Deepe Desire*":

> I do humbly crave in his behalfe, that you would either be a suter for him unto the heavenly powers, or else but onely to give your gracious consent that hee may be restored to his prystinate estate. [p. 131]

Sylvanus, both poet and undebased genius locus, intervenes on behalf of Deep Desire—Gascoigne pleading on behalf of his own prior persona, Leicester pleading on behalf of Leicester—seeking that Elizabeth redeem the cruelties of her own fictive self. It is a plea for patronage, despite a poet's offenses; for royal favor, despite a courtier's offenses; for the supercession of festive nymph by politic queen. Gascoigne's devices seek the end of all the inhibitions of pastoral fiction through a dainty critique of the very ideology of festivity. *The Princely Pleasures at Kenilworth Castle* gravitates from pleasure to the realm of necessity. And this reorientation at the level of literary plot is also a fact of literary history, for it is repeated at the level of cultural reception. The script is among the first printed texts recording royal entertainment; aristocratic revelry is reoriented in the bourgeois, public domain by Gascoigne and his printer, Jones.[27]

Let me be quite specific about the conclusion to the Kenilworth entertainments, for the event has too often been seen as quaint, artless, or uncritical, whereas both Jonson and Milton found it troublesome and stimulating. It is not surprising that Gascoigne's praise should figure the culture's enthusiasm for the queen; it is stunning that his critique should penetrate from sexual mythology to sexual politics. It is hardly noteworthy that Gascoigne should speak the interests of his patron or that he should also seek further patronage himself, but it is quite striking that as Sylvanus, he should manage to speak for both at once, rendering the appeal for Elizabeth's hand and for her purse quite literally homologous. That homology makes the conclusion to the entertainments into a dense representation of interest. Most cunning, perhaps, is the social act of printing the texts of an ideal performance, literalizing that representation of interest by making the private economy of aristocratic celebration into a public commodity. Jones and Gascoigne thus accomplish a very sober calculus of vulgarization, opening up an alternative literary nexus, a popular nexus, autonomous from the court.

The violation of the private spheres of aristocratic revelry and of the queen's sexual mystique, together with the momentary dissolution, in *Zabeta*, of any distinction between Elizabeth and Zabeta is not utterly novel, for it involves an extension of one of the crucial structural features of Renaissance masquing, a feature that came to be known in the technical parlance of the Jonsonian masque as the revels. This institution was a novelty a half-century before, in the England of 1512, when

> on the daie of the Epiphanie at night, the kyng with xi. other wer disguised, after the maner of Italie, called a maske, a thyng not seen afore in Englande. . . . These maskers came in, with six gentlemen disguised in silke bearyng staffe torches, and desired the

ladies to daunce, some were content, and some that knewe the fashion of it refused, because it was not a thyng commonly seen. And after thei daunced and commoned together, as the fashion of the Maskes is, thei toke their leave and departed, and so did the Quene, and all the ladies.[28]

The social shock of "commoning" which characterized this Italianate fashion finds ingenious manifestation in the effacement of the queen's privacy and of the privacy of the masque itself.

The poet's press toward autonomy in *The Princely Pleasures at Kenilworth Castle* can equally be discerned at the formal level in the adaptation of the continental echo-lyric to dramatic ends. Guarini, to whom Gascoigne and *The Princely Pleasures* were no doubt unknown, would make such an adaptation and make it more decisively in the following decade. *Il Pastor Fido* employs the full range of dramatic conventions not claimed for the Kenilworth entertainments—opacity of character to (professional) performer, inhibition from explicit topicality or locality (this is, of course always a matter of degree), the internalization of social occasion (marriage, transfer of power) or of biological event (birth, death) as part of a plotted Aristotelian action. In early masquing, convention dictated the easy continuity of masque and courtly context, a theatrical commoning which Gascoigne manages to extend to an unprecedented degree. But he represents the court as hostile to any commoning whatsoever:

> And since I see such sights,
>   I meane such glorious Dames
> As kindle might in frozen brestes,
>   a furnace full of flames.
> I crave (great God) to know
>   what all these Peeres might be:
> And what hath moved these sundry shewes
>   which I of late did see?

(a question wonderfully disingenuous, since the answer is either Elizabeth or Leicester or Poets)

> Enforme me some good man
>   speake, speake some courteous knight,
> They all cry mumme, what shall I do,
>   what sunne shal lend me light? [p. 96]

As always the exclusion of the Savage is a celebration of class, a defense of the value of a body of cultural knowledge that has no function other than to distinguish. But here the appeal to the audience's sense of exclusive distinction is used to authorize the speaker's license. And, in fact, the Savage Man immediately demonstrates that he has resources outside the courtly encyclopedia.

> Wel Eccho, where art thou
>   could I but Eccho finde
> Shee would returne me answere yet
>   by blast of every winde.

> Ho *Eccho: Eccho*, ho,
>   where art thou Eccho, where?
> Why Eccho friend, where dwellest thou now,
>   thou woontst to harbour here.
> *Eccho.*   Here   [pp. 96–97]

Initiating his part in a sequence of entertainments that will violate the aristocratic control of Cynthian ideology, Gascoigne suggests his own independence, a privacy that could flourish at the expense of the queen's.

The continental echo-lyric, as it had been practiced by Barbaro, Marot, Du-Bellay, Serafino, Tebaldeo, and others, projects a far "harder" form of pastoral, a world in which the voice of Echo measures not only the speaker's ignorance but his powerlessness as well.[29] But the relation between the Savage Man and his interlocutor is one of pure and mutual docility.

> Then tell me what was ment,
> By every shew that yet was seene,
>   good *Eccho* be content.
> *Eccho.*   Content.   [p. 97]

The Savage usually poses his questions as a choice between alternatives, leaving Echo the slight responsibility of indicating the latter as the correct choice. The device, then, works as an elaborate modesty topos, a means of informing the audience in the posture of being oneself uninformed. But this shift from the presentational toward the representational (albeit incomplete: the device is neither wholly oration nor wholly dialogue) suggests the possibility of fictive detachment, a world of poetic autonomy just within reach. Here, as elsewhere in the Kenilworth entertainments, metalepsis, whether of genre, mode of presentation, or ethos, denies the social protocols of royal festivity.

I shall have rather more to say about Echo's contribution to Renaissance metalepsis, particularly to the metalepsis of genre—specifically, I shall want to show how Guarini, Jonson, and Milton exploit the echoic in their various efforts to stage the pastoral lyric. Echo's assistance in the work of pastoral dramaturgy obviously derives from her various allegiances, to Virgil, to Ovid, and to Vitruvius, allegiances that I shall want to tease out later in these essays. But perhaps something should first be said about the cultural transformation that freed Echo to perform such abstract—what I should like to call "formalist"—functions.

The traditional moralized reading of the *Metamorphoses* had dictated more straitened functions for Ovid's characters, but that mythographic tradition was languishing. In her brief study of Renaissance editions and translations of Ovid, Madeleine Doran observes that the attention to moral allegory in published annotations virtually ceased in the first half of the sixteenth century; they were displaced by annotations almost exclusively philological, rhetorical, and historical.[30] Her assertion is somewhat misleading, for it suggests that the moral reading of Ovidian fable became outmoded, whereas it became quite modish. The moral tradition thrives in the iconographic handbooks—in Ripa, in Cartari, and, particularly, in Bolzani—where Ovidian *narrative* is itself reduced to the status of annotation (thus completing the Lactantian dismemberment of the Ovidian text), but where the older *allegorizations*, from the *Ovide Moralisé* and from the Ovids of Bersuire and Arnulph of Orleans, are cherished. Fable is subordinated to moral sense. The moral tradition also survives wherever the vernacular Ovids continue to be produced; Golding and Sandys maintain this tradition in England.[31] But *The Princely Pleasures at Kenilworth Castle* refrains from moralizing Echo, being intent on a mythopoesis of a far more subtle sort in the tale of Zabeta—a *modern* fable, more political than moral. The *Princely Pleasures* and, as we shall see, *Il Pastor Fido* seem to bear out the implications of Doran's study by their tendency to shift allegory from moral to formalist concerns.

Moral allegory had a hearty theatrical life in the sixteenth century, but the moralization of antique myth is much subdued by the shocks of physical embodiment, for physical immanence makes antique myth less susceptible to allegorical control. Even with that fusion of tournament, morality play, and Italian spectacle that was the Jonsonian masque, what might have presented itself primarily as psychomachia appeared, in fact, as dance. It was a near triumph of formalist allegory.

The masques are admittedly an extreme case in Jonson's career, and the transfer from moral to formal allegory is never total even there. But the pressure to aestheticize moral action is a constant in his work, making it possible to take Jonson's career as a masque-maker as perhaps the organizing principle of his intellectual biography. At any rate, we can see the displacement of the habits of moral allegory begin in Echo's lament over Narcissus in *Cynthia's Revels:*

> O NARCISSUS,
> Thou that wast once (and yet art) my NARCISSUS;
> Had ECCHO but beene private with thy thoughts,
> Shee would have dropt away her selfe in teares,
> Till shee had all turn'd water, that in her,
> (As in a truer glasse) thou mightst have gaz'd,
> And seene thy beauties by more kind reflection:
> But self-love never yet could looke on truth,
> But with bleard beames; slieke flatterie and shee
> Are twin-borne sisters, and so mixe their eyes,
> As if you sever one, the other dies.   [I.ii.29–39]

This last, purely moral, allegory splits off from antique myth. A persistent tradition of interpreting Ovid's tale, a tradition as old as the fourteenth century—we find it first in Bersuirre's *Ovidius moralizatus*—gives us an Echo who "significat adulatores," so that the structural concision of the tale, its phenomenology of reflection, appears as the complementarity of flattery and vanity.[32] This exegesis seems a bit skewed—if flattery is represented at all within the Ovidian narrative, Narcissus' image is its appropriate representative—so Jonson's dissociation of Echo and flattery would seem to be an attempt at rationalizing the traditional moral reading. Yet Jonson describes vanity and flattery as "twin-borne sisters," not simply as object and image, so that his allegory loses its dependence on much of the received Ovidian narrative; in this rationalized moralization the *formal* match of res and imago figures the social collusion of flattery and vanity. My point is that Jonson cuts Echo out of the moral allegory, leaving her to serve other functions, and he points the slackening ties of moral allegory to fable by emphasizing that *formalist* mechanisms—formal, and not narrative, relations—largely govern his moralization. That is, when Jonson asserts that the collusion of flattery and Narcissan vanity is figured by a reflection, not by a narrative, he brings the relational problem—"How is collusion like reflection?"—into the foreground by introducing a third relational term—collusion is like(?) reflection is like(?) twin birth.[33] Narrative relation thus gives way to a nearly obsessive attention to formalism, to a science of relation itself.[34]

I have suggested that when Jove (and Jonson)—

Commands, that now (after three thousand yeeres,
Which have been exercis'd in JUNOES spight)
Thou [Echo] take corporall figure, and ascend,
Enricht with vocall, and articulate power [I.ii.8–11]

—and her voice again becomes her own property, Echo's function is detached from the constraints of moral allegory. But the Echo of *Cynthia's Revels* needs further consideration.

COURT MARGINALIA I

O, which way shall I first convert my selfe?
Or in what moode shall I assay to speake? *Cynthia's Revels*, I.ii.19–20

The patronage of liminal functions seems to be Echo's most unwavering attribute in the sixteenth century. In Continental echo-lyrics of the early part of the century, Echo frequently converts the lover's despair to hope; nearly as frequently, though, she takes such common suffixes as Italian *-mento*, or *-mente*, or French *-ment* as pretexts for discrediting that hope, thus forcing a Keatsian attenuation of crisis, a being in uncertainties. In baroque drama, her offstage voice is the voice of an unabashed prompter, a voice both authoritative and marginal.[35] Such a dialogic convention had a special appeal for Jonson in 1600.

In the winter of 1599–1600, *Every Man Out of His Humour* was performed at court by Shakespeare's company, the Chamberlain's Men. It must have been particularly consoling to Jonson to find his work receive such approval. He had had a notoriously bad year and a half since his duel with Gabriel Spencer in September of 1598. Jailed and convicted for murder, but quickly freed for reciting his "neck verse," he now bore the clipped ears and branded thumb of a felon. And he was an impoverished felon: he was soon jailed again, in January of 1599, this time for debt. Henslowe apparently advanced him sufficient funds to pay off both his debts and his prison expenses, binding him (formally or informally) to continued hackwork for the Admiral's Company.[36]

Considering the novelty of public-theater economics, it is difficult to assess

Henslowe's treatment of his "gentlemen"—historians of the theater often grant him such epithets as *"reasonably* fair"—but Jonson, at least, seems to have resented this sort of virtual indenture, and none of the plays that find their way into his *Works* was sold to Henslowe's company—he would botch for Henslowe but would do little more.[37] Encouraged by the success of the Chamberlain's Company in *Every Man In* during the previous season, Jonson had gone to work on the related, but considerably less conventional *Every Man Out*, yet his responsibilities to Henslowe kept him simultaneously entangled; In August he undertook Henslowe's commission to write *Page of Plymouth* with Thomas Dekker. In September the strains of collaboration, strains that Jonson suffered badly through much of his career, were more harshly complicated when Chettle and Marston were called in to join Dekker and Jonson on another play, *The Scot's Tragedy*. Chettle was an impecunious hack, a threatening Döppelganger to inflict on an indebted journeyman; Marston may have been an even more nettling coworker, for though he seems to have admired Jonson, his *Histriomastix* seems to have nettled Jonson.

It is difficult to date *Histriomastix* very precisely—it is unlikely that it had its first performance as late as the 1599–1600 season and indeed it was probably written for the Middle Temple Christmas revels of 1598–99.[38] If the play was performed before the autumn collaboration began, it no doubt caused some friction. In his conversations with Drummond of Hawthornden in 1619, Jonson boasted that he had "had many quarrells with Marston beat him & took his Pistol from him, wrote his Poetaster on him the beginning of them were that Marston represented him in the stage"—as Chrysogonus, it is usually held, from *Histriomastix*.[39] If the portrait is broad, it is also flattering, representing Chrysogonus as "servant unto all" the Seven Liberal Arts. His service is badly rewarded; when Sir Oliver Owlet's troupe of players ask Chrysogonus for a play, they hope to get it on the cheap:

> Belch. *Chrisoganus* faith what's the lowest price,
> Chri. You know as well as I; tenne pound a play.
> Gulch. Our Companie's hard of hearing of that side.
> Chri. And will not this booke passe, alasse for pride,
>   I hope to see you starve and storme for bookes,
>   And in the dearth of rich invention,
>   When sweet smooth lines are held for pretious
>   Then will you fawne and crouch to Poesie.
> Clout. Not while goosequillian *Posthast* holds his pen.
> Gut. Will not our owne stuffe serve the multitude?
> Chri. Write on, crie on, yawle to the common sort
>   Of thickskin'd auditours: such rotten stuffs,
>   More fit to fill the paunch of Esquiline,
>   Then feed the hearings of judiciall eares,
>   Yee shades tryumphe, while foggy Ignorance
>   Clouds bright *Apollos* beauty: Time will cleere,

The misty dullnesse of Spectators Eeyes,
The wofull hisses to your fopperies.[40]

Marston and Jonson both shared Chrysogonus's principles, but Jonson may have also seen himself momentarily figured as the company poet, "goosequillian *Posthast*" (despite the fact that Posthaste was almost certainly *meant* for Anthony Munday). The grubby business of marketing what is clearly here represented as intellectual property was a sore subject with Jonson, and his annoyance sustained the so-called War of the Theaters. Johnson relieved some of this annoyance by darting some slight barbs at Marston in the person of Clove in *Every Man Out*. Still, in the face of debt and the clouding of "Bright *Apollos* beauty," this was cold comfort. Chute has suggested that when Jonson became a full member of the bricklayers' guild, probably sometime shortly after his release from Newgate, he did so out of fear that Henslowe might refuse to employ him again—Jonson had killed a valuable member of the Admiral's Company—but it is also possible that he entered the guild out of dissatisfaction with the spiritual and financial impoverishments of a theatrical career.[41]

So the success of *Every Man Out* at the newly opened Globe and its selection by the Office of the Revels for performance at court must have been consoling; no matter how strange and off-putting the play now seems, its approval for court performance argues considerable success. The Revels Office was approving the work of a playwright who not only had been jailed for sedition two years before his imprisonment for murder but was also a Catholic (and hence a potential enemy of the state), having converted during his recent imprisonment at Newgate. The success of the play must have suggested to Jonson the possibility of his own recovery from this perilous marginality. So we can find in *Cynthia's Revels*, the major work of the following year, two superficially contradictory tendencies, a withdrawal from theatricality and an effort at recovery, by means of theatricality itself, from marginality—here again is the liminal poise of echoic speech at Kenilworth. The two tendencies are finally complementary, of course, since the theatricality to which *Cynthia's Revels* commits itself is a somewhat conservative dramaturgy, detached from the sphere of the public theaters. *Cynthia's Revels* becomes an earnest of future court poetry, a prospectus for the masques.

It remains outside the scope of this essay to perform an exhaustive analysis of *Cynthia's Revels*. But attention to Jonson's use of Ovid's fable of Echo and Narcissus can direct us beyond the play's attack on vanity, its most obvious and amusing, but perhaps least interesting, feature, to what I have called the formalist tendencies of his mythographic habits. Ovid's fable authorizes a strain of antitheatricality in the play, an antitheatricality that is finally crucial to the theory of masque-making worked out in the play at large. The embodiment of Echo and her partial detachment from the tradition of the moralized Ovid will be seen as a revival of significances of echo found in those antique texts discussed in the first two chapters. Specifically, Jonson's Echo raises the problem of imitation for the first time in his career, a problem that remains central to Jonsonian poetics; here, the treatment of imitation includes its dark twin—plagiarism—making this a matter of more than private concern.[42] The War of the Theaters (only a skirmish, really—the combatants were friends again within about three years) was, for Jonson, the occasion for a public examination of the idea of originality, of poetic and moral authority in the theater; *Cynthia's Revels* is Jonson's defensive strike.

PLOT AND CURSUS IN *CYNTHIA'S REVELS*

> . . . this studiously and laboriously erratic design.
> Swinburne, *A Study of Ben Jonson*[43]

The play was written for the Children of the Chapel, a boys' company which had been disbanded for sixteen years but which was reconstituted in 1600.[44] *Cynthia's Revels* may have been the first play performed by this new company, and it is almost certainly the play that the Chapel Children performed as their contribution to the extraordinary season of court revels arranged for that winter. Elizabeth saw eight plays between Christmas and Twelfth Night; on Twelfth Night alone, when the Chapel Children made their court debut, the three major adult companies of London also gave performances. It was Elizabeth's most lavish revels, a display of flamboyant magnificence designed to demonstrate her inviolable power in the face of the slight but persistent popular allegiance to Essex, who was then under house arrest. In those words of Jonson's Cupid cited in the introduction to these essays:

> The Huntresse, and Queene of these groves, DIANA (in regard of some black and envious slanders hourely breath'd against her, for her divine justice on ACTEON, as shee pretends) hath here in the vale of *Gargaphy*, proclaim'd a solemne revells . . . in which time, it shall bee lawfull for all sorts of ingenuous persons, to visit her palace, to court her NYMPHES, to exercise all varietie of generous and noble pastimes, as well to intimate how farre shee treads such malicious imputations beneath her, as also to shew how cleere her beauties are from the least wrinkle of austerity, they may be charg'd with. [I.i.91–95, 97–103]

Jonson, of course, colludes in Elizabeth's own theatricality. The Essex rebellion was being represented as mere willful aristocratic irregularity, not a more profound and widespread dissatisfaction with price inflation, with the proliferation of monopolies, with the decay of agriculture, and with all the consequent social dislocations—a dissatisfaction that was beginning to receive perfectly lawful articulation in the House of Commons. Jonson's contribution was thus quite expedient, for its fundamental aim was merely the critique and reform of aristocratic revelry.

In many ways, this program of reform was quite conservative, as was the fashion of Elizabethan reform. Writing for the Chapel Children, Jonson chose to reproduce many of the qualities of those plays that had won the original Chapel Children such favor, the court plays of John Lyly. The reliance on a mythological frame for the plot, the paring down of plot to leave a purely paratactic dramaturgy (what Peter Saccio has called "situational dramaturgy") in which multiple exposure of characters and situations replaces development, the final transformation of mundane situation by theophany—all these point to particular Lylyan influence.[45] Yet to speak of influence may distort the matter, since the evocation of Lylyan dramaturgy is polemical. It declares the return of the Chapel Children to the glories of their old manner and advertises Jonson's abilities in this most acceptable mode. For political reasons, Lyly himself was out of favor and, by 1597, had lost hopes of reversion of the Mastership of the Revels to Sir George Buck, whose claim on the office had also languished somewhat. Some lines in Dekker's *Satiromastix* suggest that Jonson aspired (or was suspected of aspiring) to this post; much that was new to the Jonsonian manner in *Cynthia's Revels* bespeaks just this sort of pretension.[46] And yet there was much in Lyly that was easy for Jonson to adapt, for Jonson's earliest plots (as indeed many of his later plots) depend on a similar parataxis, on the juxtaposition of loosely connected scenes, on discrete character groupings in which individual behavior intensifies without any sign of transformation.[47] In *Cynthia's Revels*, Echo's cursing of the Fountain of Self-Love is followed by the moment when Amorphus drinks the waters; Amorphus purveys these waters to the court—but this line of plot is utterly fractured. Echo's curse comes in I.ii; Amorphus drinks in I.iii; in II.v, the various court pages (another Lylyan touch) go off as "yeomen of the bottles" in an antic procession to the fountain; in IV.i, the foolish ladies of the court are seen awaiting the return of the pages; the water arrives in IV.iv. And this description of the fractured line suggests an even greater focus on the waters than the play actually maintains: the references to this plot in IV.i, for example, occupy only the very first lines of the scene, providing only a pretext for the ladies' assembly on the stage. Finally, this unsophisticated sequence of actions has virtually no effect on the social behavior and organization of the theatrical court. Rather, it provides a frame for an elementary education in courtiership (Amorphus instructing Asotus), advanced classes in courtiership (Hedon and Anaides engaged in mutual instruction), and the frolics of Moria and her train. Jonson provides very little teleological promise for the play; instead of plot we have a concatenation of shows, filling but not shaping an interim.[48] This is the first of Jonson's plays to abjure the intermingling of prose and verse within the same scene, and this technical choice emphasizes the dislocations of each scenic moment from its predecessor. As in Lyly, the final coherence of these discrete shows requires a magical breach of the play's own conventions, depending upon a theophany.

One of the chief features of Lylyan drama, of course, is the use of mythological plots, usually from Ovid. Again Jonson follows the master: his Echo is explicitly that of the Ovidian story—Jonson would seem to be the first European playright to employ just this Echo—and the Echo thus evoked is specifically a pathetic one. I have shown how the antique etiologies of echo inscribe pathos upon the inhuman voice of nature, and although Jonson's scene feints toward a release of Echo from pathos into autonomy, "enricht with vocall, and articulate power" (I.ii.11), it concludes by reenacting her loss of self-possession. In Ovid's tale, Echo interests herself in the scene of Narcissus' demise, interests herself even to the point of self-abnegation; here in *Cynthia's Revels* her recovery of independence is almost complete (though her speech remains bound to antecedent discourse by anadiplosis). But the recovery is brief and she soon flees to her traditional theatrical place offstage. So the scene reenacts that aspect of the Ovidian tale which works as an etiology of pathetically passive and marginal expression.

Perhaps this reenacted etiology of the marginal is what prompted G. K. Hunter's observation that "Echo is seen as the type of the clear-eyed and eloquent scholar-satirist, condemned to be only a voice, and for most of the time a voice disregarded by those who hear her"—in effect a suggestion that Echo, as well as Crites, speaks for Jonson.[49] Hunter suggests, that is, that the scene provides a poignant opening of a theme of critical marginality that is the play's most pervasive autobiographical element. But by granting Echo new freedom of speech, Jonson does more than fulfill his own wish to be heard; he also enables her to generate that thready plot which is the play's only sign of narrative coherence. She gains this power at some cost in dignity, for Mercury recognizes that her curse on the fountain is partly motivated by anger at the Cynthian vengeance wrought there:

> Fond ECCHO, thou prophan'st the grace is done thee:
> So idle worldings (meerely made of voice)
> Censure the powers above them. [I.ii.93–95][50]

Having turned her opportunity for plaint against vengeance into her own reactive vengeance, Echo charts the potential pitfalls of transporting the techniques of comical satire into the practice of court dramaturgy.

Both the Echo-scene and the disguise of Cupid and Mercury strip the normal pattern of Lylyan theophany of its ethical power and purity.[51] Cupid and Mercury seem to revel in the "privileges" of their subordination: as Mercury puts it, "O, what a masse of benefit shall we possesse, in being the invisible spectators of this strange shew, now to be acted."[52] They continue spectators throughout; even after Cupid's fullest moment of dramatic participation (in V.vii, when he takes a part in the first of Crites' masques for Cynthia), he quickly returns to join Mercury as viewer:

> *The Maskes joyne, and they dance.*
> Cup. IS not that AMORPHUS, the travailer?
> Mer. As though it were not! doe you not see how his legs are in travaile with a measure?
> Cup. HEDON, thy master, is next.
> Mer. What, will CUPID turne nomenclator, and cry them? [V.x.1–6]

This has indeed been their function throughout the play, to observe and describe, pronouncing expanded versions of the character writing with which Jonson had augmented the list of dramatis personae of *Every Man Out*, published during the preceding year.[53] This function is most obtrusive in the second act, where their interventions provide a steady counterpoint through each of its four scenes, displacing action into empirical object. Their distance on the scene is reemphasized at the opening of II.i, when Mercury advises Cupid, "since wee are turn'd cracks, let's studie to be like cracks" (ll. 4–5). The word becomes their favorite term for their new status, a slightly unusual bit of slang and one that the child actors of the induction are also fond of applying to each other; the term ties the speech of these gods to the extrafabulous discourse of the Induction.

But Cupid and Mercury share the "benefit" of spectatorship and commentary with others. The scholar, Crites, is similarly marginal and, though less enthusiastic a spectator, similarly satiric. He passes an entire scene (III.iv) describing the multitude of theatrical fools who make up the "outer" court of Cynthia: "I have seene (most honour'd ARETE,) / The strangest pageant, fashion'd like a court, / (At least I dream't I saw it)" (ll. 3–5).[54] This is, of course, part of an extended critique of the significance or value of appearance, a critique worked out in the character grouping of Anaides and Hedon as a satire on ostentatious costume (whether of body or of phrase), in the Amorphus-Asotus group as a satire on gesture, and in the Morian group as a somewhat diffuse attack on the arts of feminine appearance (as when Philautia recapitulates Narcissan crime by swearing by her own image in a glass). The critique occasionally strikes off subtler hits, as when Amorphus makes Asotus the horribly paltry gift of his own hat—"it is a relique I could not so easily have departed with, but as the *hieroglyphicke* of my affection; you shall alter it to what forme you please, it will take any blocke" (I.iv.183–86)—and in so doing submits not only his own mutability to ridicule but also the contemporary idealization of "natural" or "necessary" signification, that ultimate overestimation of appearance manifest in the vogue of hieroglyphics.[55] Yet Jonson is clearly interested in more than a mere attack on vanity, for he has read Ovid closely. The form of vice in Jonson's Gargaphie is held close to the form of transgression in Ovid's—the overestimation of the visual.

Crites takes his station as observer far less lightly than do Cupid and Mercury:

> I suffer for their guilt now, and my soule
> (Like one that lookes on ill-affected eyes)
> Is hurt with meere intention on their follies.
> Why will I view them then? my sense might aske me:

The question opens a full range of questions about the ethics of gaze; perhaps Jonson's most Shakespearean verse, Crites' speech now takes on much of Hamlet's style:

> Or ist a raritie, or some new object,
> That straines my strict observance to this point?
> My spirit should draw a little neere to theirs,
> To gaze on novelties: so vice were one.

His reasoning then swerves wildly; ceasing to accuse his hungry eyes, he makes blindness first the sign and then the instrument of complete habituation to vice:

> Tut, she is stale, ranke, foule, and were it not
> That those (that woo her) greet her with lockt eyes,
> (In spight of all the impostures, paintings, drugs,
> Which her bawd custome dawbes her cheekes withall)
> Shee would betray, her loth'd and leprous face,
> And fright th'enamor'd dotards from themselves:
> But such is the perversenesse of our nature,
> That if we once but fancie levitie,
> (How antike and ridiculous so ere
> It sute with us) yet will our muffled thought
> Choose rather not to see it, then avoide it:

The blindness of the vicious finally shifts to vice's self-delusion of invisibility—it is the child's oddly theatrical magic trick of covering the eyes and crying, "You can't see me":

> And if we can but banish our owne sense,
> We act our mimicke trickes with that free licence,
> That lust, that pleasure, that securitie,
> As if we practiz'd in a paste-boord case,
> And no one saw the motion, but the motion.   [I.v.40–64]

Crites receives no correction in this play, is indeed one of the play's three moral authorities, yet the fascinating and subtle hysteria that laces through the imperious accusations of this speech seriously threaten that authority. To see is to be culpable; to be blind and then to believe oneself unseen is to be culpable: the vagaries of the argument are largely resistant to generalization, save that the argument manifests a pervasive ambivalence to the spectacular that endows vision and visibility with confused, but extreme, ethical import.[56] When Dekker comes to Marston's aid in "the untrussing of the humorous poet," he reacts to more than the presumption to moral authority which Jonson makes in the person(s) of "Asper, Criticus, Quintus Horatius Flaccus"; Dekker's assault challenges the *conjunction* of Jonson's critical presumption with his manifest ambivalence to using spectacle as an instrument of criticism.[57]

What distinguishes Jonson from his own critics is his eagerness to encounter methodological problems in the new practice of satiric comedy; in *Cynthia's Revels* Jonson tests the practice by subjecting spectatorship itself to spectacular treatment.[58] The final device of the play, the Lylyan theophany of Cynthia, in some way abrogates this test, for it presents itself as an ideal spectacle for a fully redeemed spectatorship. Yet when Crites introduces the famous Hesperian hymn to Cynthia, "*Queene*, and *Huntresse*, chaste, and faire," with the words,

> Now thrive invention in this glorious court,
> That not of bountie only, but of right,
> CYNTHIA may grace, and give it life by sight.   [V.v.70–72]

it is clear that the complex effects of gaze have not been simplified, for whether life is granted by the appearance or by the gaze of Cynthia remains unresolved here. Perhaps not ethically unresolved, of course, for as Cynthia herself observes,

> To men, this argument should stand for firme,
> "A Goddesse did it, therefore it was good:
> "We are not cruell, nor delight in bloud."

Yet this redemption of the spectacular from ethical ambiguity leaves a nagging question—

> But what have serious repetitions [theophany, masque; properly imitative creations]
> To doe with revels, and the sports of court?[59]

This hardly resolves the ethical problematics of satiric comedy, proposing, as it does, an alternative form of purer type. The question may or may not be a "rhetorical" one, may be a statement of absolute disjunction between comedy and masque, or may be a legitimate inquiry into whether their continuity be possible. Intended for performance in the "private" theater and at court, *Cynthia's Revels* surely means the question in both ways, registering Jonson's discomfort with the lower spectacularity of comedy and questioning his own ability to extend himself successfully into a realm of higher spectacularity. And Jonson worries here about more than mere success, for into this play he imports the anthropologist's great problem of what constitutes the critical authority of the observer. Nearly all of Jonson's observers are somehow compromised—Mercury and Cupid because of their simultaneous participation in the scene of vice and their program to further corrupt Cynthia's court by afflicting it with amorous heat, Crites because of his visual taint neuroses, Echo because her rise to power over the scene of Gargaphie grows impassioned and augments the prevailing narcissism of the court. And as we shall see, even Cynthia's power is somewhat circumscribed by the follies of her train. Thus we can say that Jonson here not only anticipates a career of masquemaking (perhaps even making a bid for the position of Master of the Revels) but also gives subtle inflection to those tragic studies in the observer's marginality which can be found in *Hamlet* and in the malcontent plays that follow from it.

Jonson shares an arresting foresight with his more honored peers, Spenser and Milton: the early work of all three poets gazes steadily toward the later products. Milton and Spenser rely, of course, on the traditional cursus of the Virgilian career, so that the *Shepheardes Calender* and "Lycidas" employ a traditional paradigm to render articulate and prophetic the youthful voices of their poets. Jonson, on the other hand, was doomed to exclusion from that traditional career, forced by social and economic pressure to make a living in the theater or remain a bricklayer—and there is no *cursus Terentii* to give inevitability to a playwright's progress. If we find in an early play, like *Cynthia's Revels*, the projection of later poetic activity, we cannot properly invoke the mysterious and implicitly typological vocabulary of foreshadowing. Almost nothing in *Cynthia's Revels* has the twilight charm of "Tomorrow to fresh fields and pastures new" (a charm at odds with the tripping fiction of the line's surface), precisely because Jonsonian anticipation is analytic and deliberate, an effortful construction.

CUPID'S COMEDY

> *Atticus.* Come, let passe, let passe, let's see what stuffe must cloath our eares: what's the plaies name?
> *Phylomuse.* What You Will.
> *Doricus.* Ist Commedy, Tragedy, Pastorall, Morall, Nocturnal, or Historie?
> John Marston, *What You Will*[60]

The later, folio version of *Cynthia's Revels* (1616) offers special evidence that the pattern of the play is intended both as a plan for the masques and as a cursus. Jonson expanded the fifth act to include what Amorphus repeatedly calls a public "Act" or "Action," a competition at courtiership.[61] Both Mercury and Crites participate as actors in these "sports of court," beating their opponents at their own games. This extended fifth act fits perfectly the clearer pattern, not of Lylyan court drama, but of Jonsonian masque—by the time the folio copy text went to the printer, Jonson had devised about a dozen masques and entertainments, and the form had achieved considerable stability—the interpolated courtly "duello" functioning as antimasque, the descent of Cynthia working as transformation scene, Crites' device taking the place of the masque proper. As deviser, Crites is redeemed from the actor's trade to which he had descended early in the act. His recovered status as spectator carries hitherto unavailable power: he is granted executive powers to match his critical ones, becoming master of Cynthia's Revels, not commentator on Moria's.

Thus the folio text traces a generic career. The diffuse comedy of the first four acts modulates to the patterned but vicious antimasque that opens the fifth act of the published version, finally unfolding into the masque of the concluding scenes. The original version of the play traces this same shift in genre (though without the antic composure of the antimasque, an aspect of the Jonsonian masque that developed only slowly and that *Cynthia's Revels* did not, in its original form, preconceive), but it traces the shift less as a simple progress from comedy *to* masque than as a disabling of comedy *by* masque. In the penultimate scene, Cupid sets about his business proper, brandishing his arrows "upon—it makes no matter which of the couples. PHANTASTE, and AMORPHUS, at you" (ll. 24–26; he does not actually shoot, fearing lest "CYNTHIA heare the twang of my bow," ll. 22–23). This action has been long deferred, purposed in the play's first scene but suspended by the dissolution of plot into "strange shows." Cynthia's descent restores the possibility of teleological structure: it begins the action anew. Cupid now takes up arms, but nothing happens:

> *Cup.* What prodigie is this? no word of love? no mention? no motion?
> *Mer.* Not a word, my little *Ignis fatue*, not a word.
> *Cup.* Are my darts inchaunted! Is their vigour gone? is their vertue—

Mer. What? CUPID turn'd jealous of himselfe? ha, ha, ha.
Cup. Laughs MERCURY?
Mer. Is CUPID angrie?
Cup. Hath he not cause, when his purpose is so deluded?
Mer. A rare *comoedie*, it shall be intitled, CUPIDS. [V.x.55–65]

The means by which Cupid's arrows have been enchanted are manifold. Crites cannot be wounded as he is already enamored of virtue, Arete, "whose favour makes any one shot-proofe" (l. 110); those courtiers who have drunk of the Fountain of Self-Love are equally impervious.[62]

There is another overarching cause for the impotence of Cupid's arrows: this larger cause is a transcendental version of the play's prevailing delusion, that clothes make the man. Mercury admonishes Cupid:

> Faith, it was ominous to take the name of ANTEROS upon you, you know not what charme or inchantment lies in the word: you saw, I durst not venter upon any device, in our presentment, but was content to be no other than a simple page. Your arrowes properties (to keepe *decorum*) CUPID, are suted (it should seeme) to the nature of him you personate. [ll. 84–90]

This radical principle of decorum provides that the theatrical signifier (name, costume) have absolute power over agency—the name has a certain preeminence here, as we should expect from Jonson—as the masque-self disables or sublimates the self of "the sports of court."

The double cause of Cupid's comedy—the masque's principle of decorum and the homeopathic protection of the fountain—is part of a larger pattern in the play, a pattern of generic rivalry between masque (*Cynthia's Revels*) and satire (*The Fountayne of Selfe-Love*). But the double cause is also sign of another pattern: throughout the play, moral restraint is conceived of as *multiple*.[63] When, for example, Crites expresses doubts in his own capacity to make such a cast "dance truely in a measure" (V.v.8), Arete reassures him that

> What could never in it selfe agree,
> Forgetteth the *eccentrike* propertie,
> And at her sight, turnes forth-with regular,
> Whose scepter guides the flowing *Ocean*.

(a transcendental, extrinsic moral authority)

> And though it did not, yet the most of them
> (Being either courtiers, or not wholly rude)
> Respect of majestie, the place, and presence,
> Will keepe them within ring; especially
> When they are not presented as themselves,
> But masqu'd like others. For (in troth) not so
> T'incorporate them, could be nothing else,
> Then like a state ungovern'd, without lawes. [ll. 19–30]

(A principle or principles of decorum again; a moral authority intrinsic to courtiership and, finally, to masquing.) The courtiers will be restrained by Cynthian magic, by courtly habit, and by the fidelity of substance to semblance: the second is an ethical power vested in the state, the last an ethical power devolving, by tradition, upon the artist; that power is analogous to, but independent of, the mystique of the state.

All this suggests grounds for rethinking the conventional appraisal of Jonsonian ethics, for though *Cynthia's Revels* shows the ethical vehemence that we are told to expect of Jonson (albeit shading off toward a critically problematic hysteria in the character of Crites), it seldom shows any *single-mindedness* about the sources of ideological authority. And because the sources of ideological authority for play and masque are manifold, the effects of such representations are necessarily manifold. It is thus not mere playfulness that motivates the sly oscillations in Jonson's dedication to *Cynthia's Revels*; rather, this dedication "to the speciall fountaine of manners: The Court" celebrates the variety of those forms of efficacy to which a representation can lay claim:

> Thou art a bountifull, and brave spring: and waterest all the noble plants of this *Iland.* In thee, the whole Kingdome dresseth it selfe, and is ambitious to use thee as her glasse. Beware, then, thou render mens figures truly, and teach them no lesse to hate their deformities, then to love their formes. . . . It is not pould'ring, perfuming, and every day smelling of the taylor, that converteth to a beautiful object: but a mind, shining through any sute, which needes no false light either of riches, or honors to helpe it. Such shalt thou find some here, even in the raigne of CYNTHIA (a CRITES, and an ARETE.) Now, under thy PHOEBUS, it will be thy province to make more: Except thou desirest to have thy source mixe with the *Spring* of *selfe-Love,* and so wilt draw upon thee as welcome a discovery of thy dayes, as was then made of her nights. [ll. 1–10, 12–23]

This is a rather complex mimetic theory. The court is first conceived of as an originator or model of behavior, but it rapidly loses this ideal, icastic function and takes on the responsibility for what Frye would call a "low mimesis" of the ethical state of the commonwealth, with Jonson's Lords described as a representation of the Commons. And the conclusion of the dedication makes it clear that Jonson's play operates under the same representational theory, providing both model and mirror.[64]

With the subliming of satiric comedy into masque, we are encouraged to think that principles of low mimesis might disappear from the play. Thus, when Cupid completes his "characters" of Moria and her train, Mercury asks, "Are these (CUPID) the starres of CYNTHIAS court? doe these *Nymphs* attend upon DIANA?" The eccentric critic responds:

> They are in her court (MERCURIE) but not as starres, these never come in the presence of CYNTHIA. The *Nymphs* that make her traine, are the divine ARETE, TIMÈ, PHRONESIS, THAUMA, and others of that high sort. These are privately brought in by MORIA in this licentious time, against her knowledge: and (like so many meteors) will vanish, when shee appeares. [II.iv.105–11]

The plots of Jonson's masques, shadowed in this passage, are primarily plots of replacement, not of struggle, preserving the tendency toward parataxis in *Cynthia's Revels*.[65] But in this early play, the struggle with the vice of spectacle is permitted to contaminate the concluding masque, and the power of Cynthia over love is shared out with the comic power of self-love. The play perpetually hedges its claims to what Saccio calls "anagogic form," the sudden supersession of the mundane by the transcendental. Thus we should interpret Cupid's prophetic history of the Morian regime carefully. When he speaks of her troop as brought in "against" Cynthia's knowledge, Jonson is, I think, being deliberately ambiguous. They are brought in secretly in order to evade a Cynthian notice that would automatically deprive them of their power; they are also brought in to oppose her, licentious folly battling against chaste knowledge. The play sustains itself both on a plot of replacement and on a plot of conflict.

The restraint of full anagogy marks even the play's most radiant moment with deft melancholy. In what may be Jonson's most famous lyric, Hesperus heralds that moment, calling for the descent of Cynthia:

> *Queene*, and *Huntresse*, chaste, and faire,
> Now the *Sunne* is laid to sleepe,
> Seated, in thy silver chaire,
> State in wonted manner keepe:
>   HESPERUS intreats thy light,
>   Goddesse, excellently bright.   [V.vi.1–6]

This is the play's most grave transition—though it is never quite complete—enacting the passage from day to night, the transfer of dramatic centrality from vice to virtue, and a shift into the lyrical mode even more extreme, perhaps, than that which begins the final act of *The Merchant of Venice*. The song finally insists on the sudden entry of the powers of nature into what has been a riot of culture at its most debased and enervated.

Yet the potent natural order here invoked is immediately entreated to slightly unnatural manifestation. In the next stanza Hesperus calls for what must occasionally involve a suspension of Cynthia's wonted manner:

> Earth, let not thy envious shade
> Dare it selfe to interpose;
> CYNTHIAS shining orb was made
> Heaven to cleere, when day did close:
>   Blesse us then with wished sight,
>   Goddesse, excellently bright.   [ll. 7–12]

Part of the charm here lies in the uncertainty that must hover around the stanza. Is the cessation of the earth's envy to be taken as apocalyptic or as a merely natural occurrence, one stage in the cycle that is the "wonted manner" of the earth? The careful emphasis placed on the earth's penumbra in changing the moon's *appearance* preserves a sense of Cynthia's essentially inviolate nature, her transcendence, but that very particular emphasis on natural causality rescinds some of the unqualified epiphanic force of the first stanza. Permanent luminousness cannot finally be manifest; envisioned, it is only momentary:

> Lay thy bow of pearle apart,
> And thy cristall-shining quiver;
> Give unto the flying hart
> Space to breathe, how short soever [ll. 13–16]

The shining is conceived as a brief arrest in a wonted hunt; the promise of pure arrest is finally excluded.[66]

Echo's appearance anticipates this restraint of Cynthian power, for like Cynthia's her appearance and power are temporary. The echo-scene bears on later scenes in other ways as well. I have already discussed the marginal pathos of Echo, a pathos that contributes to Jonson's continuing analysis of spectacle and objectifies the uncertainties of his career; I have also mentioned her emblematic control over a thready satiric plot, a plot only partly suspended by Hesperus's song and Cynthia's descent. Yet the most unsettling aspect of the echo-scene remains to be confronted: despite the thematic and narrative bonds that join it to the rest of the play, the scene possesses a remarkable detachment.[67] As Salomon Pavy describes it in the induction, the scene threatens to slip all ties to the succeeding shows:

> MERCURY, he (in the nature of a conjurer) raises up ECCHO, who weepes over her love, or Daffodill, NARCISSUS, a little; sings; curses the spring wherein the prettie foolish gentleman melted himself away: and ther's an end of her. [ll. 49–54]

This separation of the scene heightens as it isolates. Though Echo's pettish blasphemy against Cynthia joins the scene to what follows, the tonal quality of the scene, its soft pathos, particularly distinguishes it. Her song, "Slow, slow, fresh fount," with its melancholy moralizing ("our beauties are not ours"; I.ii.71) and its motif of melting and dissolution, emphasizes her own tenuous substantiality; her plea to Mercury, "Suffer my thirstie eye to gaze a while, / But e'ene to taste the place, and I am vanisht," and his counteroffer, "Foregoe thy use, and libertie of tongue, / And thou maist dwell on earth, and sport thee there" (ll. 78–81), suggest that without special and mercurial intervention, voice and even the most furtive presence must remain mutually exclusive for her.[68] To a very great extent, these, and Amorphus's boorish pursuit of the nymph as she flies the scene, efface her own verbal crime against Cynthia, helping to detach her from blame for complicity in the satiric plot; they loosen her bondage to moral allegory, preserving her as an isolate object of pity.

The complexity here may derive from a Jonsonian effort to juggle the two fables of Echo, the story of her love for Narcissus and the story of Pan's love for her. The first story was heavily moralized in the handbooks Jonson consulted; the second story, having been recovered to the literate community only lately, had received fresher, less tropological interpretations at the hands of Renaissance exegetes. In the *Dictionarium Historicum* of Charles Estienne (Paris, 1553), one of

Jonson's favorite postclassical authorities on antiquities and the chief source for the mythography of *Cynthia's Revels*, the two tales may be found in adjacent entries. In the one, Echo signifies "iactantiam, haec spreta mutatur in sonum, hoc est, in rem inanem" (boasting which, once scorned, is transformed into sound, that is, into a nullity; sig. Bb$_1$r); in the other, "[Echo] physice coeli harmoniam significare dicitur, Solis amicam, tanquam domini [these are two referents of the fictive Pan], & moderatoris omnium corporum coelestium, ex quibus ipsa componitur atque temperatur" (the physical significance of Echo is said to be the harmony of the heavens. She is the mistress of the Sun, as Lord and Master of all the celestial bodies, of which this harmony is composed and tempered).[69] The two interpretations—entering the play as stated blasphemy and demonstrated harmony—are not fully reconciled, which may help to explain both the uncertain import of the scene and the tonal privilege conferred upon it.

YET NOT PERPLEX MEN, UNTO GAZE:[70]
COURT MARGINALIA II

Despite his many debts—to Lyly, Peele, and Gascoigne; to the early English character writers; to Erasmus; to Ovid, Lucian, Martial, and Seneca—Jonson claimed real novelty for the play and hoped to found a new stage in his own career on its inventiveness:

> In this alone, his MUSE her sweetnesse hath,
> Shee shunnes the print of any beaten path;
> And proves new wayes to come to learned eares.   [Prologue, 9–11]

It does not surprise us to find hearing designated as the discriminating sense here in the prologue; in the preceding induction, the children perform for "auditors" or for an "auditorie"—Jonson indulges in his own quirky flattery by reserving the term *spectator* for those who engage in a potentially culpable form of attention. He promises "words, above action," which would make the play's intended mode of existence extraspectacular, and oddly, this promise includes so full a reification of speech that (unlike the Kenilworth entertainments) to some extent it also shuns print.[71] The virtue that Jonson claims for the play does not reside solely in this acoustic moment—he further promises "matter, above words" (Prologue, 20)— but the acoustic moment is secured as both median and mediator between scene and sense.

The privilege here conferred on sound, which records so much of Jonson's suspicion of the stage, continued through much of his career. In the *Discoveries* (first published in the 1640 folio), he generalizes from his own uneasy disposition when he remarks that "wee *praise* the things wee heare, with much more willingnesse, then those wee see."[72] When Mercury reinstitutes the Macrobian Echo, figure for *harmonia coeli*, by calling for airy concert with her song, the harmonies provide an alternative to the spectacular world that Amorphus carries with him and that can never properly transcend the ethical, as the acoustic can. Echo's music is her chief claim on our sympathy, and it lifts her out of the realm of judgment. Unlike Spenser or Lyly, Jonson endorses an acoustic sublime.

Yet we may still wonder why Echo is betrayed to the spectacular, why she is embodied. In part, the embodiment is proof of the novelty to which Jonson lays claim in his prologue; he braves the challenge of Ausonius's epigram and thus perhaps grows guilty of the play's signal vice—"Vane fictor." Jonson's echo-scene employs theatrical embodiment to figure such contemporary metaphors of cultural history as revival, recovery, and renaissance; as the next essay will show, it is a theatrical figure that Jonson might have learned from Guarini. But unlike Guarini, Jonson gives this master trope of the theater over to ethical critique, questioning whether the embodied past will necessarily lead toward virtue and showing that, granted theatrical presence, the revived Echo stoops to convert her tragically deferred mourning to petty hybris.

Moreover, for perhaps the first time in the Renaissance, Echo again engages that complex of issues accumulating around the Echoes and echoes of Aristophanes, Longus, and Ovid, the problem of literary imitation. And it is the complexity of this problem that finally authorizes the complexity of Jonson's echo-scene. Her first "free speech" renews a voice constrained for three thousand years:

> His name revives, and lifts me up from earth.
> O, which way shall I first convert my selfe?
> Or in what moode shall I assay to speake? [I.ii.18–20]

Her perplexity figures Jonson's, for Echo, having just recovered from a purely nominal existence, speculates on a problem both psychological and grammatical: the question of mood is the satirist's problem par excellence. Is Juvenal's *saeva indignatio* or Horace's gentler manner more in order? Or, to shift from psychological to grammatical mood, does the moralist in the theater speak indicatives (mirror), jussives (model), or, if this last were possible, imperatives? We can shift still again, from these broader rhetorical questions to more particular issues in practical poetics. What is the proper mode of reviving antique genre and antique tale? How may the modern writer usefully convert prevenient utterance? (And one must, after all, convert the prevenient: the tenor of Echo's complaint against hoarding of beauties extends to literary property, as we shall see shortly.) Flat repetition is seen as bondage in this scene, and Mercury's induction to Echo's appearance, with its allusion to the tragic pressure to achieve mourning, together with Echo's resistance to silencing once the scene is underway, foreground her appetite for this conversion or recreation of self. This conversion is strenuously performed in Echo's every speech; we see her work through repetition to a fully expressive independence of speech as she breaks the bonds of anadiplosis which tie each speech to Mercury's. With each speech she gains anew the power of self-representation.[73]

The theoretical problems of artful imitation receive a particularly grubby reinforcement later in *Cynthia's Revels*, when Anaides tells Hedon how best to mount an attack on Crites. The cherished idea of imitatio intrudes, scornfully represented as plagiarism:

Ile instruct thee what thou shalt doe . . . .: Approve any thing thou hearest of his, to the receiv'd opinion of it; but if it bee extraordinarie, give it from him to some other, whom thou more particularly affect'st. That's the way to plague him, and he shall never come to defend himselfe. S'lud, Ile give out, all he does is dictated from other men, and sweare it too (if thou'lt ha' mee) and that I know the time, and place where he stole it, though my soule bee guiltie of no such thing. [III.ii.54–63]

Hedon's hostility to Crites is everywhere marked by hysteria; here he is outraged that Crites hasn't noticed him (Anaides will later devise further revenge by encouraging the court to deprive Crites of their gaze). Yet in fact Crites has at least overheard their plot, and he responds with wily aptness: his soliloquy in the next scene is indeed dictated from other men, and the place where he stole it is Seneca's *De Remediis Fortuitorum* (VII.i) when it is not the *De Constantia* (xiii). The Senecan moral bombast that Jonson so often and so freely drew on throughout his career is here imported not simply for its content but because the appropriation of Seneca can serve as an *example*. The speech demonstrates the difference between the composite surface of courtiership and the imitative integration carried on in wisdom's self-construction.⁷⁴ The charges of plagiarism are shown to be irrelevant (or at least that is Jonson's aim), not because Crites has demonstrated his independence from influence, but because he has managed to perform that perfect imitation which is "to make choise of one excellent man above the rest, and so to follow him, till he grow very *Hee*" (*Discoveries*, ll. 2469–70).

The strategem of accusing Crites of plagiarism is the device of courtly bad conscience, as Amorphus's advice on courtiership makes clear. He tells Asotus to acquaint himself with Crites in order to steal his phrases:

Amo. A quick nimble memory will lift it away, and, at your next publique meale, it is your owne.
Aso. But I shall never utter it perfectly, sir.
Amo. No matter, let it come lame. In ordinary talke you shall play it away, as you doe your light crownes at *primero*: It will passe.
Aso. I shall attempt sir.
Amo. Doe. It is your shifting age for wit, and I assure you, men must bee prudent.
[III.i.43–52]

Phrases become coin in a court economy. Asotus is encouraged, though, to test his own credit as well. "See what your proper GENIUS can performe alone, without adiection of any other MINERVA" (III.v.99–100), says Amorphus on another occasion, but he seems hardly to suggest the test in true earnest, for when a faltering Amorphus resorts to citation from Kyd's *Spanish Tragedy* (following the example of his master), he is applauded: "O, that peece was excellent! if you could picke out more of these *play-particles*, and (as occasion shall salute you) embroider, or damaske your discourse with them, perswade your soule, it would most judiciously commend you" (118–22).⁷⁵

The issue of plagiarism cuts considerably deeper than these slight examples of courtly pretense perhaps suggest. Similar concerns with verbal theft are manifest in the induction, outside the fictive scene of Gargaphie, in the "real" scene of the mere stage. Pavy, hurt that the Author has given the prologue to another actor, decides to "tell all the argument of his play aforehand, and so stale his invention to the auditorie before it come forth" (ll. 35–37). He suggests that the audience is oddly obsessed with novelty, a suggestion he soon makes more explicit in his impersonation of a gallant who comes to sit on stage, rails at the company, and then demands to see the playwright "in the general behalfe of this faire societie here" (l. 173):

> They could wish, your *Poets* would leave to bee the promoters of other mens jests, and to way-lay all the stale *apothegmes*, or olde bookes, they can heare of (in print, or otherwise) to farce their *Scenes* withall. That they would not so penuriously gleane wit, from everie laundresse, or hackney-man. . . . They say, the *umbrae*, or ghosts of some three or four playes, departed a dozen yeeres since, have bin seene walking on your stage heere: take heed, boy, if your house bee haunted with such *hobgoblins*. [ll. 176–81, 194–98][76]

This is the tenor of much of Marston's attack on Jonson in *What You Will* and of Dekker's assaults in *Satiromastix*—that his plays are composites of phrase and of genre, particularly of classical phrase and genre.[77] Marston and Dekker had not yet made such criticism a matter of public record by the time of the queen's Christmastide revels of 1600–01, but these men were Jonson's colleagues; the place of these flytings on originality in the ensuing War of the Theaters suggests that they were aware of Jonson's particular sensitivity to the matter and that they may well have twitted him about his cherished imitatio already, arguing that such matters did not pertain to the theater. But the war established their pertinence.[78]

In any event, *Cynthia's Revels* already manifests some defensiveness about the attractions and dangers of renovation and innovation. Indeed, the play dismisses the spectacular pursuit of perpetual novelty as folly, even while maintaining its claims for its own novelty. Property and nervous pride, then, may explain the considerable detachment of this echo-scene from the atmosphere and action that follows it. This detachment, together with the suppression of the moralizations of Echo, frees the echo-scene to represent a very tenuous materialization of voice, the conversion of poetry into a commodity within a modern theatrical marketplace. More poignantly, the isolation of the scene registers the pathos attendant on the invention of a self constructed out of the words of others.

4
THE MASQUE OF MEMORY: ECHO AND AUTHORSHIP IN JONSON'S MASQUES

> They live, againe, these beauties to behold.
> And thence in flowry mazes walking forth,
> Sing hymnes in celebration of their worth.
> Whilst, to their songs, two fountaines flow, one hight
> Of *lasting Youth*, the other *chast Delight*,
> That at the closes, from their bottomes spring,
> And strike the ayre to *eccho* what they sing.
>
> *The Masque of Beautie*, 142–48

Readers familiar with the major events of Jonson's later career will have recognized the critique of theatricality in *Cynthia's Revels* as a slight and composed prologue to that series of furious little outbursts that make up the quarrel with Inigo Jones. The rivalry of spectacle and word in the dispute would be easier to describe as a reenactment of the agon between Narcissus and Echo, were it not that the exponent of the word is so obviously the more afflicted with vanity. Jonson's professional Narcissism is not all that prevents a simple identification between himself and the *reasonabilis nympha*, for the chief means by which he asserts the preeminence of the acoustic is to print the texts of the masques, and as we have seen, Ovid's Echo had maintained a doomed resistance to the visual technologies of the page. Still, the myth had helped Jonson probe his resistance to spectacle in *Cynthia's Revels*, and the idea of the echoic would continue to inform his meditations on masquing.

It is difficult to say when Jones and Jonson began to irritate each other, when Jones's scenic virtuosity became central to Jonson's uneasy imaginings of the theatrical. Signs of friction begin to show as early as 1609, when, in the text of *The Masque of Queenes*, Jonson describes the House of Fame as "Mr *Jones* his Invention, and Designe . . ."

> which I willingly acknowledge for him; since it is a vertue, planted in good natures, that what respects they wish to obtayne fruictfully from others, they will give ingenuously themselves. [ll. 683, 706–709]

The edge here is unmistakable, a sure indication that Jonson had found Jones unwilling to accede to the poet's preeminence in the creation of the masque. The quarrel probably did not approach full heat until the collaboration was more than a decade old, but the quarrel was in a sense "plotted" even before the slight petulance of Jonson's nod to Jones in *Queenes*.

In the preface to *The Masques of Blacknesse and Beautie* (performed in 1605 and 1608—*Blacknesse* was the first Jones-Jonson collaboration), we find Jonson justifying publication on the grounds that "little had beene done to the studie of *magnificence* in these, if presently with the rage of the people, who (as a part of greatnesse) are priviledged by custome, to deface their *carkasses*, the *spirits* had also perished" (ll. 5–9); the "bodily part" (ll. 90–91) of masque is already described as near-carrion.[1] The insinuation in *carkasses* develops a more fundamental Jonsonian topos from the preface to *Hymenaei* (first performed in 1606, after *Blacknesse*, but the first published of all the masques)—the masque performed is a soul embodied—

> It is a noble and just advantage, that the things subjected to the *understanding* have of those which are objected to *sense*, that the one sort are but momentarie, and meerely taking; the other impressing, and lasting: Else the glorie of all these *solemnities* had perish'd like a blaze, and gone out, in the *beholders* eyes. So short-liv'd are the *bodies* of all things, in comparison of their *soules*. [ll. 1–7]

The privilege or "advantage" of the appeal to understanding lies in its durability, and that is why the privileged acoustic moment of *Cynthia's Revels* reappears as the privileged text of the masques. Though the durable text must not be confused with "the things subjected to understanding" (i.e., "the most high, and heartie *inventions*" [ll. 14–15] appropriated to the Senecan ethical subject), the two are analogous: they are both durable properties, freed from the temporal constraints of occasion.[2] The present chapter will treat of this getting-free for it is an important episode in the social history of authorship.

The famous phrase used to describe masque-devices in the preface to *Hymenaei*—"More remov'd *mysteries*" (ll. 18–19)—has often been misconstrued: "remov'd" is not rendered tautologous by "*mysteries*" and does not simply mean "esoteric"; it means "detached from 'present occasions.'" Printing can represent, but does not *itself* constitute, that removal. The Platonic poetics of the preface to *Hymenaei*, the implied celebration of the ecstatic removal of the masque from an occasional body, may help us to understand the issues at stake in the Jones-Jonson controversy.

What has not been noticed in the various histories of the quarrel is that, while the reference to "carkasses" in the preface to *Blacknesse and Beautie* does in fact slight the "bodily part," it does not slight Jones; nothing in the careful description of the spectacle in *Blacknesse* is aimed at denigrating Jones's work. Jonson eagerly describes the "extravagant order" (l. 65) of Jones's machines and patiently explains Jones's perspective effects—this was part of a long campaign to educate the English eye, which persisted in its inability to apprehend those pictorial conventions that on the Continent were the accepted marks of recession.[3] In fact, only the term *carkasses* registers that ambivalence toward the spectacular already manifest in *Cynthia's Revels*. So we need no longer marvel at the eventual hostility to Jones; it would be more fruitful to inquire initially into how Jones's particular scenic art managed to hold Jonsonian ambivalence in check. Even "holding in check" may underestimate Jones's achievement. Jonson was so beguiled by the architect's devices for their first production that he went further than he ever had or ever would toward an endorsement of gaze. *Blacknesse* is based on a Pican metaphysics of light, making it perhaps the most emphatic of all Renaissance celebrations of the visual.[4] Here we may begin to articulate the appeal that Jones's style held for Jonson.

First, it required the education of the eye. Though the reverse may seem true to the viewer habituated to it, the novelty of perspective and the difficulty of its cultural apprehension dissipated the affective power of accepted spectacular practice. Because vision had become more "objected to sense," Jonson could conceive of spectacle as "meerely taking." More important, Jones provided a figure for the Platonic ideal of masque-poetics; though actually no deeper than that of the public theaters, Jones's stage presented an image of infinite regress, of a systematically attenuated presence, and so stood as a constant visual reminder that occasional space and time were part of a larger continuum. And finally, in the extensive foreground, the conventions of perspective made the spatial continuum of Jones's stage into an hierarchical space, a figure of control. The court stage was not the democratic place of the public stage, not a homogeneous space in which the pretensions of an Amorphus might flourish.[5]

The hierarchical space was finally necessary to the special exigencies of Jacobean masquing, for (in a move that harks back three-quarters of a century to Henrician masquing) the queen herself, and soon thereafter the prince, chose to participate in Jonson's first masque. She joined not simply as a dancer within the revels—which suspend (without dissolving) Tudor masquing—but as a participant within the fictive space and (occasionally) fictive time of the device itself. The royal intrusion upon the theatrical space made it possible to give that space greater ideological power; the intrusion also deprived Jonson of that ultimate authority he had hoped to gain over the courtly stage, and it made the denial of occasional constraints an uphill battle. This is precisely why Jones won the quarrel with Jonson: whereas the poet's aims were often tangential to those of the royal masquers, the architect's were always congruent with them, and the space that aggrandized the masque aggrandized Jones.

My purpose here is to explore the relations that obtain between Jonsonian echo and this imperial space.

VISION AND CONTINUITY IN *THE MASQUES OF BLACKNESSE AND BEAUTIE*

> Now, under thy *PHOEBUS*, it will be thy province to make more.
> Dedication to Cynthia's Revels

We can construct a crude historical typology of Jonson's masques thus: the Jacobean masque reveals royal power; the Caroline masque conceals royal impotence. Stephen Orgel has noted that "when a pastoral scene appears before 1616 it always comes at the beginning, after 1616 it always comes at the end."[6] Though I shall soon need to qualify these generalizations, they help us rough out the two spatial patterns, progress toward court and vacation from it, that distinguish the two phases of Jonsonian masquing. His first court masques, the paired *Masques of Blacknesse and Beautie*, are patterned as a romance quest which makes Britain the universal center and goal; this spatial pattern has its temporal correlative in progresses from night to day and from winter to spring, plots of natural time which may also be taken as historical, as a plot of modernization.

As is customary in the masques, the action is simple—though it is noteworthy that *Blacknesse and Beautie* is among the more elaborate of Jonson's masque-plots—and its germ was Queen Anne's decision to perform in a masque of "Black-mores." Niger has gone in search of evidence to confute "the fabulous voices of some few / Poore brain-sicke men, stil'd *Poets*" (ll. 155–56), for the poets hold dark skin in low esteem; he wants to bolster an argument on behalf of his daughters, impersonated by the queen and her ladies, "that, in their black, the perfectst beauty growes" (l. 144). His search is thwarted—only the fair are "made queenes of all desires" (l. 176)—but hard on his sad discovery has come an apparition of the moon-goddess, Æthiopia, who sends his daughters in search of a land where the sun which mars their beauty is replaced by "a greater *Light*, / Who formes all beauty, with his sight" (ll. 194–95).

The masque presents the end of their quest, the discovery of "Britania." Though the revels unite these Daughters of Niger with the men of England, the masque finally divides them with an echo-song, leaving these nymphs of fresh water, like Alpheus, suspended as "the Ocean's guests," lost to their native lake, but parted from their new-found land. The closing speech of Æthiopia foretells the bleaching of their skin in a year-long ritual bathing and the drying of their faces in the British sun a year hence, all of which will enable them to rejoin their terrestrial suitors in perfect beauty. Thus *Blacknesse*.

Beautie was postponed two years, for the marriages of Essex to Lady Frances Howard and of Lord Hay to Honora Denny demanded special wedding masques (Jonson's *Hymenaei* and Campion's *Lord Hay's Masque*); hence, one of the special functions of the plot of *Beautie* was to explain the delay of the Daughters of Niger. Moreover, Jonson had to adapt the situation to accommodate four new Daughters. Proteus informs the original dozen that Night has jealously abducted these new sisters and has imprisoned them on a floating island, so the errantry begins again. The search is only reported—first, by Boreas, blustering and insensitive to the magnificence before him (he opens the masque with the unceremonious question, "Which, among these, is ALBION, NEPTUNES sonne?" [ll. 27–28]), and finally, by the suaver Vulturus, who announces the Daughters' discovery of the island. The transformation scene then reveals the island to the audience, with an echo-song describing this as a figure both of Platonic creation, Love's genesis of the world out of Chaos (ll. 282–84), and of dawning.

Beautie nicely illustrates the centrality of the revels to the significance of masque. Its dancing, hardly a dissipation of meaning, is quite clearly magical in function: the "commoning" of dance fixes the island, "*beauties* perfect *throne*," so that it is "now made peculiar, to this place, alone (l. 386–87).[7] A final choral song marks the end of all wandering, closing the scene with a double echo:

> So all that see your *beauties* sphære,
> May know the'*Elysian* fields are here.
> *Ecch.* Th'*Elysian* fields are here.
> > *Ecch. Elysian* fields are here. [ll. 406–09]

As in Virgilian pastoral, the resonance of the place signals its docility, its pure receptiveness to human dominion; as in those entertainments that draw on the echo-device of the Kenilworth festivities—the more elegant, more spectacular, and less subtle Elvetham entertainment (1591); the plain, but vigorous devices for the progress to Bisham Abbey (1592); the very impressive Gray's Inn masque, *Proteus and the Adamantine Rock* (1959)—the natural reverence of a particular landscape for the monarch effaces the specific power of the pastoralist as the motive for echoing. In the year before the production of *Beautie*, Campion had used Jones's stage at Whitehall to bring this slight tradition to a head with the *Lord Hay's Masque*.[8] A riot of echo-song is foretold when Zephyrus seconds Flora's gifts:

> *Flora.* Such are her presents, endles, as her love,
> And such for ever may this nights joy prove
> *Zeph.* For ever endles may this nights joy prove,
> So eccoes *Zephyrus* the friend of love.[9]

Night then ordains a magical concert of Orphean song which makes the trees of Flora's grove dance. The song is repeated thrice, transforming the trees, three by three, into masquers. Campion explains:

> This *Chorus* was in manner of an Eccho seconded by the Cornets, then by the consort of ten, then by the consort of twelve, and by a double *Chorus* of voices standing on either side . . . and as soone as the *Chorus* ended, the violins, or consorte of twelve, began to play the second new daunce, which was taken in form of an Eccho by the cornetts, and then catch't in like manner by the consort of ten, . . . which kind of ecchoing musicke rarely became their *Silvan* attire.[10]

Two more such echo-songs conclude the masque, confirming the association of the form with the locus of courtly celebration, yet depriving the form of analytic force. Though *Beautie* concludes with a similar representation of the amenity of landscape, its plot of difficult progress maintains precisely the analytic power that Campion's masque relinquishes.

Blacknesse is a masque of Discrimination in nearly every sense of the term. It opens with a song welcoming "Fayre Niger," an immediate challenge to analytic vision which constitutes the first stage in a program to subject the element of the spectacular to ethical control. The praise of the Daughters of Niger is both a compliment to the queen and her ladies and an effort to "prove that beauty best, / Which not the colour, but the feature / Assures unto the creature" (ll. 106–08)—this latter a proof intended to teach the eye to discriminate, to resist confusions.

Niger exemplifies such resistance, preserving himself, to Ocean's astonishment, free from brackish admixture throughout his maritime wanderings. His models in this engaged purity are souls, which "mix with their bodies, yet reserve for ever / A power of separation" (ll. 125–26). Yet his quest entails a countervailing drive toward unity. Searching out a land "whose termination (of the *Greeke*) / sounds *TANIA*" (ll. 189–90) and whose climate is controlled by a new Phoebus, he aims to reassemble the name of the island. Britannia was a new name, chosen by James to mark the unification of England and Scotland and the realignment of political boundaries with natural ones. The image of the unified kingdom, magically embodied in the reunified name (there is a great deal of such word magic in Jonson's masques), is a distant goal, prefigured in the dance that joins the blackened ladies and their admiring audience and finally achieved in the celebration of Harmonia in *Beautie*. But synthesis depends upon the prior reification of boundaries. Thus:

> With that great name BRITANIA, this blest Isle
> Hath wonne her ancient dignitie, and stile,
> A *world, divided from the world:* and tri'd
> The abstract of it, in his general pride   [ll. 246–49]

Many aspects of the philosophical stance of the Jonsonian masque may be found here in miniature. The Neoplatonic habit of thought, which posits levels of microcosm and macrocosm linked by various forms of magical correspondence, makes the island into the separate, functional image of an integral world. We may further note that the *name* of the island has some sort of instrumentality ("with that great name") in this system of representation, replacing all the apparatuses of correspondence (influence, resemblance, synecdoche) with the single apparatus of denomination.[11] Perhaps more striking than this linguistic Neoplatonism is the way in which it is infused with the Stoicism that everywhere dominates Jonsonian ethics. Britannia's separation makes it a place of retirement of the Senecan, not the Ficinan sort, for it is a place in which the world may be "tri'd." Britannia thus enters a conservative tradition of Utopian thought in which private reflection, both juridical and empirical, claims privileged access to knowledge of the world at large. The crucial point here is that the relation of the island to the world is not mechanical, not part of the structure of a cosmos layered from its creation: *abstract* is a verbal noun, an activity of trial, of renaming; it is a conceptual struggle to be won.

We here confront what I should like to designate as the phenomenology of the proscenium. I shall have more to say of the Italianate proscenium and how it influenced Jonson, but for the moment it will suffice to notice the way the proscenium confers spatial unity on the stage and functions as a visual ceremony by which the stage is abstracted from the phenomenological world of the audience. The abstraction of Britannia is patterned on this abstraction of the integral stage. It is hardly surprising, then, that Jonson has contrived considerable resistance to the revels in *Blacknesse*, insisting that the breach in the proscenium convention threatens the ideal of reserve or abstraction that controls the masque;

the Daughters of Niger dance on the shore of Albion (marked, I take it, by the plane of the proscenium), but:

> *Their owne single* dance *ended, as they were about to make choice of their men: One, from the sea, was heard to call 'hem with this* charme, *sung by a tenor voyce.*
>
> SONG
> Come away, come away,
> We grow jealous of your stay:
> If you doe not stop your eare,
> We shall have more cause to feare
> *Syrens* of the land, then they
> To doubt the *Syrens* of the sea [ll. 291–300]

Something tense and precious is at stake here, as the charged evocation of the Sirens' song makes clear, but that something is difficult to define.[12] Jonson would seem to have *designed* the difficulty: the song is not sung in *character* and its advocacy is beyond personal interest. Though generally "oceanic," the voice is not that of Oceanus; it sings beyond the genius of the sea. But the Daughters of Niger persist in their intent to dance, so a second song reiterates the call to abjure the revels. Impersonal double echoes answer this impersonal call; as in *Beautie*, they hollow out an offstage site, though this time the site is the auditorium—"several parts of the land" (l. 304)—not some inaccessible spot concealed beyond the proscenium. As the sea-voice sings, the echoing land appropriates and subverts its words:

> Daughters of the subtle floud,
>   Doe not let earth longer intertayne you;
> 1. *Ecch.* Let earth longer intertayne you.
> 2. *Ecch.* Longer intertayne you. [ll. 306–09]

The double echo is a voice of conjunction, of "intertaynment." As in the Ovidian tale of Echo, the repetition of words has coital implications; in the context of the revels, this is entirely appropriate, for it complements the erotic dimension of the dancing. Ovid enables us to gloss the passage further, for the sea-voice sympathizes with the Narcissan ideal of self-possession.

The largest aim of this masque has been to describe the boundaries of political and personal form and so isolate the essential unities of the nation and of the subject, but the "intertaynment" of dance and echo-song gravely threatens those boundaries. We can see them waver as the sea-voice, relenting in its advocacy of absolute, virgin withdrawal, argues that a demure retirement is, after all, only prudent courtship:

> If they love,
>   You shall quickly see;
> For when to flight you move,
> They'll follow you, the more you flee.
>   1. *Ecch.* Follow you, the more you flee.
>   2. *Ecch.* The more you flee. [ll. 315–19][13]

The echoes no longer need to convert the import of the prior utterance, for their damage has been done. This is Jonson at his most powerfully witty: though tidal motion may cause the chaste withdrawal of the seas, the ardent land will persist in flirtatious contact. The shore that figures the stability of the subject thus grows inconstant and fluctuating.

The masque, ending at this subtly fluctuating national and personal shore, has none of the closure that critical tradition asks us to expect of the Jonsonian masque. Its ideal of defined subjectivity is challenged by the very center of the performance, the ritual dance, which is the masque's archaic motive (as the royal will is its immediate motive). Nor does the challenge conduce to a final resolution; the Daughters of Niger retire convinced of their own imperfection—a surface imperfection, perhaps, yet one that is no longer to be dismissed by the educated eye. Instead, the Daughters themselves are charged with effacing that imperfection ("You shall your gentler limmes ore-lave, / And for your paines, perfection have" [ll. 345–46]). This purgation of blackness, moreover, is as much a threat to definition as is the tide: the ritual baths in "that purer brine / And wholesome dew, call'd *Ros-marine*" (ll. 339–40) may have a certain dainty elegance, but they effectively destroy the miracle of the Daughters' untainted travel through the domains of Oceanus. Jonson's marginal gloss on the lines in which the miracle is first mentioned is telling: "There wants not inough, in nature, to authorize this part of our fiction, in separating *Niger* from the *Ocean*, (beside the fable of *Alpheus*, and that, to which *Virgil* alludes of *Arethusa* in his 10. *Eclog. Sic tibi, cum fluctus subterlabere Sicanos, Doris amara suam non intermisceat undam*), etc."[14] We could say that Jonson expiates his bad conscience for earlier unauthorized fiction in this masque; *Blacknesse* might be named *The Triumph of the Reality Principle*. Its final affirmations, that blackness is indeed a problem and that patience—not vision—can solve that problem, are rather homely, though just what one would expect from Jonson, whose ambivalence to the visionary so fully informed his first essay in the theory of the masque, *Cynthia's Revels*.

There are signs of a change, though, a relief of the ambivalence. In the courtly context, Jonson seems willing to make his peace with hieroglyphics, as long as they have demonstrable authority.[15] The hieroglyphics that appear on the fans of the Daughters of Niger are accompanied, it should be added, by the Daughters' names, so the nonreferential symbology is restrained. Moreover, Jonson insists that decorum also dictated the use of hieroglyphics, "which manner of *Symbole* I rather chose, then *Imprese*, as well for strangenesse, as relishing of antiquitie, and more applying to that originall doctrine of sculpture [scripture?], which the *Ægyptians* are said, first, to have brought from the *Æthiopians*" (ll. 270–74). The antiquity of these symbols recommends them, not merely because of Jonson's famous antiquarianism, but more particularly because they date the masque (and because their provenance is particularly appropriate). Finally, this emphasis on Ethiopian antiquity takes its place in that scheme of modernization that is one of the overarching plots of *Blacknesse and Beautie*.

The *Masque of Blacknesse* takes place under the influence of Aethiopia, a Cynthia made alien. The lunar and aquatic symbolism of the masque—its hieroglyphics of water, the mysterious writing on the moon which is reflected in the lake at the source of the Niger (ll. 180–95), the tidal figure that closes the revels—lack the swelling power that such figures muster in Elizabethan regicentric poetry, but that is, I think, precisely Jonson's point.[16] We observe, here, the afterlife of the Cynthian, the fictions of Elizabeth reduced to a tenuous restraint, capable only of effecting a brief withdrawal, a year's purgation which will release the nymphs into a myth of Jacobean union. Thus, like the Cynthia of *Cynthia's Revels*, unable to provide more than a moment of serene glory ("space to breathe how short soever") and gracefully suffering invidious compare to "a lasting *plenilune*," Aethiopia submits her deity to natural compulsion: "Inough, bright *Nymphs*, the night growes old, / And we are griev'd, we cannot hold / You longer light" (ll. 325–27).

I am not suggesting that the masque is simply nostalgic or that it manifests any resistance to the present. Rather, *Blacknesse* is a conservative fiction; it argues that the proper celebration of Anne and the women of her court must convert the mythology of earlier celebrations. The echoing voice is not the voice of withdrawal, for it calls upon the nymphs instead to remain; it provides a model for the deferred conversion of Cynthian restraint into decorous coition—dance, national union, the dalliance of land and sea. But it is only a model, and the masque is shaped to acknowledge the human labor required to accommodate past to present.

Perhaps I should have used *travail* instead of *labor* and so have exploited that most Jonsonian of puns. The form chosen—quest, transformation scene, revels, withdrawal—returns the masquers to a disequilibrium, and this disequilibrium reappears at the opening of *Beautie* as a continued imperative for effortful journey, for travail. In the second masque, which ends the travail, the implications of that travail are extended: the quest is more vagrant, for the Daughters are seeking a wandering island, and it takes on a more fully articulated temporal dimension. That is, the implicit historical allegory of *Blacknesse*, represented as the journey from an Ethiopia imbued with antique and nocturnal lore to a modern, daytime Britain, is enriched. This second journey is presided over by Januarius, genius of spatial and seasonal passage; it too narrates a passage from night to day (and one far more emphatic than that of Blacknesse); and it deals explicitly with problems of spatial and temporal vagrancy, linking the themes of error and of delay.

This enrichment of the earlier allegory is particularly clear in the speeches before the transformation scene, where Jonson adopts a manner considerably more dramatic than that of *Blacknesse*. Where, for example, a diffuse tidal force had retarded and deferred full union at the conclusion of the 1605 masque, in 1608 Jonson opens with a fully realized antagonist: Night, whose overt envy of beauty and union rises aggressively to block fruition, enforces the wandering with "malice and her magicke" (l. 84). As the struggle of quest grows more dire, so too does the goal grow in both synchronic and syncretic power. When Vulturnus announces the recovery of the floating island, he informs the audience that the Daughters of Niger have been joined there by Linus and Orpheus. The song of transformation during which the island is revealed raises the plot of modernization to what seems an ultimate extreme:

> When *Love*, at first, did moove
> From out of *Chaos*, brightned
> So was the world, and lightned,
> As now! *Eccho.* As now! *Eccho.* As now! [ll. 282–85]

The fit of present to past is both stated and figured here—figured, that is, in an echo-song that recalls the earlier fiction of *Blacknesse*. In the earlier masque, the echo-song had advocated coition *in opposition to* chaste and discriminating withdrawal; here echo-song is endowed with purely affirmative force.

The celebratory purity of this affirmation does not, of course, exhaust Jonson's attitude to theatrical anachrony. Indeed, Jonson carried on continuous efforts to rationalize the synchrony and syncretism of the "As now" of *Beautie*'s first echo-song or of the concluding declaration (the spatial equivalent of the "As now"), "Th'*Elysian* fields are here." In the speeches for the queen and prince's progress to Highgate (1604), Maia gives an offhand, but still apologetic explanation to the visitors: "This place, whereon you are now advanced (by the mightie power of *Poetrie*, and the helpe of a faith, that can remove mountaynes) is the *Arcadian* hill CYLLENE" (ll. 60–63). Rather graver in tone—and lacking the appeal to "faith"—is the paragraph that follows the description of the dozen heroines of *The Masque of Queenes* (1609):

> But, here, I discerne a possible Objection, arising agaynst mee, to which I must turne: As, *How I can bring* Persons, *of so different* Ages, *to appeare, properly, together?* Or, *Why* (*which is more unnaturall*) *with* Virgil's Mezentius, *I joyne the living, with the dead?* I answere to both these, at once, Nothing is more proper; Nothing more naturall: For these all live; and together, in theyr *Fame;* and so I present them. Besides, if I would fly to the all-daring Power of *Poetry*, Where could I not take Sanctuary? or in whose *Poëme?* [ll. 670–79]

Queenes renders the problems of theatrical anachrony explicit, thus carrying on that crucial Elizabethan debate (to which Sidney gives classic expression in the *Apologie for Poetry*) on the relation of poetry to history. This inquiry into the dynamics of historical continuity surpasses his *celebration* of progress in *Blacknesse and Beautie* by advancing a *theory* of progress. He is not the first Renaissance poet to have done so nor even the first to use echo to figure the difficult conversion of past to present. Before I turn to the Jonsonian theory of progress, a larger look at theatrical anachrony—a look at the historical conversions of Italianate dramaturgy—will be in order.

RICONOSCIUTA ARCADIA

> Exercise, loftily, your visions
> Where the mountainous distance

Echoes its unfaltering speech
To mere outcry and harrowing search.

                                Geoffrey Hill, "Metamorphoses: II"[17]

I need not insist, yet I suspect that when Italianate theatrical conventions influence the Jonsonian masque, that influence is not always mediated by Jones. Jonson may have been more interested in Continental dramaturgy than is often allowed. I would guess, for example, that Guarini as much as Virgil stands behind the device of Niger's untainted sea passage. As Niger's appearance opens the *Masque of Blacknesse*, so Alfeo's opens *Il Pastor Fido*. He tells the story of how a river pursued a naiad, Aretusa, and by this storytelling identifies himself:

> Quel son io: già l'udiste, or ne vedete
> prova tal, ch'a voi stessi
> fede negar non lice.
> Ecco, lasciando il corso antico e noto,
> per incognito mar l'onda incontrando
> del re de'fiumi altéro,
> qui sorgo, e lieto a riveder ne vegno
> qual esser già solea libera e bella,
> or desolata e serva,
> quell'antica mia terra ond'io derivo.
> O cara genitrice! O dal tuo figlio
> riconosciuta Arcadia.[18]

> [That Brook am I. Though what you have been told
> Ye may, your eyes ye cannot doubt. Behold!
> Leaving my loved Nymph, and thridding back
> That well known way where I had made a track
> Through the great waters, I in person rise
> And view (with tears of gladnesse in mine eyes)
> That ancient and that venerable earth
> From whose cold entrails I receiv'd my birth,
> Not thrall'd and plundred (as of late) but free
> And beautifull as it was wont to be.
> O my deer mother! O Arcadia, known
> By me thy son.]

The Senecan device in which the antique arises from underground is invoked often enough in the sixteenth century, giving uncanny power to the idea of a *renaissance* in drama: here its power is somehow both necromantic and cheerful, and it works to define the generic novelty of this play. Pastoral drama is here summed up as a drama of pastoral presence, of Arcadian *visibility* ("già l'udiste, or ne vedete / prova tal, ch'a voi stessi / fede negar non lice. / Ecco . . ."), the modern incarnation of a tradition of lyric, of voice radically without presence.

Guarini's plot of modernization in *Il Pastor Fido* is thus more radical than that of *Blacknesse*, for it involves a renovation-by-transformation of pastoral itself. The unsettling force of Guarini's play is something to be learned not only from the texts themselves but from the large body of critical literature with which the Ferrarese literati greeted these productions. *Il Pastor Fido* was for so long in so celebrated a process of composition that critical reception seems to have preceded its completion: the work was printed in 1590 and first performed in 1592, but as early as 1586 it fell under published attack by Giason Denores. (In 1588, Guarini published a rebuttal and then, one assumes, got back to work on the play.) But perhaps the play's most canny monument to its own novelty may be found in its echo-scene (IV.viii), for there echoing represents the genesis of drama from lyric, a representation that hovers at the uncertain border between eclogue and tragicomedy.

Structurally, the play is a "cross-wooing": in order to dispel the antique curse on Arcadia, it has been arranged that Amarilli be betrothed to Silvio; Mirtillo loves Amarilli, who conceals her reciprocal devotion; Dorinda loves Silvio, whose only love is hunting. The first stage in the triumph of Eros which is the largest plot of the drama is the recovery of Silvio to a world of desire, a social world. His devotion to hunting and his nearly pathological resistance to the erotic link him to Adonis and to Hippolytus, but in Act IV, scene viii, Silvio's crime is specifically represented as Narcissism, for Echo appropriates his words.[19]

He opens this famous scene—it was one of the most influential formal achievements of Guarinian dramaturgy—in soliloquy. Soliloquy is this play's theatrical gesture of either great vice or grave vulnerability, and his insistent blasphemy against Venus ("O dea che non se' dea" [goddess and no goddess], "sordida dea" [base goddess], "nemica di ragione, / macchinatrice sol d'opre furtive, / corruttela de l'alme" [enemie / of reason, plotter of sweet theevery], etc.) suggests that both apply.[20] Within the roughly contemporary context of Elizabethan state mythology, Zabeta's choice between Juno and Cynthia is nearly a no-lose situation, but in the Neoplatonic ideological context that prevails in Italian pastoral drama, Silvio's exclusive allegiance to "Cintia, mia sola dea" is culpable. He confuses Echo's voice with that of Amor, which has the happy effect of implying that linguistic behavior objectifies his inner amorousness and so effects a return of the repressed. It is the Callimachan turn that reappropriates and transforms speech into a *lapsus linguae*: Echo's frustrating literalism betrays the frustrations of the speaking subject. Thus the confused annoyance when Silvio asks how this "Amor" will conquer him:

>   E con qual armi? E con qual arco?
> Forse col tuo?
> Eco.   Col tuo.
> Silvio. Come "col mio"? Vuoi dir quando l'avrai
>   con la lascivia tua corrotto?
> Eco.   Rotto.
> Silvio. E le mie armi rotte
>   mi faran guerra? E romperailo tu?
> Eco.   Tu.
>
>   [and with what Arms? and with what bow?
> Shall it be happily with thine?   With thine.

Thou mean'st perchance, when by thy wantonnesse
It is unbent, and the nerve broken? *Broken.*
Shall my own bow, after 'tis broken too,
Make war on me? and who shall break't? thou? *Thou.*]

As in Ovid's *Cadmeans*, Echo speaks out against repression (as she does in *Daphnis and Chloë*, though there the attack on oppressive *mathesis* is a defense of chastity). Only with his capitulation to love does Silvio manage to correct his confusion, recognizing that the "terribil garzon" had not spoken directly, but "tra quelle frondi / in suon d'Eco indovina" (from yonder grove / In a prophetick Eccho!; IV.ix). Echo is discovered as intercessory prophet to an Amor who is restored both as transcendental principle and as internal mover—"nume, domator d'uomini e dei, / già nemico, or signore / di tutti i pensieri miei" (thou high / Conqu'rour of Gods and men, once enemy, / Now lord of all my thoughts! IV.ix).[21] His final question to Echo—"Ma dimmi / dove fien queste maraviglie? Qui?" (IV.viii)—enables her to promise ("Qui") that the *frondi* from which she speaks will be the very site of Silvio's conversion; that is, the plot will pivot on that site of incipient presence from which she speaks—nearly onstage, nearly embodied, nearly social. Immediately thereafter, Silvio sees what he takes to be a wolf moving within the brake and, hoping "in un dì solo/trionfar di due fère" (in one day a pair / Of such wilde beasts to triumph ore), shoots the often scorned Dorinda. He wounds her in the thigh, pities and then loves her; so the wounding, like his words, is opened up to polysemy. The private act of hunting becomes the prelude to more sociable behavior and thus recapitulates the pattern in which monody is converted, by Echo, to dialogue.[22]

This plot of conversion is also an act of considerable historical self-consciousness.[23] Pastoral was relatively new to drama, or at least that was the contention of Guarini's critic, Denores. He claimed that Guarini had taken elements of the eclogue and "improvisamente le hanno ridotte alla grandessa della comedie, & della tragedie con cinque atti," a distortion precisely because the pastoral mode was being riven from its traditional lyric genres.[24] Denores's argument was certainly open to challenge. One can faithfully generalize that, for a variety of reasons, Continental pastoral underwent a steady process of "dramatization" from about the eighth century. What seems to have happened is a steady revaluation of the formal convention of writing eclogues *in alterni versi*.[25] If only a third of Theocritus's *Idyllia* are dialogic, half of Virgil's *Eclogues* are so, and during the early Middle Ages the Virgilian pastoral may have been more influential as a formal influence than as a modal one; it is possible to trace a thread of direct influence from the *Eclogues* to the Carolingian *conflictus* and thence to the scholastic and courtly *débat* of the High Middle Ages.[26]

The link between pastoral and dialogue is considerably complicated by the appearance in the twelfth century of the *pastourelle*, a lyric form, stable in plot (knight attempts to seduce shepherdess), dialogic in form, and rustic in setting. Whether or not the pastourelle is itself an actual descendant of the classical eclogue, it certainly influenced the *perception* of the eclogue by opening the pastoral milieu up to narrative (and well before Boccaccio's *Ameto*, often cited as the first modern pastoral narrative).[27] It was not long before the pastourelle plot began to appear in dramatic form, and when popular religious dramatists, enriching their work by drawing on the allegorical tradition of reading Virgilian pastoral, began to specialize in shepherds' plays, the fundamentally lyric and textual status of pastoral was further eroded. The shepherd speaks so often in the dramatic performances of the fourteenth and fifteenth centuries that it is hardly surprising that dialogic form became a predominant feature of nearly all late fifteenth-century pastoral compositions.

Thus dialogue came to seem virtually necessary to pastoral, one of its constituents, and it took the celebrated recovery of the Greek romances in the sixteenth century to alter this to any significant degree. In his *Art Poetique Francoys* (1548), Sebillet defines the Greek term, *dialogue*, by marshaling some exemplary forms: he lists three—"Eclogue, Moralité, Farce." This goes as far as one could go toward articulating a common ground of the dramatic.[28] W. W. Greg notices that the earliest examples of *ecloghe rappresentative* from the fifteenth century are identical in form with those written for literary circulation, which suggests the haze that hovered at the boundary of eclogue and drama. The decades that follow Poliziano's *Orfeo*, often taken as the first full pastoral drama, saw the "dramatization" of pastoral completed.

It is quite true that the history of pastoral had conduced to the invention of pastoral drama by making the pastoral mode and dramatic form seem particularly well suited to each other. Yet there was a corrective development in the mid-sixteenth century, for the widening familiarity with Aristotle's *Poetics* straitened the European conception of what was properly dramatic; even as pastoral was at its most assimilable to dramatization, the formal "receptiveness" of European drama suddenly declined. There was, by this time, a flourishing Italian tradition of pastoral court drama, but the revival of Aristotelian poetics disrupted the apparent dramatic aptitude of pastoral, and it made pastoral drama seem somehow slightly daring. For Denores the genre seemed downright objectionable.

Denores's attack is actually a double one. He objects to the generic confusion of tragedy and comedy *and* to the modal intrusion of pastoral on dramatic representation. Guarini devotes the major part of his prose defense, the *Compendio della poesia tragicomica*, to the first charge, answering the second charge with the rather perfunctory claim that pastoral is merely accidental to the genre, adjectival, as it were. He does take time, though, to praise his great Ferrarese predecessor in the genre, Agostino Beccari. It is for its novelty, its ingenuity, that Beccari's *Sacrifizio* is praised:

> Hassi dunque a sapere che la poesia pastorale, benché, 'n quanto alle personne introdotte, riconosca la sua primiera origine e dall'egloga e dalla satira degli antichi, nulladimeno, quanto alla forma e ordine, può chiamarsi cosa moderna, essendo che non si truovi appresso l'antichitá di tal favola alcuno esempio greco o latino. Il primo de' moderni, che felicemente ardisse di farlo, fu Agostin de'Beccari, onorato cittadin di Ferrara, da cui solo dé' riconoscere il mondo la bella invenzione di tal poema.[29]

[Yet therefore one should know that, with respect to the sorts of characters introduced, pastoral poetry finds its first origins in the eclogues and satyr plays of the ancients. Nonetheless as for form and structure, on the other hand, pastoral may be said to be a modern invention, since antiquity offers no Greek nor Latin examples of such fables. The first of the moderns who, happily, dared to write such a piece was Agostino de'Beccari, honored citizen of Ferrara, and one must be indebted to him alone for the wonderful contrivance of such a poem.]

Felice ardimento: the phrase describes a somewhat transgressive charm and thus points to a specifically modern creativity, one that found perfect expression in the union of eclogue and satyr play, the *concordia discors* of tragicomedy, and the "presentation" of pastoral eclogue in the form of this Arcadian drama.[30]

It is a felice ardimento that brings Arcadia into the spatial and temporal presence of the Ferrarese theater, for the appearance of Alfeo in the prologue has a wit to it that is anything but naive.[31] When Alfeo bursts out in delight, "qui surgo, e lieto a riveder . . . quell' antica mia terra ond'io derivo," he is mistaken, disoriented in every sense. His departure from the Sicily of the past, "lasciando il corso antico e noto," leaves him deluded, for his argument is not that Arcadia has moved (though he will eventually suggest that the *otium* of Arcadia is now wholly entrusted to the *disinvoltura* of the Ferrarese court) but that theater of Ferrara *is* Arcadia.

> Queste son le contrade
> sì chiare un tempo, e queste son le selve
> ove 'l prisco valor visse e morìo.
> In questo angolo sol del ferreo mondo
> cred'io che ricovrasse il secol d'oro,
> quando fuggìa le scelerate genti.
> Qui non veduta altrove
> libertà moderata e senza invidia
> fiorir si vide . . .   [Prologue]
> [These be the streets once so renown'd, these be
> The woods where the old russet honestie
> Did live and die: unto this onely nook
> O' th'iron world, when she her flight had took
> From sinfull men, the golden age retir'd.
> Here (that which elsewhere is in vain desir'd)
> Freedome unstrain'd, and from suspicion free,]

"Queste," "questo," "qui,": the rhetoric has an insistent quality. The demonstratives assert identity, whereas analogy is the logically appropriate relationship. The insistent rhetoric requires that the normal irony of the courtly spectator, a normal irony about the power and limits of cultural fiction, become analytic, with the analysis focused on the illusionist claims of the theatrical locus and on what might be called the "generic hyperbole" of pastoral drama, the practice of giving bodies to the personal *figures* of Arcadia, of making the likes of Alfeo, Amarilli, Mirtillo, Silvio, and Dorinda appear in the flesh.[32]

So what is striking about Guarini's echo-scene is that it not only initiates that realignment of desire which is the fundamental plot of Guarini's play, it also celebrates the generic realignment of the pastoral mode. The scene superbly conjures Silvio's boundary-state, a suspension between constricted selfhood and social being; but it also articulates a formal boundary-state between private monody and dialogue. We can trace in the interrruption of Silvio's address to the absent goddesses, Venus and Cynthia, by an Echo who hovers at the border of theatrical presence the same pattern of emerging presence that took place in the history of pastoral—the turn from lyric presentation, addressed to an absent reader, to dramatic representation, addressed to an audience which is always an incipient presence in the phenomenological world of court performance.

The pressure to bring Arcadia into theatrical presence leaves traces throughout the play. Thus, Mirtillo's first entrance reproduces and embodies the original moments of the Virgilian career; he is a Tityrus reincarnate:

> Cruda Amarilli, che col nome ancora,
> d'amar, ahi lasso, amaramente insegni!
> Amarilli, del candido ligustro
> più candida e più bella,
> ma de l'àspido sordo
> e più sorda e più fèra e più fugace,
> poi che col dir t'offendo,
> i' mi morrò tacendo;
> ma grideran per me le piagge e i monti
> e questa selva, a cui
> sì spesso il tuo bel nome
> di risonare insegno. [I. ii]
>
> [O Amarillis, Authresse of my flame,
> (Within my mouth how sweet now is thy name!
> But in my heart how bitter!) Amarillis,
> Fairer and whiter then the whitest Lillies,
> But crueller than cruell Adders far,
> Which having stung (least they should pitie) bar
> Their ears, and flie: If then by speaking I
> Offend thee, I will hold my peace and die.
> I'll hold my peace, but what will that do good,
> If hils and dales roar for me, and this wood
> Which thy deer name can nere forget, from me
> So often heard?]

The plaint combines the Tityran power over the resonant landscape with the powerlessness of a Corydon ("O crudelis Alexis"; *Ecl.*, II.6). One of the subplots of the play is the invigoration of the weak and suffering aspect of resonance: from here we progress to the articulate intrusion of Echo and thence to the final jubilant moment when "risuone il monte e 'l pian, le valli e i poggi / del pastor fido il glorioso nome" (The laund, the dale, the mountain, and the plain / Resound *the faithfull shepherd's* glorious name; V.viii).³³ Mirtillo's most touching complaint comes at the very center of the play when he bemoans the sorrow of speaking unheard; the dramatization of pastoral provides an audience for the figures of eclogue.

The specific source of Mirtillo's plight, the obstacle to the full realization of the locus amoenus, is a tyrannous prohibition of the Oracle stipulating the yearly sacrifice of a "vergine o donna," sacrifices that can only be suspended by the marriage of Silvio and Amarilli. This law, with its demand for repeated sacrifice, is associated with repetition itself: the grave cruelty of Diana's law manifests itself dramatically in the frequent repetition of tags from that law during the course of the fifth act, a canon of law. So there is a vicious form of repetition in the play, as there is a hideous, tragic form of pastoral resonance when Cynthia is angered:

> Suda sangue la dea, trema la terra,
> E la caverna sacra
> mugge tutta, e risuona
> d'insoliti ululati e di funesti
> gemiti. [V.ii]
>
> [The Goddesse sweats cold drops of blood, the Earth
> Is Palsey-shook; the sacred Cavern howls
> With such unwonted sounds as tortur'd souls
> Send out of graves.]

In order to free the land from the curse of tragic repetition and tragic resonance, a comic repetition must be discovered and established.³⁴

Its model is to be found in the echo-scene. The benign repetition in the subplot, the echoes by which the straits of Narcissism are violated, provides a pattern that can be pressed into the service of the main plot. Consider Echo's technique once more. Guarini uses both of the two technical means of echoic semantic transfer, aphaeresis (dropping initial phonemes) and antanaclasis (punning). The latter creates that fundamental confusion which controls the dialogue of Silvio and Echo:

> *Silvio.* Eco, o più tosto Amor, che così d'Eco
> imita il sòno?
> *Eco.* Sono. [IV.viii]
>
> [What art thou that reply'st? Eccho? or Love?
> That so doth imitate the same? *The same.*]

Confused about the identity of his interlocutor, Silvio takes this *sono* as an affirmation that he is indeed addressing Amor, but Echo's response is also a scholarly self-identification. That is, *sono* may correct *imita*—"non imito, ma *sono, il sòno*"—which would give us an etymologizing Echo, one who renovates the meaning of ἠχώ: in this neat response, *sono* can function as either noun or verb with no alteration of meaning, for each correctly identifies the speaker. The punning is not confined to this dialogue: it resurfaces in the main plot, where it loosens the archaic constraints on erotic fulfillment within the play. Thus Montano reminds Tirenio—

> che, senza violar la santa legge,
> non può ella a Mirtillo
> dar quella fè che fu già data a Silvio

and Carino intervenes—

> E a Silvio fie data
> parimenti la fede, ché Mirtillo
> fin dal suo nascimento ebbe tal nome,
> se dal tuo servo mi fu detto il vero;
> ed egli si compiacque
> ch'io'l nomassi Mirtillo anzi che Silvio. [V.vi]
>
> [*Montano.* That faith which formerly she gave away
>   To Silvio, she cannot now withdraw
>   And give Mirtillo, without breach of Law.
> *Carino.* 'Tis Silvio still, Mirtillo was call'd so
>   At first (thy man told me) and Silvio
>   By mee chang'd to Mirtillo, to which hee
>   Consented.]

The troth plighted to Silvio is transferable precisely because of the name's arbitrary breadth of reference; Tirenio's comment is both emphatic and wonderfully flat-footed—"il dubbio era importante." As in the echo-scene, verbal opportunism is the chief agent of comic closure, helping to persuade the hunter to love and then freeing the couples to marry as they will.

It is a generic resolution as well. The blocking force of the play (everywhere identified with Cynthia) is a sacral version, a tragic version, of the fathers of New Comedy—the ancient law of the wrathful goddess. In *Il Pastor Fido*, a New Comic resolution, dependent on a tricksy verbal opportunism, frees Arcadia from the repetitive structures of antique law. An ingenuity purely verbal in kind thus frees the play from various forms of tyranny: not only the tyranny of the antierotic, but also the larger tyranny of cultural tradition as well as the specific generic tyranny of tragedy. *Il Pastor Fido* finally succeeds in making a comedy of cultural history, its verbal sleight of hand creating a space of cultural freedom in which formal proprieties lose their power so that pastoral may emerge in a new medium, comedy may combine with and then overcome tragedy, and Arcadia may overlap Ferrara.

I take it that the echo-scene has an emblematic force here, since it marks the boundary between the tragic drama of fatal isolation and private consciousness and the comic drama of erotic union and social intercourse. It is a scene that cherishes boundaries: between monologue and dialogue, private and public, onstage and off. When Echo tells Silvio that his conquest will take place "qui," she is marking out an area of spatial, generic, and modal liminality which would come to be the very soul of pastoral tragicomedy.[35]

The *qui* of Echo's hiding place, the *qui* of Alfeo's prologue—if they are not effectively the same locus, they share a delightfully paradoxical theatrical status. I suspect that Guarini is insisting on the aesthetic raciness of his enterprise and doing so boldly to flout the pure formalism urged by the likes of Denores. That is the point of his prologue, in which Alfeo argues that Ferrara *is* Arcadia (that most utopian of topoi), that the present *is* the Golden Age, that the antique has been made impossibly new; that is the point of his echo-scene, in which the privacy of Silvio and the phenomenological isolation of the bucolic voice shimmer at a theatrical brink of communal Presence.

THE VOYCE OF FAME

Helpe, helpe all Tongues, to celebrate this wonder:
The voyce of FAME should be as loud as Thonder.
   Her House is all of *echo* made,
     Where never dies the sound;
   And, as her browes the cloudes invade,
     Her feete do strike the ground.

Queenes, 723–28

Echo preserves profound ties to this scenic Presence, this oddly translated Arcadian spot. The lore that accumulated around Echo in the sixteenth-century annotations to Virgil and Ovid, and in the dictionaries and the handbooks to mythology, nearly always include a considerable proportion of topographic material. These books catalog the famous echo portals of antiquity—one in Thrace and another, called the Heptaphone, near Olympia—as well as the modern loci echoici—one in Pavia and one in Milan, another at the Capo di Bove in Rome, still another at the Tuilleries, and one, the most famous of them all, at the church at Charenton. So Echo has a continuing status as a genius loci. We might even reverse the terms of Raphael Regio's comment on Ovid's lines, "'heu frustra dilecte puer!' totidemque remisit / verba locus, dictoque vale 'vale' inquit et Echo" ("Alas, dear boy, vainly beloved!" and the place gave back his words. And when he said, "Farewell!" "Farewell!" said Echo too; III. 500–01), for where Regio glosses "locus" as "Echo qu[a]e in illo erat loco. Continens enim pro contento per metonymiam positum est" (Echo, who was in that place: the container given for the contained), sixteenth-century mythographers tend to treat Echo as "ille locus in quo erat Echo: contentum pro continente positum" (that place in which Echo was to be found: the contained given for the container).[36]

I have already suggested, however, that Vitruvius, not Virgil or Longus, is largely responsible for the interest of sixteenth-century thinkers in echo as a local phenomenon: the Echo of *Il Pastor Fido* derives her unusual significance from her function as the genius of a specifically theatrical locus. Yet a certain irony attends on the relocation of an Arcadian echo upon the Vitruvian stage. The local status of Echo always has a furtive immanence, one that the newly recovered *Daphnis and Chloë* shrewdly exploits, for there Echo is both present and, maddeningly, just out of range. Gascoigne's Echo is the genius of just such a locus, a place of pure proximity, inaccessible to any transgression that could utterly transform the immanent into the here and now. His Echo argues for the impermeable presence of the pleasance, a dramatic space that, like the printed text, denies its dependence on courtly sustenance.

Yet early in *his* career as a masque-maker, Jonson uses the figure of Echo quite otherwise: the echo-song of *Blacknesse* opposes the withdrawal of the theatrical from the courtly space of the dancing floor. The crucial echo-song of *Beautie* triumphs, on the other hand, in the announcement that the alien and the ancient can be brought into the communal here and now of the revels. In what must seem a curiously Hegelian solution, the oppositional terms of *Blacknesse*, so carefully restated and overstated in the antagonisms of the opening of *Beautie*, are finally rendered complementary, subsumed in the celebration of creative concord.

D. J. Gordon has already had much to say about the debt of this masque to Ficino and to Neoplatonic theory of creative Love in general: the other esoteric gods of the world—Phanes and Pan—are assimilated to this Erotic demiurge. We may support Gordon by observing that Harmonia is chosen as the presiding figure in the constituent instruments of love's power (the attributes of beauty). Jonson is "aestheticizing" the already considerable aestheticist nature of Ficinan cosmogony, and he complements the power of Harmonia by his recourse to echo-song. All three of the major mythographers who stand behind this masque—Giraldi, Cartari, and Comes—recover the Macrobian gloss on Echo as "harmonia coeli." So echo-song is redeemed and integrated into the masque, where it finds its place in a cosmology in which it represents "the world's *soule*, true harmony" (l. 374).[37]

Echo here is not the sly echo of Callimachus nor even the easy echo of the docile Virgilian landscape; this is a redeemed Ovidian Echo, a coital voice which opposes nothing but the Nothing of chaos itself. (This would no doubt have earned the particular approval of one member of the audience, Sir Francis Bacon; the following year would see the publication of the *De Sapientia Veterum*, where Echo would be taken to represent an ideally mimetic philosophical discourse.) Whereas in *Blacknesse* the echo-song provided only a formal model for decorous coition, in *Beautie* it claims the achievement of that coition, confirming the prophetic powers of the earlier repetitive voice, as it adjusts the slightly unseemly erotics of that earlier voice to a nobler modernity.[38] Thus, one of the two fountains from which the echoes issue is rightly called "chast Delight" (l. 146).

Later in this chapter I shall have more to say about this moment of triumphal echoing; I shall want to show how the larger structure of the masque recovers the impermeability of the Italian theatrical pleasance. For the moment, suffice it to say that the most important feature of *Beautie*'s echo-song is that it recovers the allusiveness of echo, its diachronous mimesis. The echo of *Beautie* is a sign that the echo of *Blacknesse* has been made an object of full reflection.[39] We will again find an analogy in publication: as the printed text frees the soul of the masque from its bondage within the occasional bodily part, so this representation of allusiveness figures the release of one masque device into another. The great formal innovation of *Blacknesse and Beautie* lies in Jonson's assault on what we may call the unconstructiveness of revelry, the inability of court revelry to constitute more than a momentary breach in normal time. Thus, the occasion of *Beautie* as Jonson represents it is not so much a function of the audience as it is a function of an imperative originating in *Blacknesse*; the historical occasion itself has been transformed, abstracted into a locus amoenus responsive to the authoritative cry of *Blacknesse*. The echoic allusion, like publication, extends the moment of masquing in time: hence the second echoing fountain is called "lasting Youth."

Pleasure and chastity, youth and endurance: these provide the conceptual dialectic of Jonson's masques. On these coordinates we can graph the Comus and Hercules (as well as the originating Rabelais and Virgil) of *Pleasure Reconcil'd to Vertue*. The dialectic reappears in *The Vision of Delight* as Wonder and Fant'sy (categories in which Jonson was finally able to articulate a distinction between ideal and dangerous spectacle—a subtle moment in Jonson's theorizing of the form, coming just before a collapse of theory into spleen, when painting and poetry become the crudely opposed poles of his thoughts on masque making). Later the Cook and Poet of *Neptunes Triumph for the Returne of Albion* reconstitute this dialectic as the generative opposition of participation and understanding. Jonson perfected the masque as a dialectical genre—and Milton would be much in his debt.

In the Christmastide masque next after *Beautie*, the extravagant and coruscated *Masque of Queenes* (1609), Jonson would give that conceptual dialectic a clearer formal structure: antimasque and masque.[40] (The new emphasis on the formal, on the *shape* of the ethical, thus recapitulates the formalist shift in sixteenth-century mythography noted above.)[41] The dialectic remains subtle enough: antimasque is no more the simple image of vice than youth or pleasure are the vicious opposites of longevity or chastity. Only of *Queenes* did Jonson remark that the antimasque passed away "scarse suffring the memory of any such thing" (ll. 358–59), and even there the issues raised in the dance of the hags persist in refined form within the masque proper. The courtly measures of masque always recall the antic motions that precede them.

The formal innovation of the antimasque (an innovation that Jonson downplays: he refers priority to the brief and minor "*Anti-masque* of Boyes" in *The Haddington Masque*) is not the most striking development in *Queenes*. Having already written expanded accounts of the union of pleasure and chastity in his two early hymeneal masques, *Hymenaei* (1606) and *The Haddington Masque* (1608; also known as *The Hue and Cry after Cupid*), Jonson turned to examine a historiographic problem, the union of youth and endurance; the remarkable House of Fame of *Queenes* was the result. This dialectical solution to the Sidneian opposition of history and poetry involves an extreme case of theatrical anachrony, pertinent to our inquiry as the first step in Jonson's discovery and exploitation of the potent ironies of the resonant stage.

We return to Jonson's defense, in the published text of *Queenes*, against such potential objections to his anachrony:

> As, *How I can bring* Persons, *of so different* Ages, *to appeare, properly, together? Or, Why (which is more unnaturall)* with Virgil's Mezntius, *I joyne the living, with the dead?* I answere

to both these, at once, Nothing is more proper; Nothing more naturall: For these all live; and together, in theyr *Fame*; and so I present them. Besides, if I would fly to the all-daring Power of *Poetrie*, Where could I not take Sanctuary? or in whose *Poëme*? [ll. 670–79]

It is difficult to establish whether the anachrony sustains an apology for poetry or whether the prestige of poetry sustains the anachrony; they seem to rely upon each other for mutual defense. Here in the explanatory preface Jonson tips his hand, glossing the implicit argument of the transformation scene—glossing, too, the *felice ardimento* that is the spirit of Jones's and Jonson's transformations. The gloss is salutary, for when the dancing hags of the antimasque disappear and Heroique Virtue displays the antique queens whom Fame preserves, his speech is as mysterious as the scenic miracle it accompanies.

The difficulty of the transformation speech (ll. 367–445) lies in its variety of purposes. The foundation of the speech is a celebration of Queen Anne, whom the famous queens of antiquity have chosen to occupy "the soveraigne Place / of all that *Palace*" (ll. 420–21)—the House of Fame. Yet the speech contains a great deal more: an allegorical genealogy of Fame ("When *Vertue* cut of *Terror*, he gat *Fame*" [l. 375]), a veiled but pragmatic account of the genesis of this masque (Queen Anne "hath agayne brought forth / Theyr Names to Memory, and meanes this night / To make them, once more, visible to light" [ll. 427–29]), and a Neoplatonic allegory of kingship and marriage (James is the light that creates the queens', particulary his own queen's, luster [ll. 430–31]).[42] And finally, Jonson adds a theory of courtly trope in order to take on the problem of figuring the royal Virtue: Fame "can give no'increase"

> to you that cherish every great Example
> Contracted in your selfe; and, being so ample
> A Feild of honor, cannot but embrace
> A *spectacle*, so full of love, and grace
> Unto your Court: where every *Princely Dame*
> Contendes to be as bounteous of her Fame,
> To others, as her Life was good to her.
> For, by their lives, they only did confer
> Good on them selves, but by theyr fame, to yours,
> And every Age, the Benefit endures.   [ll. 434, 436–45]

James's satisfaction with the masque must derive from the special way in which it adumbrates his nature: the masque is an emanation which becomes an erotic object. In this spectacular image of himself, the king contemplates what Angus Fletcher has called an "opulent optative," an image poised between model and mirror; given such a spectacle, the problem of Narcissism can never be far away.[43]

This myth of emanation-turned-erotic-object is the myth of the genesis of Eve, reexamined in a courtly setting. Like Milton after him, Jonson displaces the problem of Adamic narcissism upon the female emanation, but Jonson treats Bel-Anna more leniently than Milton treats his Eve. Anne embraces the honor conferred upon her by the antique queens "with a vertuous joy, / Farre from *selfe-love*, as humbling all her Worth / To him that gave it."[44] "Farre" here is also optative, for actually the joy that royalty takes in its own ideal image is dangerously close to narcissim: Ficino's Narcissus is divided by a very fine line from the ideal Neoplatonic lover, whose enthusiasm for the image leads him past it. The speech of Heroique Virtue keeps us close to the boundary line between an ennobling attitude to spectacle and a vainglorious one: he carries the shield of Perseus, a mirror—potentially either a mirror of Narcissus or a moral *speculum.*

The basic means by which the king is protected from narcissistic spectatorship lies in the use of the *queen* as the chief performer. Jonson had a tendency to use the cooperative queen or prince to figure the virtues of *king*ship, and this device is more than a response to the exigencies of the occasion, to the fact that the king was watching and not participating; usually, as here, Jonson emphasizes the *derivation* of the spectacle. By doing so, he both points to his own figurative energies and shows the king the many ways in which what he watches is distinct from himself. In Heroique Virtue's speech, the genealogy of Fame, the practical genetics of masque, and the theory of courtly trope all work to concentrate attention on the action of deriving the masque device. And, finally, they all aim at answering the question of how the representation of virtue can be made *useful.*

There are two answers—one simple and one mysterious—and they may be summed up as two ways of construing what it would mean for the field of honor to "embrace" this spectacle (ll. 438–39). First, the spectacle may be received into the sociable embrace of the court, where the glories of fame will inspire the noble viewers to virtue. Taken thus, the spectacle of Fame does not so much benefit James as it benefits the Jacobeans. But James, too, embraces the queenly spectacle, and the embrace is a closer and more curious knot. Both the progenitrix and the emanation of Virtue, Fame becomes a spectacle which, through Bel-Anna, inspires the king to love. The tangle of figures in this speech creates a mysterious system in which Virtue and Fame engender each other even as they incite each other to congress. What preserves the system of spectacle and spectatorship from narcissism is the simple fact of sexual difference. Though the life of virtue is self-referential, bound in person and time ("they only did confer / Good on them selves"), if it be entrusted to history, it develops the allure of Fame (an allure represented in the special exposure of the queen to James and of the ancient queens to the modern court). Differentiation of sex replaces differentiation in time and so relieves the sterile isolation of temporal discontinuity: Jonson's fame is an erotic principle in history.

Thus, for James (indeed, for both members of the royal couple), the utility of the spectacle lies in the way it aligns all forms of desire, making the appetite for fame congruent with a sexual appetite, both of which are purged of the taint of narcissism: the masque dramatizes the adroit conversion of the desire for self-perpetuation into object-love. The triumph of fame is a triumph of Ovid's Echo, as the triumph of Beauty had been. As in *Beautie*, Ovid's Echo appears freed of the censure of early mythography; this is also the favored Echo whom Arnulph describes as *bona Fama*, as well as an eroticized version of Macrobius's harmonia *coeli*.

Yet *Queenes* involves curious suppressions of literary memory—and in this sense the Echo of *Queenes* is emphatically not that of Ovid, who uses her voice to align sexual desire with the desire for literary continuities. This is not to suggest that Jonson departs from his imitative program in *Queenes*, that the device is in any sense "unauthorized." The hags of the antimasque and their behavior are carefully documented from all available sources—the antimasque of the published text of *Queenes* is awash in annotation—but when the hags vanish, challenging "the memory of any such thing," the annotation thins remarkably.[45] The historical sources concerning the queens of antiquity are provided, but the iconography of the House of Fame, and of Fama herself, is powerfully distorted. The celebration of historical memory suffers at its center.

Jonson attributes the entire design of the House of Fame to Jones, who in turn "profest to follow that noble description, made by *Chaucer*, of the like place" (ll. 692–93). In the long iconographic history of Fama, from Virgil to Ovid to Chaucer to Jones and Jonson, no more benignant representation can be found than Jones's. Having seen the implicit connection between Virgil's *Fama* and the prophetic site at Cumae, Ovid had created a *domus Famae* that assimilated the two Virgilian descriptions each to each.[46] Chaucer's House of Fame is based on Ovid's, but he contrives an alternative building, the ramshackle whirling house of twigs, where rumors are fantastically propagated, and the contrivance draws some of the blame off from the House of Fame; though injustice thrives in the House of Fame, sheer inaccuracy begins elsewhere. Jones continues the purgation of Fame by depicting only the splendors of her house. He ignores, for example, any of the iconography of *Fortuna* that also touches the Chaucerian house: the glittering cliff of ice that provides the uncertain foundation for Chaucer's house and that would have made for just the sort of spectacle on which Jones's stagecraft throve figures nowhere in his design.

Jonson's Fame seems equally uncompromised; yet Jonson took greater risks, for as he maintains Jones's and Chaucer's tendency to redeem the figure of Fama, he restores features of both Ovid's and Virgil's descriptions—the thunderous resonance of her house (from Ovid, *Metamorphoses*, XII.46–47, 51–52) and her size (from Virgil, *Aeneid*, IV.176–77). Jonson does not annotate his description of the House of Fame, but it would have been unnecessary as both passages, particularly the passage from Virgil, would have been familiar to all but the most unlettered readers and spectators. Jonson engages here in an obtrusive misrepresentation of Fama as the bona fama of Heroique Virtue's speech, with the result that the first triumphal song of the masque proves guilty of precisely that superficial imitation condemned in the final song:

Th'*Assyrian* pompe, the *Persian* pride,
Greekes glory, and the *Romanes* dy'de:
  And who yet imitate
Theyr noyses, tary the same fate.   [ll. 766–69]

This only makes the problem more acute. In a masque designed to reveal the moral power of knowledge in general, and of historiographic memory in particular, a masque in which emulation and imitation are both idealized and made the natural corollaries of chaste desire, casual imitation would seem a signal vice.

The specific imitative lapse—inflating the relative benignity of Chaucer's Fame to absolute benignity—has the effect of an oddly bitter joke, for it hints that, under the occasional pressure of royal entertainment, antique authority is purely decorative. Alongside his declaration that good Fame is eternal and self-sustaining, Jonson asserts that Anne has herself caused the return of the virtuous queens to modern memory; he thus casts severe doubts on the connection between Fame and Virtue. The contradictions imported into the theory of Fame—its allure and its susceptibility to neglect, its self-perpetuation and its need for modern sustenance—show Jonson again resisting an unqualified assent to royal power as a source of ethical stability. Virgil's *Fama* had attacked the erotic life of heroic virtue, had succeeded, finally, in interposing a sea between Dido's soft Carthage and Aeneas's vigorous Rome; the difficulty of reconciling pleasure and virtue remains the guilty Virgilian secret of Jonson's Fame.

The Masque of Queenes represents a limiting case of Renaissance synchrony: its argument for the easy continuities of history and the availability of the past leads to a near-collapse of temporality. Jonson's ingenious substitution of sexual for temporal difference thus has something desperate about it. His notes justifying the collocation of the living and the dead make an unnecessary defense (since Heroique Virtue also explains Anne's place among the queens of antiquity); they suggest that Jonson himself suspected he had gone too far with his anachronics. Henceforth the modernization of antiquity will be a comic device:

> *Venus.* I am *Cupids* Mother, *Cupids* owne Mother, forsooth; yes forsooth: I dwell in Pudding-lane; I forsooth, he is Prentise in Love-lane with a Bugle-maker, that makes of your Bobs, and Bird-bolts for Ladies.
> *Christmas.* Good lady Venus of Pudding-lane, you must go out for all this.
> *Venus.* Yes forsooth, I can sit any where, so I may see my *Cupid* act; hee is a pretty Child, though I say it that perhaps should not, you will say: I had him by my first Husband, he was a Smith forsooth. [*Christmas his Masque*, 117–26]

Here, in 1616, Venus's contemporaneity is of a piece with the incongruity of her demotion in social status. The comic anachrony finds its place only in a parodic masque (an extended antimasque, really), a device unrelieved by transformation. Venus's entry as spectator parodies the transformation scene of masque proper in which a god or godlike figure appears poised along that visual axis which links the royal spectator to the vanishing point. Instead of honoring the hierarchical structure of perspectival space and time, Venus's intrusion shatters this structure and restricts this entertainment to jesting.

Only one record of the contemporary reaction to *Queenes* survives, a few sentences written by the French ambassador, who pronounced it "plus superbe qu'ingenieux."[47] *Queenes* is something of a descent to apprenticeship for both

Jones and Jonson, after their surefooted work in previous seasons. Henceforth, Jonson will establish greater continuity between masque and antimasque and will restore temporal *perspective* to his masques. The entertainment for the next year, *Prince Henries Barriers*, is in fact a history of England, recounted by Merlin, whose memory links the chivalric past with a mercantile present. The act of memory is, crucially, *labored*, for time thickens within the masque. Merlin must be resurrected in order to speak, and he is shocked by the novelty of his surroundings; the history of *Barriers* develops a perspectival continuity which is manifestly lacking in *Queenes*. Indeed the absence of such continuities is recorded within the very revels of *Queenes* itself, as if Jonson wished to admit the risks of headlong synchrony: in the course of his curiously self-negating celebration of Fame, he distinguishes between the natural resonance of true fame ("never dies the sound") and the imitative revival of the mere "noyse" of greatness. The acoustic afterlife of Virtue demands tempered continuity; if it be interrupted, it is naught. Jonson may be subtly repeating the appeal of *Cynthia's Revels*, suggesting that royal fame requires the continuous employment of a poet-chronologer. But Jonson's quest for a sustained and sustaining career went on in other spheres; much as he coveted such employment, he remained avid for his own autonomy. Hence, perhaps, his interest in Echo, who has the last word.

THE *SCENE* CLOS'D

> They yeild to Time, and so must all.
> As Night to sport, Day doth to action call,
>   Which they the rather doe obey,
> Because the Morne, with Roses strew's the way.
>
> *The Vision of Delight*, 244–47

The quest for autonomy, we shall soon see, informs the very structure of the masques, for like Gascoigne's entertainment they frequently resist the authority of aristocratic occasion.[48] As Jonson explored the resources of the Italianate theater, the impermeable presence of stage to audience, he discovered new techniques for demonstrating his autonomy: again and again, the masques represent the power of syncretism as a power exclusive to the poet. But the poet's autonomy is not simply a structural motive within the masques; it motivates their very material existence. Before considering the closural patterns within the masques, a glance at the facts of their publication will be useful.

Jonson published his first few masques without dedications, partly because the texts themselves paid homage to their patrons, but largely because the printing of masques, as with most dramatic publications, was extrinsic to the systems for compensating the poet, and dedication would seem a cheeky redundancy in a deviser of masques (on the other hand, much nondramatic literature, even when such literature was commissioned by a stationer, was published as part of a speculative campaign for further aristocratic patronage). Jonson ceremoniously ascribes the inhibition to the patrons themselves—"because *Princes* (out of a religious respect to theyr modesty) may wiselye refuse to be the publique patrons of theyr own actions."[49]

Plays, as opposed to masques, traditionally went undedicated as well, but for the simple reason that copy texts were usually sold to stationers by their rightful owners, that is, by an acting company as a whole or by a major shareholder in the company. Nonetheless, after 1607 (the publication date of *Volpone*), we often find dedications attached to the quarto versions of Jonson's plays: the poet claims the attention of the privileged even for his work in the public theaters. For the 1616 folio, even those plays not dedicated in quarto are commended to particular individuals or groups: in that volume, Jonson reasserts a special authority over all the plays.[50] He began his recovery of the plays as dedicable objects with the publication of *Volpone*, which he dedicated to the universities; it is not an appeal for monetary patronage, but for the continued scholarly approval of these "most learned ARBITRESSES" (l. 103) for the practice of dramatic poetry. It is Jonson's defense of poetry or, to attend more closely to Jonson's language, a declaration of the plenitude of the Poet—"a Name, so ful of authority, antiquity, and all greate marke" (l. 96). Composition seems based on just such plenitude: a year later he writes to Prince Henry of "a work of some difficulty to mee to retrive the particular *authorities* (according to your gracious command, and a desire borne out of judgement) to these things, which I writt out of fullnesse, and memory of my former readings."[51] This letter appears in the quarto text of *Queenes*—it is the only masque with a dedicatory letter in one of its printed texts—yet it does not violate the convention of *not* dedicating masques: Jonson dedicates, not the work of composing the masque, but the work of *annotating* it. Henry becomes more a patron of scholarship than of masque-making, rather like the universities of the *Volpone* dedication.[52] But Jonson founds the accumulating authorial propriety which culminates in the folio *Works* on this very scholarship, on the "fullnesse" of his literary production.

He also develops his authorial propriety by a scrupulous editorial intrusion between the rightful owners of copy texts (the players) and the rightful owners of copy per se (the stationers). We do not know how his printer, William Stansby, managed to secure all the copyrights to himself, but he indulges Jonson in some rather lengthy revisions (the most notorious being the complete overhaul given to *Every Man In*), permitting the poet, as *dramatist*, an utterly exceptional encounter with the text. As Jonson mediates between performance and printing, he revises the very nature of authorship.[53]

I have suggested how Gascoigne exploited a similar relationship with his printer; one of the most important determinants of the difference between the texts of plays and those of entertainments may be found in the specially privileged control conventionally maintained by the deviser of courtly entertainments. With the elimination of the acting company as middleman, the masque-maker comes one stage closer to those functions of the printers' guild that generate the "work," and this, more than the state censorship which, according to Michel Foucault, generates the author in his or her modern form, is the primary source of the Jonsonian assertion of "authority" in the 1616 folio; the devising of masques habituates Jonson to a control which he subsequently strives to impose on his plays. The publication, in 1604, of the entertainments for the royal family's arrival at London and for the queen and prince's visit to Althorp, as well as the publication of *Hymenaei* in 1606, of *The Masques of Blacknesse and Beautie* with *The Lord Haddington's Masque* in 1608, and of *The Masque of Queenes* in 1609— these are the crucial landmarks in Jonson's progress toward the notorious *Works* of 1616, itself perhaps the single most important event in the social history of English authorship before the Statute of Anne (1709). Indeed, when this statute designated authors and not publishers as the true source and owners of copyrights, it simply ratified that accumulation of personal power of author over book that Jonson did so much to create.

The social history of authorship may be one of the crucial contexts for evaluating Jonsonian echo. The echo-song that, by allusion, links *Beautie* to *Blacknesse* is a sign that their shared plot coheres, that it slips the constraints of public occasion and restores it to its place in Jonson's own literary biography.[54] Like the folio *Works*, it affirms the idea of an oeuvre, a sequence of artifacts whose unity is potentially extrinsic to performance: as the folio denies the diffuse theatrical life of Jonson's plays in favor of the material unity of the volume, so the allusive echo of *Beautie* denies the diffuse life of court revelry, positing fiction and author as the source of coherence.[55] The entry song of *Queenes* confirms not only the continuities of Famous royal history, but also the fact that Jonson had come to think of the echoic coherence of oeuvre as the very foundation of his own reputation: Fame's "House is all of *echo* made."[56]

Thus the syncretism of *Beautie*—summarized in the "As now!" of the masque's first echo-song and in the declaration that "Th'*Elysian* fields are here" of the second echo-song—a syncretism that ends wandering and honors the present state of the commonwealth also honors the overarching control of the author, who transcends his position as royal servant in the very act of acknowledging the power of the sovereign. This contradiction in the work can explain certain of its formal anomalies.

I have already pointed out how the bland tensions of *Blacknesse* are reenacted as hostilities in the opening of *Beautie*, this to emphasize the triumphal structure of the second masque, its crowning achievement of harmony. Yet considering Jonson's intention to effect concord from extreme discord, we might expect him to have repeated the structural choices, not of the "deferential" *Blacknesse*, but of the "consequential" masques of 1606 and 1607: *Hymenaei* and Campion's *The Lord Hay's Masque*. In these hymeneal masques, which divide *Beautie* from *Blacknesse*, the achievement of the revels is to blend the artifice of the transformation scene into the evening's festivities.[57] In the text of *Hymenaei*, Jonson twice describes this as a "dissolution" (ll. 340, 433)—the term seems to be used without pejorative connotations. Campion's diction is less ambiguous. After describing all the dances of the revels, he notes that "at the end whereof the Maskers, putting off their visards and helmets, made a low honour to the King, and attended his

Majestie to the banquetting place."[58] This is not a paradigm confined to early stages of Jacobean masquing, for as late as 1625 we find a structure of "dissolution" in *The Fortunate Isles*; the Chorus that announces the beginning of the revels describes their "endless" plot:

> Spring all the *Graces* of the age,
>   And all the *Loves* of time;
> Bring all the pleasures of the stage,
>   And relishes of rime:
> Add all the softnesses of Courts,
>   The lookes, the laughters, and the sports,
> And mingle all their sweets, and salts,
> That none may say, the *Triumph* halts.   [ll. 559–66]

The conclusion records the pangs implicit in the alternate, "enclosed" structure—pangs not utterly excluded in this late masque. Though the structure of this masque is essentially one of dissolution, it does include a ceremonial departure, not of the dancing masquers, but of the speakers who had accompanied them when they appeared during the transformation scene.

The Fortunate Isles is also a hymeneal masque, to which the structure of dissolution—a structure in which the ideal image merges permanently with the world of social fact—has an obvious appropriateness, yet this masque is really only the merest rewriting of the unperformed *Neptune's Triumph for the Returne of Albion* which, celebrating as it does the collapse of the proposed Spanish alliance, is anything but a hymeneal masque.[59] Both of these late masques are based on the device of *Beautie*, the fixing of the floating island, with Jones providing the scenes and machines (in 1608, the task of devising these sets had fallen—to Jonson's dismay—to William Portington). Like the hymeneal masques of 1606 and 1607, these two late masques employ just the sort of unfolding into "normal" festivity that would have seemed an ideal conclusion to *Beautie*.[60] The arrival at a unified Britain, the devolution of past into present, would seem a perfect narrative occasion for the dissolving which adjusts fictional spectacle to the active life of those who had contemplated it. Yet *Beautie* ends with a withdrawal into the machine, a return to that inviolable presence we have found in Guarini's Arcadia: "*they danc'd their last dance, into their Throne againe: and that turning, the scene clos'd with this full song.*"

SONG.
> Still turne, and imitate the heaven
>   In motion swift and even;
>   And as his Planets goe,
>   Your brighter lights doe so:
> May *youth* and *pleasure* ever flow.
>   But let your state, the while,
>   Be fixed as the Isle.
> CHO. So all that see your *beauties* sphære,
>   May know the'*Elysian* fields are here.

> *Ecch.* Th'*Elysian* fields are here.
> *Ecch.* *Elysian* fields are here. [ll. 396–409]

The paradox of fixed motion recalls the gentle oppositions of *Blacknesse* and pronounces even those (along with the harsher oppositions of the first half of *Beautie*) extremist; the chaste pull toward separation and the amorous urge toward union that provide the poles of action in the first masque are, finally, suavely conjoined in this song.

In *Il Pastor Fido*, echo-song is enlisted on behalf of pleasant modernity, in service of a theatrical event which is conceived as a break with the generic language of the antique past. Echo emerges as a genius of difficult transition. This function has a visual complement in that most novel of developments in Renaissance theatrical architecture, the proscenium. The function of the proscenium, finally, is not to conduce between audience and stage, but to render the distinction between the two realms ceremonial. It is, in effect, the visual equivalent of Echo's and Alfeo's *qui*: certainly it participates in their spatial paradox. Neither precisely barrier nor passageway, the proscenium celebrates the boundary between the phenomenal world of the play and that of its audience, so that the two spaces persistently *verge* on each other. Jones's and Jonson's devices transmute this paradox, making of the proscenium an architectural *rite de passage*, by means of which the two spaces, once unblinkingly present to each other, lose their integrity. Thus the Jonsonian revels institute the transgression of this boundary, restoring its impermeability when they conclude. The Italianate proscenium had made possible a scenic abstraction more extreme, perhaps, than any previously mustered in the history of the theater; Jonson's great achievement in *Beautie*, then, was to elaborate that abstraction, to emphasize the theatrical dynamics that lead to the final, poised achievement, when "*the* scene *clos'd.*" The moment of celebratory union carries with it that discriminating impulse that *Blacknesse* had instigated. Thus the "here" of "Th'*Elysian* fields are here" is a challenge of sorts, for the closure of the scene makes the throne on the stage and the throne in the audience distinct. Here is one of those particular instances in which the proscenium stage served the poet's particular purpose, for its closure brings the audience up short, forcing the court to recognize the celebration of harmony as a fiction, a flight "to the all-daring Power of *Poetrie.*" *Blacknesse* had foretold a fiction of national union, but the echoes of *Beautie* convert that expected action: the syncretic "now" and "here" of *Beautie* are represented as indigenous only to a formally autonomous object.

Nowhere in the entire corpus of Jonson's masques is the fictive locus granted greater authority relative to that of the courtly audience than in *The Golden Age Restored* (1615). As printed in the folio of 1640 and in the late states of the 1616 folio, the masque ends with a "dissolution."[61] Pallas has withdrawn, leaving Astraea to reign over the revels:

> I had not more
> Desire to leave the earth before,

> Then I have now, to stay;
> My silver feet, like roots, are wreath'd
> Into the ground, my wings are sheath'd
>   And I cannot away. [ll. 222–27]

The earthly stasis, here represented as a wreathing fixity (recalling the fixed motion of *Beautie* as well as the vocabulary of figure-dancing), has slightly sinister connotations, somewhat relieved by the mazy dancing that accompanies it. But that relief can be overestimated: the masque was probably not performed this way. Earlier states of the folio place Astraea's speech, and the galliards and corantoes that make up the last stages of the revels, *before* Pallas's departing words.[62] Herford and Simpson suggest that, in performance, Pallas's speech would have come last, and surely that best explains the reference of her "here," "what," and "hither:"

> 'Tis now inough, behold you here,
> What JOVE hath built to be your shore,
>   You hither must retire.
> And as his bountie gives you cause
> Be readie still without your pause
>   To show the world your fire.[63]

This calls an end to the revels. Its "hither" is "the Scene of Light" (140 n.) discovered in the transformation scene: the masquers are exhorted to withdraw. This conclusion relieves the darker side of Astraea's fixity, but at the expense of her continued integration within the scene of courtly dancing. As with the union of *Beautie*, the restoration of *The Golden Age* is emphatically momentary. And yet not so in print: by means of a hasty revision (in the later text, the "here" and "hither" are somewhat confusing), the evening ends with dancing. The late, printed version—and it is the concluding text in the *Works*—is a script for the union of stage and audience, achieving permanence for the restorations of masque. It is a permanence conferred in print and not in performance.

Jonson had been working without Jones for three years when he wrote *The Golden Age Restored* and was freer to assert the preeminence of poetry in the invention of the masque. In this plot of modernization, the reification of the present that takes place with the transformation scene is not allowed to stand unmediated as it did in *Queenes*. Pallas calls:

> You farre-fam'd spirits of this happie Ile,
> That, for your sacred songs have gain'd the stile
> Of PHOEBUS sons: whose notes the aire aspire
> Of th'old Ægyptian, or the *Thracian* lyre,
> That *Chaucer, Gower, Lidgate, Spencer* hight,
> Put on your better flames, and larger light,
> To wait upon the age that shall your names new nourish. [ll. 113–19]

The service of poets is hardly subservient, since their call is necessary for the awakening of the new age; the poets, not some abstract version of Fame, are the means to revival. (Even in the vernal bowers of Jonson's last masque, *Chloridia*, when Jonson reevaluates the relation of Fame to Virtue for this, the only masque in which the *new* queen would participate, the apotheosis of Fame requires the support of personified figures of Poetry, History, Architecture, and Sculpture.)

Sometimes he is less insistent on the preeminence of poetry, but Jonson seldom concludes a masque without enforcing a perception of the transcendental (and, therefore, extraoccasional) reference of the revels. Consider *Pleasure Reconcil'd to Virtue*, in which Jonson comes closest to affirming the self-sufficiency of the occasion. The masque songs are given to Daedalus, through whom Jonson attains the cherished position of instructor to the court, a position that, once attained, he maintains with a stern warmth of singular grace. Daedalus is a dancing master, and he contrives that the revels focus the concerns of the masque rather than disperse them:

> Come on, come on; and where you goe,
>   so enter-weave the curious knot,
> as ev'n th'observer scarce may know
>   which lines are Pleasures, and which not.   [ll. 253–56]

Then comes the characteristic exhortation to discriminating sight:

> so let your Daunces be entwin'd,
>   yet not perplex men, unto gaze.
> But measur'd, and so numerous too,
>   as men may read each act you doo.   [ll. 263–66]

This is virtue reconciled to pleasure, the combination of an ethics and an aesthetics of *mensura*.

But the masque, which begins in the pleasance of a Rabelaisian Comus, must revert to the chillier locus of Virgil's Mount Atlas. "Theis, theis are howres, by Vertue spar'd / hirself, she being hir owne reward. . . . You must returne unto the Hill, / and there advaunce / with labour" (ll. 328–29, 333–35). Even this ascent, which can be represented on Jones's stage, is only an anagogic sign: Daedalus speaks of heaven, not this local purgatorial mount:

>   There, there is Vertues seat.
> Strive to keepe hir your owne,
>   'tis only she, can make you great,
> though place, here, make you knowne.   [ll. 345–48]

The last line—it is the final line of the masque—with its very artful pun ("place, here" doubling as a slightly gallicized, and thus too gallant, "pleasure") again marks the absolute limit of courtly representation. The curious knot of dance, we are reminded, can only *refer* to virtue; no matter how great the participant's "place," or status, he or she cannot embody the wisdom to which the masque directs him.[64] Here again, Jonson gives the fugitive presence of the Italianate, Guarinian stage an ethical value.

I have been concentrating on the conclusions of the masques simply because Jonson does, because the end of the revels in nearly all the masques receives special attention. Usually, the syntax and prosody of the exit songs are particularly intricate, foregrounding the craftsmanship of the poet. The departure of the masquers need not have been plotted—*The Lord Hay's Masque* and *Hymenaei* make this clear—yet it nearly always *is* plotted, and the plot is usually protracted, often involving the arrival of another god or demigod to call the masquers home. The end of any occasion of social dancing puts special pressure on the wit and tact of the dancers, but Jonson arrogates these strains to his own text, so that the talents of individual courtiers are allowed rather little play. Jonson guards the coherence of the event even more closely than he guards its celebratory function.

THE PASTORAL AUDITORIUM

The guarded closure of the masques is one aspect of their subtle resistance to occasional constraint, and it complements their coherence as oeuvre. The allusive echoes of *Blacknesse* and *Beautie* suggest the possibility of a sonorous and self-sufficient continuum of Jonsonian control over the genre's fate. This continuity is a simple fact of literary history, for from 1605 to 1625, Jonson was in the steady annual employ of James's court: with the exceptions of 1607 and 1619, Jonson provided one or two masques a year. In 1616, James granted Jonson a pension, a royal notice of a prestige that Jonson publicly claimed as an author of *Works*.

I have already drawn on Orgel's observation that after 1616 the pastoral scene becomes the goal of the fictive progress within the masque, whereas before 1616 natural settings had provided the point of origin for a quest for a central, edified court. Orgel argues that the late plots of vacation are obfuscatory, efforts to divert attention from the embattled royal seat: "Thus the ruler gradually redefines himself through the illusionist's art, from a hero, the center of a court and a culture, to the god of power, the center of a universe. . . . Such productions . . . are offered not to him but by him, and they are direct political assertions."[65] I take it that by "political" Orgel means something like "ideological," since he is arguing that the late masques set out to *obscure* attention to practical politics— the "heroic," as opposed to the divine aspect of kingship. Orgel's attention to the ideological function of masque has always been illuminating, yet he incurs some slight risk by suggesting an inherently impractical, "apolitical" (as opposed to anideological) nature for pastoral. The practice of Virgil and Mantuan as pastoralists, or of Spenser, Milton, and Marvell, provides sufficient correctives.[66]

More important, the assertion that "when a pastoral scene appears before 1616 it always comes at the beginning, after 1616 it always comes at the end" needs some slight adjustment. The transformation scenes of the early *Masques of Blacknesse and Beautie* involve the arrival of pastoral islands at the British shore; and when the transformation scenes of two late masques, *Neptune's Triumph* (1624) and *The Fortunate Isles* (1625), recapitulate these arrivals, the main masque in both concludes with the further revelation of the fleet—hardly an attempt to conceal the instrumental aspect of royal power. We may perhaps modify Orgel's observation and speak instead of the increasing importance of pastoral conventions for the developing seventeenth-century masque. But Jonson's late dramatic fragment, *The Sad Shepherd*, testifies to his *generally* burgeoning interest in pastoral, an interest not confined to the masque in particular. The *Aminta* and *Il Pastor Fido* had suggested the means for a lyricization of the public drama at the turn of the century; the pastoral became an increasingly public language in seventeenth-century England, exerting its influence in a variety of cultural productions. And if the ideological assertions of these various productions are not always direct, it seems fair to argue that the mere employ of pastoral does not always imply the evasion of the political. Indeed, pastoral is often adopted in order to subject the heroism of politics to critical scrutiny.

Consider that most "through-composed" of Jonson's pastoral fictions, *Pan's Anniversary*, which opens with a floral strewing—"Thus, thus, begin the yearly rites / Are due to Pan on these bright nights" (ll. 5–6)—and ends with the gently Mantuanesque warning not to be too trustful of hirelings:

> See, yond' they goe, and timely doe
> The office you have put them to,
> But if you often give this leave,
> Your sheepe, and you they will deceave.   [ll. 275–78]

The conclusion proposes a pragmatic attitude to generic allegiances: pastoral is recommended as properly momentary—the model for this is the so-called greenworld dramaturgy. The masque itself, a celebration of James's fifty-fourth birthday in 1620, works out its customary antioccasional closure in unusually reflexive manner: the stated limitations of the audience are also the stated limitations of the fiction. The final song announces the overestimation of pastoral vacation as dangerous—again, hardly a politic occlusion of the political.

The antimasque of *Pan's Anniversary* wreathes a subtler maze than those of the earlier masques. That Jonson was being judged by his antimasques we can see from contemporary comments on *Pleasure Reconcil'd*; in the later masques he accommodates himself to court tastes, for he uses antimasque more as a leitmotif than as a stage in the dramatic sequence of the masque. A braggadocian fencer and his Boeotian comrades twice intrude on the Arcadians, each time offering bellicose challenges to a dancing competition. Ridiculous as the Boeotian troupe is, it does represent the heroic values that have been abjured for the occasion: abjured, but not excluded—the masque enacts both a banishment and a transformation of the heroic and, concluding, offers a critique of that treatment.

In romance, invading belligerence is conquered (though sometimes after great delay) and invading chivalry is accommodated, garlanded; here the sense of generic rivalry is far greater. Again, such emphasis on ethos, as in the entertainments at Kenilworth or Althorp, cannot be taken as an obfuscation of the political. An idyllic and apolitical world is, in fact, the masque's premise, but it is soon revealed as a naive one. The hostility between the Boeotians and the Arcadians is formally obtrusive, for the masque begins without a hint of the hostility; it disrupts, not only Arcadia, but the formal paradigm of the precedent antimasque established in earlier Jonsonian masques. Before the masquers can make the first move from their ranked poise in the opening machine, the bumptious Fencer intrudes "flourishing," and with a cry for "room" that affiliates him with the comic entries of specifically English folk drama. (This is the same nearly mechanical joke of stylistic anachronism so perfectly exploited in the Venus in *Christmas his Masque*.) The addled modernity of the "boys of Boeotia" is easily vanquished by Arcadian classicism, but it must be vanquished twice. The second vanquishing is, curiously, not another expulsion; instead, just after the revels, when the Fencer announces that his "boys" "looke for some sheepish devises here in *Arcadia*," the Shepherd offers the flat counter, "They have their punishment in fact. They shall be sheepe" (ll. 233–34, 239–40). Jonson thus gives us two comic versions of the misuse of pastoral. The Fencer's first entry shows us a bellicose disdain for the apparent fragility of pastoral order; his second shows us an indulgence in pastoral conventions so overenthusiastic that the Boeotians resign their heroic armor in order to put on, not the garlands of repose, but sheep's clothing.[67] As is customary, the antimasque tests the tolerance of the main device, not so much articulating the bounds of generic decorum as insisting on the persistence of such bounds through the festal topsy-turvy of the antimasque. The persistence is offered, of course, as proof of the magic of aristocracy, of an aristocracy privy to exclusive codes. (The codes of decorum remain inarticulate: the masques represent the *idea* of coding.)

The antimasque tests social tolerances, whereas the masque itself challenges fictive tolerances, tests the ability of masquers and audience to enter and remain in fictions that, as in earlier masques, finally exclude them. The first entrance of the antimasquers of *Pan's Anniversary* may be compared to the conclusions of earlier masques: as this Boeotian rabble is too citified, too tied to comic realism to enter the Arcadian world, so the courtiers of earlier masques had been shown finally incapable of complete adaptation to the ideality of the masque world. The second entrance poses a subtler problem, for the sheepish Boeotians suddenly show themselves too sympathetic with Arcadian rusticity; the closing song of the masque matches the second antimasque with its caution against immoderate adaptation to the masque-device. Jonson thus returns to the central theme of *Cynthia's Revels*, the perilous ethics of festivity.

It is not surprising, then, that the entrance song of *Pan's Anniversary* should recall that initiatory production in Jonson's career as courtly maker: the shepherd encourages the masquers to dance "Till the applause it brings, Wakes Eccho from her seate"—and as at Mercury's invocation in *Cynthia's Revels*, she proves surprisingly ready to hand—"The closes to repeate / (*Ech*. The closes to repeate)" (ll. 216–19). This is again the redeemed Echo of *Beautie*, an Echo who reconciles the coital energies of the Ovidian nymph to the chastity of the nymph claimed, since

Moschus, as the harmonious "belov'd of Pan, the Valleyes Queene." The entrance song should perhaps be given in full:

> If yet, if yet
> *Pans* orgies you will further fit,
> See where the silver-footed Fayes doe sit,
> The Nymphes of wood and water,
> Each trees, and Fountaines daughter.
> Goe take them forth, it will be good
> To see some wave it like a wood,
> And others wind it like a flood;
> In springs,
> And rings,
> Till the applause it brings,
> Wakes Eccho from her seate,
> The closes to repeate.
> (*Ech.* The closes to repeate)
> Eccho, the truest Oracle on ground,
> Though nothing but a sound.
> (*Ech.* Though nothing but a sound.)
> Belov'd of *Pan*, the Valleyes Queene
> (*Ech.* The Valleyes Queene)
> And often heard, though never seene,
> (*Ech.* Though never seene.) [ll. 206–26]

Jonson uses *orgies* in that morally neutral sense pointed in his notes to *Hymenaei*; the term refers to all rites, not merely to Bacchic ones. The philological nicety is a test of the sober sanctity of the pastoral mind, a challenge to those who will "further fit" the Arcadian world. The unspotted sophistication of this decorous "fittedness" is figured in the specifically antiscenic harmonies of this locus amoenus. It is worth pointing out just how subtly Jonson has figured the superiority of dance and song to spectacle here, proof that the quarrel with Jones was not carried out exclusively in outbursts of spleen. The choice of Echo, "often heard but never seen," as the queen of the valley dance floor is variously determined, but here, for the first time, her furtive presence is made to complement that of the royal auditor rather than to challenge the audience with notice of the inaccessibility of the theatrical scene. The cooperative, unironic voice of Echo suggests, if only momentarily, the easy accessibility of the two worlds to each other, suggesting that Pan's orgies *can* be fit.

Jonson thus manages to demystify the world behind the proscenium; indeed, he contrives that the dancing act as a dynamic replacement of the setting itself, for the dancing imitates the physical features of the landscape—"some wave it like a wood / And others wind it like a flood." But finally—"in springs / And rings"—the fountains and fairy rings of the staged locus amoenus are absorbed in the linguistic and gestural magic of pun and figure-dancing.[68] Jonson's old suspicion of a scenic spectacularity that perplexes unto gaze is assuaged in *Pan's Anniversary*, first of all because the scene is not allowed to arrest the mind with merely visual ideality, and second of all, because there is a visual reciprocity operating in the masque, one that matches the acoustic reciprocity of echo.[69] Even before the masquers direct their attention to potential partners among the "silver-footed Fayes" of the court, the audience has been made the object of gaze; when the Shepherd calls the masquers from the machine, he first reminds them that they have been

> taught
> By PAN the rites of true societie,
> From his loud Musicke, all your manners wraught
> And made your Commonwealth a harmonie. [ll. 159–62]

and then urges them to

> Daunce from the top of the Lycaean mountaine
> Downe to this valley, and with nearer eye
> Enjoy, what long in that illumin'd Fountaine
> You did farre of, but yet with wonder spye. [ll. 167–70]

The masquers seek a vision of the king, perhaps more eagerly than the king seeks a vision of the masquers. The exhortation to take a closer look at the audience—to "enjoy" and not "to spye"—arrests any overestimation of Jones's settings and makes the king, raised above the audience on a dais that works as a second stage, a more proper object of attention. Unusually early, the masquers are asked to resign their purchase on a scene that distances them from the court.

The argument is both subtle and simple: the demystification of the stage and the mystification of voice makes narcissistic spectatorship impossible. Mimesis here is not visual, but auditory; the fictive site cannot be watched, though it can be heard and inhabited—it is as if, at the midpoint of the masque, an echo chamber, and not a mirror, were being held up to nature. In this pastoral auditorium, as at the death of Narcissus in Ovid's epic, the techniques of a lost acoustic mimesis make a momentary return.

The pastoral has not yet been placed off limits: that is not why the masquers are called away from the machine. Indeed, they are urged forth on the pretext of the pastoral identity of the audience itself; the ladies are nymphs and James is Pan. This seems to move us in the direction of a praise of royalty more fulsome than is to be found in any earlier masque; yet the praise that bursts forth is equally an homage to Spenser:

> Of *Pan* we sing, the best of Shepherds, Pan
> That keepes our flocks, and us, and both leads forth
> To better pastures than great *Pales* can.
> Cho. Heare, O you groves, and hills, resound his worth.
> And while his powers, and praises thus we sing,
> The valleys let rebound, and all the rivers ring. [ll. 184–89]

The hymeneal rhetoric of the *Epithalamion* is here wedded to the vocabulary of the *Calender* (particularly of the December eclogue); the attenuating metrical marker is the crucial sign. All of this mediates the influence of Virgil; in his gloss to the December eclogue, E. K. notes Spenser's imitation of Virgil's "Pan curat ovis oviumque magistras" (*Ecl.*, II.33), a line that Jonson imitates even more closely here; the reference to Pales is taken from the *Georgics*; and though the rhythm and language of the invocation of pastoral resonance is, of course, Spenserian, the line points back past the *Epithalamion* to the Virgilian locus classicus of such resonance. The nature of the tribute is difficult to ascertain. Jonson's Pan, "that taught us swaines, how first to tune our layes" (l. 173), is a deified Tityrus, a divine version of Virgil, of Spenser's Chaucer, and, finally, of Jonson's Spenser.[70] James becomes the object of praise only by virtue of being assimilable to a place within this tradition of poetic indebtedness.

We have seen the pattern before. Indeed, it is difficult to find an instance of echoing, of literary repetition imitative of acoustic reflection, that is not attended on by some form of allusion: here the allusions create a literary locus amoenus in preparation for the conjuration of Echo in the main masque. *Pan's Anniversary* thus shows lingering traces of preliterate composition, of a mimesis in which the primary object of imitation is an earlier imitative act and not a phenomenal object, not a something "out there" that the work of art represents as having metaphysical priority. The advantage of echoic mimesis is its categorical adequacy to the object of imitation; the mirror held up to nature must always distort, whereas the acoustic reflection is always an imitation in kind.

The precise nature of Jonson's homage is difficult to assess because, for Jonson's meditations on the calendrical recurrence of royal birthdays have led him—via the *Shepheardes Calender*—to a celebration of the recurrent initiatory moment in poetry, the moment of pastoral beginnings. We cannot make sense of the admonition that opens the masque—"All Envious, and Prophane, away, / This is the Shepherds Holy-day"—if we fail to recognize the function of this masque as an enactment of poetic initiation. Sacral, even virginal purity is part of the traditionally initiatory ethos of pastoral making, an ethos exploited on the poet's own behalf. The catalog of flowers that follows from this ritual admonishment to the impure is, again, less a birthday custom than an evocation of pastoral for its own sake.

A Jonson so concerned with the innocence of poesy may surprise readers who have been accustomed to descriptions of the poet's unremitting tough-mindedness or who are unfamiliar with the occasionally delicate self-doubt and circumspection of his devotional verse. The familiar Jonson reasserts himself at the close of *Pan's Anniversary*, no doubt, as well as in the antimasques, but the language of the main masque has nothing of the Martial (or Mantuan) in Jonson, nothing even of the Horatian Jonson of earlier main masques. The authority of the fictive maker is not claimed as a specifically moral authority. In *Pleasure Reconcil'd to Virtue* the dancing is bound to both a poetics and an ethics of mensura, but in *Pan's Anniversary*, on the other hand, the dancing is a moving conjuration of pastoral—the poetics make no overt claim to ethics. We can see how the claim of an amoral power for the main masque, a self-authenticating power based solely on the tradition of pastoral purity and pastoral charm, might lead to an assertion of the apolitical force of *Pan's Anniversary*, though such an assertion would somehow slight the crucial rivalry embodied in the masque as a whole.

The competition between Boeotian energies and Arcadian ease has a far more dialectical function than had maintained heretofore between antimasque and main masque. Orgel has himself commented on the way the antimasque becomes the theoretical component within the later masques; as the antimasque becomes less diverting and less frivolous, its authority increases, and this despite the persistence of manifest folly within the challenges of the antimasquers. Here the competition for authority is figured as a struggle between heroic and pastoral, politics and poetics. And insofar as pastoral is allowed a momentary victory it is an assertion of Jonson's authority in the face of the king's.[71]

This assertion may seem odd at first, since the Pan of the main masque is so obviously a figure for James himself. Pan traditionally constitutes the chief authority in the pastoral world and so figures a whole range of extra-Arcadian authorities—God, or king, or pope, or nature, or the epistemological field at large. This range of potential reference generates considerable uncertainty in the *Shepheardes Calender*, as E. K.'s glosses to the eclogues for April, May, and July show, and this uncertainty reaches a crisis in the December eclogue.[72] This eclogue, on which Jonson depended for much of the language of *Pan's Anniversary*, also provides a teleology (or a feint toward teleology—it depends on the degree to which we accept Spenser's claim in the envoy that "I have made a calendar for every year") for the calendrical cyclicality and pastoral self-sufficiency of its context. Pan is apostrophized as "God of shepheards all," but his godhead is abruptly denied in somewhat enigmatic lines that unite Pan and Cupid, usually at odds, in league against Colin:

> The shepheards' God (perdie God was he none)
> My hurtlesse pleasaunce did me ill upbraide,
> My freedome lorne, my life he lefte to mone.
>   Love they him called, that gave me checkmate,
>   But better mought they have behote him Hate. [ll. 50–54]

The disingenuous "perdie" punctures the neoclassicism of the *Calender*, suggesting that the union between the Skeltonic and the Virgilian has become insupportable; the breach is only one stage in a program of dismantling that concludes with the litany of adieus at the end of this eclogue. Colin resigns soft pastoral as winter takes control of the landscape, and he relinquishes his clownish reliance on pagan deity as youth fades into age; he may suffer within his pastoral environment, but he musters his revenge on the environment by dismissing it. Of all the gods, Pan suffers the dismissal most greatly, since his deity itself is denied; I suspect that he receives such treatment because of his special association with indolence, that component of pastoral which Spenser held in the highest suspicion—that suspicion is a central cause, finally, of Spenser's enduring ambivalence to the pastoral mode.

In *Pan's Anniversary*, this most Spenserian of the masques, Jonson anatomizes that ambivalence. He had perfected the art of exclusive closure in the masques, having repeatedly devised bravura public displays of fictive privacy. Increasingly, he figures that closure as a Spenserian "green cabinet" (*December*, l. 95) proper to poetry and occasionally proper to royalty. The cabinet is not erected to exclude the political so much as to argue that ideological claims *on* the masque must be subordinated to the intrinsic fictive claims *of* the masque itself. This argument was not new to Jonson. Orgel has commented on problems, as early as *Oberon* (1611), in reconciling the intrinsic fictive monarch and the extrinsic observing monarch, and his observation is useful, though, I submit, imperfectly *valued*: the disparity between the real king and his image is in no way a defect.[73] In *Oberon*, it has a double power. First, the disparity contributes to the ethical suasion of the masque; in earlier masques, like *Oberon*, the perfection of the masque is an assertion in the subjunctive (Fletcher's "opulent optative"), a future goal couched as a description. Second, the disparity delimits the king's realm and marks his sway as modal; in the masque world, government must be based on poetics.

In *Pan's Anniversary*, the emphasis shifts, for the ethical function of disparity is absorbed into this assertion of modality. The king's purchase on the role of Pan is described as momentary, even subtly culpable; insofar as it is temporarily allowable, the identification of James with Pan is as contingent as is the reference of Pan in Spenserian pastoral, as contingent as the divinity of Pan in the December eclogue. The identification of James with Pan is achieved by a collaboration between poet and king, Echo *and* Pan. So the earlier alignment of ethics and poetics in *Pleasure Reconcil'd* has been transformed as Jonson makes the mystery of masquing even more removed; ethical discrimination is reduced to the discrimination between genres and to the discrimination between the fictive and the real. The echoing center momentarily opens and includes its audience; its final closure is its only moral.

5

"TRANSLATED TO THE SKIES": ECHOIC SILENCE IN *COMUS*

> Un Anglais, qui voyageait en Italie, recontra sur sa route un écho tellement beau qu'il voulut l'acheter. L'écho était produit par une maison isolée. L'Anglais la fit démolir, numérota toutes les pierres, et les emporta avec lui en Angleterre, dans une de ses propriétés, où il fit rebâtir la maison exactement come elle avait été. Il choisit pour emplacement un endroit de son parc qui était à une distance du chateau égale à celle où l'écho avait été distinct en Italie. Quand tout fut prêt, l'heureux propriétaire résolut de pendre la crémaillère de son écho d'une manière solennelle. Il invita tous ses amis à un grand dîner, et leur promit l'écho pour le dessert. On mangea bien: l'histoire ne dit pas si l'on ne but pas mieux. . . . Quand on fut arrivé au dessert, l'amphitryon annonça qu'il allait inaugurer son phénomène, et se fit apporter sa boite aux pistolets. Après avoir chargé lentement les deux armes, il s'approcha de la fenêtre ouverte et tira un coup. Pas l'ombre d'un écho! Alors il prit le second pistolet et se brûla la cervelle.
> "Echo," *Grand dictionnaire universel* (Larousse)[1]

At the moment of revels, in the space of the dancing floor—at the time and place in which performers and witnesses are most fully present to each other, breaching pastoral ideality in order to recreate it—then and there the masque transforms the locus amoenus into a slightly more secret "valley." And Echo is "the Valleyes Queene." But at this hallowed occasional spot, at this wavering occasional moment where worlds of experience merge, Echo reenacts the withdrawal from presence that she has always performed on the Renaissance stage: "often heard, though never seene," withdrawn from Jones's and James's imperial line of vision, she establishes herself in a line of literary tradition. Recollective, like the gongs at Dodona or the caves of the Cumaean sibyl, she grows capable of prophecy. Thus, as "the truest Oracle on ground," Echo restores the core of mystery, the transcendental impulse, to pastoral.

In the Silenan song of Virgil's sixth eclogue, the impulse is tied to the secretive infolding of the pastoral locus:

> Omnia, quae Phoebo quondam meditante beatus
> audiit Eurotas iussitque ediscere lauros,
> ille [Silenus] canit, pulsae referunt ad sidera valles;
> cogere donec ovis stabulis numerumque referre
> iussit et invito processit Vesper Olympo.   [*Ecl.*, VI.82–86]

[All the songs that of old Phoebus rehearsed, while happy Eurotas listened and bade his laurels learn by heart—these Silenus sings. The re-echoing valleys fling them again to the stars, till Vesper gave the word to fold the flocks and tell their tale, as he set forth over an unwilling sky.]

Silenus's song is more ambitious, of course, than any of Jonson's pastoral musings,

133

a song of cosmology and metamorphoses, compressed, twisting, and dark. Such verse was out of Jonson's range; more important, it is arguably outside the range of any dramatic verse (even the Shakespearean line takes on some bluster when, in the late tragedies, it approaches this huge secrecy; mystery does not approach Virgilian *scale* without overreaching Virgilian *pitch*). And we must trace Jonson's chariness about theatrical uses of pastoral to his recognition that dramatic verse was inadequate to any conception of pastoral that could accommodate the spacious mystery of Silenus's song.[2]

"Here's PASTOR FIDO," says Lady Would-Be in *Volpone*. "All our English writers . . . Will Deigne to steale out of this author" (II.iv.86–89). It is an Erasmian trick; we can barely gauge Jonson's attitude to Guarini through this voice of pretentious folly. Still, the condescension of this particular lady suggests that Jonson thinks it folly to sell pastoral short. Milton may have been the first masque writer to turn the Circes and Proteuses of the English masque to the task of recovering Silenan mysteries, the first to redirect the formal transformations of masque plot to figure the terrors of metamorphosis. True, in *Pan's Anniversary* Jonson warns his audience away from the pastoral dancing floor; he shows that the uninitiated, stumbling there, would find themselves transformed into beasts; he even repeats the alternation of antimasque and revelation and so suggests the uncertain purchase of order on the world. But only Milton would so tangle the antimasque in the plot of the main masque that the processes of noble transformation become nearly confounded with the debasements of Circean metamorphosis. And only Milton would similarly tangle the amenity of Tityran pastoral with both the keening terror of Orphic lament and the *mysterium* of Silenus's song. If Jonson *made* the masque, Milton made the masque adequate to the range of Virgilian pastoral. Yet this Miltonic tangling of amenity with mystery was only momentary; in Milton's handling of such topoi as that of pastoral resonance, pastoral amenity shows itself fundamentally frail.

There is no echo-song in the masque Milton wrote for the installation of the Earl of Bridgewater at Ludlow Castle. The evasion of resonance is a resistance to a signal characteristic of both Virgilian pastoral and Jonsonian masque. Such a repression would not seem so odd were it not that the echoing moments in other, less generalized influences than Virgil's and Jonson's are equally being repressed. Take, for example, *The Old Wive's Tale* of George Peele, often named as one of the sources for the plot of *Comus*. Peele provided Milton with a model for the transformation of Spenserian chivalric quest-romance into what we might call a *family* quest-romance:

> There was a Conjurer, and this Conjurer could doo anything, and hee turned himselfe into a great Dragon, and carried the Kinges Daughter away in his mouth to a Castle that hee made of stone, and there he kept hir I know not how long, till at last all the Kinges men went out so long, that hir two Brothers went to seeke hir.[3]

In Peele, Echo marks the threshold of success in the brothers' quest, for she functions as an orienting voice:

> *Thelea.* Call out Calypha that she may heare,
>   And crie aloud, for Delya is neere.
> *Echo.* Neere.
> *Calypha.* Neere, O where, hast thou any tidings?
> *Echo.* Tidings.
> *Thelea.* Which way is Delya then. or that, or this?
> *Echo.* This.
> *Calypha.* And may we safely come where Delia is?
> *Echo.* Yes.[4]

As in the Elizabethan vacation entertainments and in the *Masques of Blacknesse and Beautie*, the voice of Echo announces the arrival at a threshold where the reasonable and flat acoustics of England open onto the imaginative resonances of Faerie; it marks a juncture between the real landscape and the landscape of the mind. A few years after *The Old Wive's Tale* was written, Dekker would open *Old Fortunatus* with an awesome comic exchange that searches this echoic tradition to the quick:

> *Old Fortunatus.* Tel me how thou cal'st this wood
> *Echo.* This wood. [I.i.5–7]

It is the Wandering Wood, the *selva oscura*, the wood found everywhere that there is mind. The reflections *of* this wood can only become reflections *on* this wood when the hero's wandering becomes self-consciousness, and he has discovered the lesson of Ausonius's Echo: "Auribus in vestris habito penetrabilis Echo." Old Fortunatus is simply impenetrable, being both self-absorbed and unself-conscious, and so his Echo only mocks. This mockery predicts a narrative of antiheroic self-discovery, a fairy-tale narrative like that of the three (abused) magical wishes; we can see such a folk narrative given the proper aristocratic form in the Jonsonian masque, for in masque the transformation scene gives local habitation to the monarch's political and imaginative appetites for ideality, while the closure of the masque reinstates an intransigent reality. This rhythm of transformation and reinstatement exposes the origins of masquing in appetite and, in so doing, makes regal consciousness available to itself. The masque is folktale wishing on a grand scale.

This romance-questing for consciousness is a family romance in both *The Old Wive's Tale* and *Comus*, achieving the representation of a family to itself; in *Comus* the representation is attended by a spirit of musical (and literary) education who announces:

> Noble Lord, and Lady bright
> I have brought ye new delight,
> Here behold so goodly grown
> Three fair branches of your own. [ll. 966–69]

The figure of the family tree reminds us that the recognition of the wood and the recognition of the self are nearly one and the same thing. Echo makes possible a sylvan objectification of self; that is, Echo is a pastoral analogue to those objectifications made possible through the family, in which child functions as parent's second self, and brother or sister works rather like Jung's animus or anima. In Peele's play, Echo marks the site of the family's reunion, but the brothers do not free their sister Delia immediately; before they can earn the reconstitution of the family, they are forced to labors more strenuous than mere outcry. In Peele, to halloo the name of Delia to the reverberate hills is not enough to hallow the hills; it only begins a process by which the family can make itself at home in unenchanted woods.

But the Egerton family found itself bereft of even this initiating power: "I can not hallo to my Brothers," says Alice Egerton. Instead, she shows her naive wit by an effort to *invoke* the orienting Echo, calling on the uncalled for. Bookish and musical, she makes the mistake of thinking that she can compel the response of that Echo who restores or relocates us in the woods. Echo's address to the disoriented had heretofore come at the nymph's, or God's, own whim. Thus, Echo confers resounding *grace*, to use the Lady's words, and the words focus the Lady's peculiar intellectual predicament. John Hollander points out the charming baroque turn here, the play of the massive theological meaning of *grace* against the trim musical one; Alice Egerton is quite capable of such verbal subtlety (of which more later), but she sweetly deludes herself to think that such graces can be compelled.[5] Her folly is both youthful and aristocratic: in the slight compass of her song to Echo she claims omnipotence. For this, the masque closes her out with the quick assurance of dogma.

She is Corydon; she is Milton at his most uncertain, for unlike Tityrus, she vainly scatters her songs to a largely indifferent landscape. Yet the landscape has offered her at least one suggestion of its docility. Just before her invocation of Echo, the Lady had sought, or perhaps observed, other attendants:

> O welcome pure-ey'd Faith, white-handed Hope,
> Thou hov'ring Angel girt with golden wings
> And thou unblemish'd form of Chastity,
> I see ye visibly, and now believe
> That he, the Supreme good, t'whom all things ill
> Would send a glist'ring Guardian, if need were,
> To keep my life and honor unassail'd.   [ll. 214–20]

The welcome resembles a Jonsonian exultation at the splendid moment of a masque transformation, but Ludlow Castle afforded no such spectacle. "I see ye visibly," says the Lady, displaying the power of her own spiritual vision and not the ingenuity of an architect. But what was called enthusiasm in Milton's day subsides into what is *now* called enthusiasm, naive enthusiasm, and that vision loses its purchase even on the mind's eyes. Indicative shades into subjunctive: "the Supreme good . . . *would* send . . . if need were." Need *is*, but what is sent seems a sorry reduction from the full trinity of cardinal Miltonic virtues, faith, hope and chastity:

> Was I deceived or did a sable cloud
> Turn forth her silver lining on the night,
> I did not err, there does a sable cloud
> Turn forth her silver lining on the night. [ll. 221–24]

These are notorious lines, though it is curious how quickly critics write them off as simply bad; we see here what wondrous risks Milton was willing to take in his masque. The impoverishment of the verse points the impoverishment of what masque can show. Milton had greater doubts about the mimetic power of scenic art than even Jonson had, and here he insists on the inadequacy of the scene to his trinity: the revelations of the stage are petty, mechanical. This scene is not so much docile as momentarily solicitous, and the solicitude is facile. Nonetheless, the Lady's repetition, clumsy record of nature's generosity toward human need, has the further function of jogging her memory, for it recalls the traditional device by which masquers had oriented themselves. She remembers Echo:

> SONG
> Sweet Echo, sweetest Nymph that liv'st unseen
> Within thy airy shell
> By slow *Meander's* margent green,
> And in the violet-embroider'd vale
> Where the love-lorn Nightingale
> Nightly to thee her sad Song mourneth well.
> Canst thou not tell me of a gentle Pair
> That likest thy *Narcissus* are?
> O if thou have
> Hid them in some flow'ry Cave,
> Tell me but where,
> Sweet Queen of Parley, Daughter of the Sphere,
> So mayst thou be translated to the skies,
> And give resounding grace to all Heav'n's Harmonies. [ll. 230–43]

There are several reasons for the Lady's failure to rouse Echo, but an account of those reasons may profitably begin by honestly acknowledging the scenic bathos of the sable cloud. It need not be considered a defect; occasionally something of Keaton flashes out in *Comus*. Here, as when the two Egerton boys, aged nine and eleven, rush onto the stage brandishing swords and so dispel the rout of monsters, we contemplate the inadequacy of Ludlow Castle to the assured displays of Whitehall. Conventional court masquing had become too sophisticated for this stage, and Milton took considerable liberties with its conventions. Dialectic makes up for the visual dazzle of spectacle; solos replace conventional choral songs; the element of antimasque becomes a vice and a rabble, thus obviating the need for skilled comic actors. Most important, three aristocratic masquers do what courtly masquers nearly never do—they speak.

Milton works an eerie humor into this aesthetic surprise. The burden of the masque, to make men mindful of the crown that virtue gives, is a burden that has been placed on the very young. In the earlier masques of the century, the mark of virtue is an elegant silence, a moving grace, an overwhelming gestural power; in *Comus*, noble masquers speak, the central figure is rendered immobile, and gallant saviors rush incompetently to her rescue—this masque is a dance of half-measures. The nine-year-old's famous exclamation, "How charming is divine Philosophy," may stand as a kind of posy of the stylistic will-to-fail in the masque. Indulgent criticism explains away the tender bathos here either by urging that we make allowances for Milton's youth or by suggesting that, as he wrote, the poet engaged in some sort of willful repression of occasional constraints. The folly of the first assertion is obvious. "L'Allegro" and "Il Penseroso" had been written three years before *Comus*, so, although Milton can *pose* as a poetic novice (a favorite pose), he cannot actually be *taken* as one. The other explanation deserves slightly more generous consideration.

I argued in the preceding essay that some hostility to the occasional had been characteristic of Jonsonian masque-making, though I have never postulated a willed *forgetting* of the scene at hand. Nor can the script of *Comus* sustain any such postulate. A moment after the nine-year-old's fervent exclamation, the children's music master enters doubly disguised (he portrays the Airy Spirit in the assumed likeness of a shepherd); the youngest child bursts out, "O brother, 'tis my father's shepherd sure," thus sustaining and dissolving the fiction in a single line. Henry Lawes has assumed a role twice removed, yet the roles describe nearly a complete circle, for the role of singing caretaker of wandering lambs is an easy pastoral translation of Lawes's proper function: this second exclamation identifies the actor as well as the role, remarking the cry of the occasion.

The young Milton was obsessed with occasion, with the fit of poem both to its audience—hence his early fondness for the verse epistle—and to its season—hence the frequent recourse to calendrical themes, the odes of Nativity, Circumcision, Passion. The circle of Lawes's disguises all but restores persona to personator and so works as a formal prelude to that representation of the child actors to their parents which will take place just before the revels. The setting itself circles slowly round to the occasional spot when, at this late moment of representation, it "changes, presenting *Ludlow* Town and the President's Castle" (l. 958), again nearly completing a full spatial involution of the masque upon itself. The cursus of the masque may take the long way around, but its occasional wariness should hardly be challenged, even by the most apologetic of Miltonists. Even its true title, *A Mask, Presented at Ludlow Castle, 1634*, etc., goes out of its way to be seasonable. Since the 1610s this sort of title had been displaced by thematic titles, so Milton's conservative attention to occasion is immediately evident in the text of the masque. The decorum of *Comus* is so firm that the awkwardnesses of style and tone need to be faced more squarely. If we acknowledge that the lapses and failures that dog the Egerton children form a consistent pattern in the masque, we can recognize the Lady's inability to rouse Echo as part of that pattern. Such failures are crucial to *Comus*, particularly crucial to the way the masque fashions out its own place in a tradition of English masquing.

From the very beginning, the English masque intends a sanctification of place, hence its constant invocation of genii loci; the exposure of voices or revelation of figures in a landscape had certainly been the most common method for so valorizing place (in Elizabethan royal celebrations Echo often replaces or "ingeminates" the genius loci). Most of the surviving texts of Elizabethan celebrations are "progress-devices," inventions for a mobile court in which the host could aggrandize himself by suggesting a particular affinity between royal presence and noble seat, the presence of a genius loci often acting as the sign of the monarch's evocative power. The Jacobean masque is more domestic. James saw most of his masques at home, so he often performed the function of genius loci himself, while the sonorities of the place tended to revert to disembodiment, as in *Blacknesse and Beautie*. The conservative early Jacobean masque draws on the resources of the public stage to provide narratives of travel, narratives that replace the actual fact of Elizabeth's vacationing—again, the early *Blacknesse and Beautie* provides a good example of such a quest-fiction. The paradigmatic plot of these masques is the *Odyssey*, hence their Proteuses and Circes; hence, too, the hovering at the shore in *Blacknesse*, *Neptune's Triumph*, *The Fortunate Isles*, and *Love's Triumph Through Callipolis*, moments of dancing suspension each of which works as a quintessence of odyssey. Milton's debt to these quest-masques is obvious, for the circular progress of *Comus* recalls the search for a stable English locale that is the most archaic plot of English masquing. If Jonsonian masque affixes the monarch to a privileged spot—a spot whose privilege is limited by *both* monarch and deviser—Milton, historian of royal festivity par excellence, treats that stasis as a sign of the audience's degeneration. The Lady in Milton's masque transfixed in the Comic chair is the ironic image of the monarch enthroned in the royal seat, enthralled by baroque perspective, unable to move lest he destroy the *visae imago formae*.[6] Both Jonson and Milton preserve the quest-plot within the masque (and thus manifest a persistent nostalgia for Elizabethan festivity), but Milton makes arrest a crucial sign of lapse. Alice Egerton's disorientation is one thing; getting stuck is another, marking as it does the possibility of a thorough enervation of quest.

Enervation, arrest—the plot of *Comus* derives from books IX and X of the *Odyssey*, the tales of the Lotos-Eaters and of Circe. A tradition of allegorical interpretation had rendered these tales curiously similar to each other; they were both taken as accounts of the corruption of the will. The choice of source suggests that Milton had contrived to take the cry of this occasion personally, making of *Comus* a masque of delay. By masque of delay, I mean a fiction both of protracted quest (like *Blacknesse and Beautie*) and of quest begun too late—congenial subject for a poet whose every great poem claims the burden of "catching up" with the occasional imperative of its production, whether that occasion be the death of a friend, the perceived impatience of a generous father or Father, the birth of Christ, or the Fall of Man. The *Mask Presented at Ludlow Castle* is an act of memory as well as of commemoration: Bridgewater had been appointed lord president of Wales and the Marches in 1631, and his installation at Ludlow had taken rather longer than it should have. Milton may have found in this deferred assumption of responsibility an analogue to what he conceived of as his own poetic inaction.

In the opening of "Lycidas," the poet's embarrassment over protracting his apprenticeship manifests itself in exclamations on the disastrous effects of precipitous action. *Comus* makes similar protestations, and not only in the histrionic awkwardness of childish declamation. Comus's appeal to the Lady, once she is bound in his magic chair, is twofold: he first argues against temperance in general (ll. 706-36) and then narrows his attack to the folly of virginity. In the Egerton MS, our best text for the acting version of *Comus*, the Lady Alice succeeds in rebutting only the first of his arguments. (Her defense is fuller and more authoritative in the published version: the expanded text attained a gravity that the delicate humor of the performance abjures. As Jonson occasionally does, so Milton reserves his most sage and serious doctrines for print, where he trims away the antic diffusions of performance.) She gives a staunch defense of temperance, but the enchanter interrupts her, rails briefly on her folly, and then is himself interrupted; the Brothers break in, drive out Comus and his rout, and break his glass. The Brothers not only curtail the debate; they fail in their second charge, neglecting to snatch away Comus's charming rod. The masque ultimately aims to enact a triumph "O'er sensual Folly and Intemperance," so the Brothers' intrusion results in one of the masque's half-measures: rushing in, they preclude the Lady's rhetorical defense of virginity—virginity hardly seems to need physical defense here—and leave the enchanter still armed with his charming phallic rod. It is a badly botched job, this rescue, and that is Milton's point: triumphing (somewhat) over sensual folly the Brothers' action remains marred specifically by intemperance. That is, Milton has clearly taken the imperfection of the children's skills in performance and built it into the very plot of the masque. The overhasty entrance of the two boys (they precede the Attendant Spirit, fighting alone) fails to produce physical freedom for either their sister or the audience. Both remain rooted to their chairs; the revels, undoubtedly expected to ensue from the expulsion of the comic threat, are postponed until the entrance of Sabrina. None may rise and dance.

Thus, when the Spirit does bring on the revels, his summary of the action is far more dense than is often credited: he speaks of a "timely trial," a test directed specifically at their youth, an inquiry into the particular temporality of virtuous action. The rich irony of the occasion demonstrates the difficulty of rendering action timely, the imperfect and unripe performance celebrating a political moment that had been long overdue.

I have already suggested that the failure of the Lady's appeal to Echo is one of the first signs of the actors' immaturity. Seeking Tityrus's stature by beseeching the presence of Echo, the Lady hopes to find in the wandering wood a voice both foreign and her own. An answering voice would be a sign of self-sufficiency, the sufficiency of an extended self, a manifestation of some kind of magic intrinsic to aristocracy or virginity. So Milton's graceful refusal to let the Lady "awake the courteous Echo" can be taken both as an occasional refusal and as a warning, sounded throughout his poetry, against vain credence, not merely in the idea of self-sufficiency, but in the very idea of the intrinsic.

Thus Milton's own reluctance to assume the posture of Tityran prowess, his wariness of the impulsive aspect of pastoral is hardly surprising. In the year before the earl of Bridgewater received his commission as lord president of Wales, Milton had attempted an "Ode on the Passion," a poem intended as a companion piece to the Nativity Ode, but this timely trial was an acknowledged, even a flaunted, failure: "This Subject the Author finding to be above the years he had, when he wrote it, and nothing satisfied with what was begun, left it unfinisht." We can see the thing begin to slip in the Clevelandizing of the penultimate completed stanza—

> For sure so well instructed are my tears
> That they would fitly fall in order'd Characters. [ll. 48–49]

—but the failure of the piece is not confined to this sort of stylistic lapse. The final stanza has much less of this flamboyance (though it does again veer *toward* it); indeed, it opens in a restrained, somewhat neoclassicized, version of the "authentic" Miltonic voice:

> Or should I thence [i.e., from the Sepulcher] hurried on viewless wing,
> Take up a weeping on the Mountains wild,
> The gentle neighborhood of grove and spring
> Would soon unbosom all their echoes mild,
> And I (for grief is easily beguiled)
>   Might think the infection of my sorrows loud
> Hath got a race of mourners on some pregnant cloud. [ll. 50–56]7

Milton's imaginings of echoic response tend to recall, not Tityran exuberance, but the lamentations of Bion and Moschus. To some extent, this seems an effort to chasten the idea of resonance and the idea of pastoral itself. Thus in "Lycidas," Milton will distinguish between strict pastoral meditation of a thankless muse, and indulgent sport with Amaryllis in the shade; Milton polarizes the pleasant virtuosity of a Tityrus, making pleasure and (virtuous) pastoral virtuosity exclusive alternatives. (More could be said of this: Tityrus sports with Amaryllis in name alone, whereas here the polarizing Milton represses the possibility of a purely nominal *jouissance*. This repression functions as a kind of self-deluding flight from the poem's central horror and central guilt—that the corpse of Edward King is lost to the poet so that only a nominal representation, the name of "Lycidas," remains.) Tityran resonance is thus suppressed in favor of echoing of a purely mournful kind:

> Thee, shepherd, thee the woods, and desert caves
> With wild thyme and the gadding vine o'ergrown,
> And all their echoes mourn. [ll. 39–41]

Milton knew the tradition of celebratory echoing, of course. A draft for his great hymn to the (somewhat incestuous) wedding of the "harmonious sisters, Voice and Verse" describes a heavenly consort in which saints and angels join in song "While all the starry rounds and arches blue / Resound and echo Hallelu," but the lines were rejected.[8] I think the rejection can be explained in two ways, and both explanations pertain as well to the silence of Echo in *Comus*.

The first has already been hinted at. Milton's associations with echo have an odd morbidity, as if he recognized only the lamenting strain in the traditions of echo. He seems to have been particularly obsessed with Plutarch's tale (*De Defectu Oraculorum*, xvii) of the genius of the shore who burst forth in resonant mourning at word of the death of Pan, so that for Milton echo came to signify a graceless response to the loss of the dying god. Indeed, so graceless did echo become for Milton that, in *Paradise Lost*, it becomes the most grimly reductive of lamentations, the infernal clamor at the birth of Death; at the sight of her monstrous newborn offspring, Sin

> fled, and cried out Death;
> Hell trembled at the hideous name, and sighed
> From all her caves, and back resounded Death.   [II.787–89]

This paradox, the celebratory mourning over the nascence of Death, is reasserted after the Fall of Man, when Adam radicalizes the nostalgia implicit even in Virgilian pastoral:

> Why comes not Death,
> Said he, with one thrice ácceptable stroke
> To end me? Shall Truth fail to keep her word,
> Justice Divine not hast'n to be just?
> But death comes not at call, Justice Divine
> Mends not her slowest pace for prayers or cries.
> O Woods, O Fountains, Hillocks, Dales and Bow'rs
> With other echo late I taught your Shades
> To answer, and resound far other Song.   [X.854–62]

That prelapsarian indoctrination of the landscape, a transcendental version of the Tityran situation, has been lost, just as, soon, the paradigmatic locus amoenus is to be lost. Tityran resonance gives way to the grim and ironic Callimachan repetitions of "Death." Here in *Paradise Lost*, Milton rationalizes the repressions of echo in his early poetry. This repression, unproductive in 1633, begins to yield a sublimated and specialized notion of echo in the *Mask* of 1634; the rationalized loss of the Tityran is thus paired with a new and specialized notion of echo, an echo "translated to the skies." This compensatory principle of echo merits some considerable scrutiny, both for its own sake and because it will lead us to the second explanation for the original repression of resonance in "At a Solemn Music" and the final rationale for the unresponsiveness of Echo in *Comus*.

Imitation d'elle mesme rien ne peut faire.⁹

In 1571, Alessandro Farra wrote an analysis of the myth of Echo and Narcissus which integrates Ficino's interpretation with a theory of Christian prophecy. Ficino's exegesis had made Narcissus' lapse a crucial breach in an ideal Neoplatonic semiotic. Ficinan epistemology esteems the world of signs, conceiving them as essentially bound into a chain of referents, but it grounds the esteem on the fact that the signs possess an intrinsic power to *impel* transcendental reference. Narcissus' crime lies not, for Ficino, in his esteem for the *image*, but in his apparent obliviousness to its transcendental impulse. Thus any lover whose desire arrests the dynamic of knowledge commits Narcissus' crime; the fable is singled out because self-love *figures* an appetite that remains "horizontal," one that, failing to register the transcendental, gives itself over to "the vanity of worldly things." Farra accommodates this modernized moralization to a specifically Christian discourse by associating the transcendental impulse with the divine spirit itself: "questi muove la mente, indi eccita la ragione, & toccata la imagine o idolo riflette, & per i medesimi gradi ritorna all'unità intellettuale."¹⁰ This Plotinan rhythm of descent (the devolution of spirit to matter) and return (the epistemological ascent of the human soul) is figured as the reflex of Echo; thus the Ovidian Echo is linked to her Palestinian counterpart, the scriptural *Bat kol* ("Daughter of the Voice"), in the middle ground of *prisca theologia*:

> questa riflettione chiamano i Theologi simbolici Echo & i Cabalisti Bathchol, cioè, figliuola della voce. . . . L'Echo innamorata di Narciso significa esso divino spirito discendente alla illustratione dell'animo nostro. . . . Ci consiglia dunque Pitagoro con questo simbolo ad adorare Echo, cioè, ad acconsentire allo spirito della divina gratia, il quale rifflettendo, & ritornando indietro alla somma unità ci rivolge.¹¹

> [The symbolic theologians call this Reflection Echo, the Cabalists call it Bat kol, that is, the Daughter of the Voice. . . . Echo, enamoured of Narcissus, signifies the divine spirit, descending to enlighten our souls. . . . By this symbolic utterance Pythagoras teaches us to pray to Echo, that is, to attend to the spirit of divine grace, which, reflected and returning, returns us to the ultimate Unity.]

Thus, it is against the background of a syncretic exegesis of Ovid that one of Milton's plots of the Fall is enacted. Eve's first action is to recapitulate the enamorment of Narcissus—the eroticizing of a shadow of an image which thus destroys the proper dynamics of love and self-knowledge—and she is first corrected by a disembodied warning voice:

> What thou seest,
> What there thou seest fair creature is thyself,
> With thee it came and goes: but follow me
> And I will bring thee where no shadow stays
> Thy coming.   [IV.467–71]

For reasons very different from Jonson's, Milton favors the acoustic over the visual; Milton's faith, like St. Paul's faith, is "by hearing."¹² The disembodied voice corrects Eve from her allegiance to the voiceless image and leads her to her proper place in an erotic and epistemological hierarchy. *Paradise Lost*, for all its bookishness, is after all an oral composition, and the poem aspires to a voice so fully reified that it might approach the autonomy of the voice that walks in the Garden. Much of the poem is an investigation of the *Dinglichkeit* of the spoken word, even of the *personality* of the Word.

So Milton gains more than the ominous comparison of Eve to Narcissus by appropriating the Ovidian situation here. He also recovers the pathos of Echo's existence, her shadowy subsistence at the border between an autonomous personality and a derivative, mechanical state. The status of the Word, the degree of its peril, depends upon the extent to which Ovid's narrative fits the history of our first parents' conduct. The word stands in danger of reversion to impersonal reflex throughout the poem, but nowhere more so than at the moment of temptation:

> Serpent, we might have spared our coming hither,
> Fruitless to me, though fruit be here to excess,
> The credit of whose virtue rest with thee;
> Wondrous indeed, if cause of such effects.

(a bestial version of pastoral vocality having been offered as proof of the fruit's essential power)

> But of this tree we may not taste nor touch:
> God so commanded, and left that command
> Sole daughter of his voice; the rest, we live
> Law to ourselves; our reason is our law. [IX.647–54

Milton here figures the vitality of the commandment, its poise against mortality, in the personal genealogy of that commandment. The Daughter of the Voice is not a repeater: to revert to the rough distinction with which these essays began, she is a *resonator*, an utterance powerfully extended in time. Only with the Fall does Law acquire its discontinuity with the present, its archaism; only with the Fall does the Law become an adversary voice. At the close of book X, a principle of repetition intrudes on the poem, a principle utterly impersonal, providing a harsh standard of postlapsarian behavior: the repentant Adam intuits mercy as the divine complement to justice:

> What better can we do than to the place
> Repairing where he judged us, prostrate fall
> Before him reverent, and there confess
> Humbly our faults, and pardon beg, with tears
> Frequenting, sent from hearts contrite, in sign
> Of sorrow unfeigned, and humiliation meek? [X.1086–92]

The adequacy of Adam's will to his pious intent is then quickly measured:

> So spake our father penitent, nor Eve
> Felt less remorse: they forthwith to the place
> Repairing where he judged them, prostrate fell
> Before him reverent . . . [X.1097–1100]

Repentance inhibits invention: the pair returns to the place of judgment, perfectly fitting deed to prediction. The repetition limns the basic structure of legality, the development of impersonal verbal formulae to which actions must accord themselves. Here the accord is total, the repentance complete; even in the context of lapse, Adam and Eve can still live as Law to themselves, though necessity will slowly strip them of this power, further alienating the Law. Only a reincarnation of the Word can redeem the tyranny of that legal alienation.

Milton's transcendental principle of Echo, the Daughter of the Voice—and thus sister to Christ—is, of course, as unavailable to the Lady of *Comus* as the prelapsarian echo is to Adam. Milton even chooses to exclude so pure a transcendental principle from the epithalamium to voice and verse. Just as "Lycidas" splits pastoral musing into strict meditation and frivolous sport, dividing pastoral into idioms of grace and idioms of nature, so *Paradise Lost* divides the transcendental Daughter of the Voice from a more death-marked echo. In the case of *Paradise Lost*, the division is specifically a *periodization*, a discrimination between pre- and postlapsarian echo. Something very much like the anatomy of pastoral musing in "Lycidas" and the periodization of echoing in *Paradise Lost* takes place in *Comus*.

The Lady's appeal to Echo, her desire for personal extension in a docile landscape, is founded on the misconception of the self as source—as source of voice (which is from God, who creates us by inspiration), as source of the organizing power over landscape that Stevens pretends to discover in the jar placed in Tennessee, as source of the potential benefits to the unseen nymph:

> So mayst thou be translated to the skies,
> And give resounding grace to all Heavn's Harmonies.   [ll. 242–43]

By the last line of the song, the structure of benefits has been much confused, for Echo can hardly be the (mediate) source of grace in heaven (with the Lady's impulse as the First Acoustic Mover). The pun that binds musical to theological grace is no less dangerously casuistical than the charm that will soon bind the Lady to her seat. The wit of the song confirms the fullness of the Lady's error, and the silence of Echo prophesies her punishment.[13]

The nature of her error is, specifically, its Nature. The natural confidence of Tityran pastoral, the internal sufficiency of the resonant *locus amoenus*, the childish Arcadian illusions of omnipotence—all of these come in for criticism at this moment, when the Lady's maturation reaches a crisis of impotent isolation. The Lady is not to be saved by the blithe swelling of the self.

Rather she is to be saved within a community of impotence, restored to a family that is little more sufficient to its redemption than is the Lady alone. The Egerton family is, after all, the family of the Castlehaven scandal: it can commission masques of purification, but it cannot institute its own purification.[14] Milton and Lawes strengthen the force of the implicit admonition here by representing the force of redemptive grace as extrinsic, extrinsic even for Lawes. The Attendant Spirit, partly because he is clothed in the natural flesh of Thyrsis, is insufficient to the task. The Attendant Spirit defers to Sabrina.

In this masque of delay, the ascent of Sabrina comes as the supreme example of postponed response. Angus Fletcher points out that "Lawes composed his songs so that, without precise musical duplication, the song to Echo and the Spirit's song to Sabrina are echoes of each other, since the falling interval of a fifth in the Lady's 'Sweet Echo' is doubled by an identical falling fifth, more cadential to be sure, in the phrase 'listen and save.'"[15] Milton, too, contrived a purely technical link between Echo and Sabrina: the final line of the Lady's song to Echo is an alexandrine, the only alexandrine in the masque, and the lengthening here works as an allusion to the distinguishing metrical feature of the *Faerie Queene*, source text for the tale of Sabrina (Milton had so used metrical lengthening to clinch a Spenserian allusion once before, at line 121 of *Il Penseroso*, the conclusion of the Melancholy Man's history of the Chaucerian-Spenserian tradition of English romance).[16] When Sabrina bursts her watery tomb she redeems the subjugated virgin, the Spenserian tradition, and Echo in a single instant.

Curiously enough, her rising also constitutes a traditional animation of place, for Sabrina is a genius loci who paradoxically frees the family in order to establish it in its new and proper fixity at Ludlow Castle: just as there are aimless and purposeful motions—error and progress—so there are vicious and virtuous immobilities—paralysis and poise. The masque develops by binary discriminations, perhaps the most intriguing of which is the discrimination in the category of the echoic, between Echo and Sabrina. Certain aspects of that discrimination are obvious: Echo is Greco-Roman, Sabrina native; Echo is eroticized, Sabrina chaste; Echo is contingent, Sabrina above contingency; and, of course, Echo is Euripidean, Longan, Ovidian, Virgilian, while Sabrina is Spenserian—Milton's masque intrudes authorial will on literary genetics.[17] The discrimination also works on traditional functions of the echoic, breaking down the long-standing association of allusion and reflection.

In my first essay, I remarked on the odd inappropriateness of using echo to figure allusion: the figure is a lie against time, for it ignores temporal gap and represents all texts as present to each other, more or less. The lie particularly beguiles the lyricists of the Renaissance, who exploit the figure to deny the historical disjunction that divides a Petrarch from a Cicero. But lost time weighs too heavily on Milton for him to sustain such a fiction: here is his post-Renaissance modernity writ large. If *Comus* is nostalgic—an attempt to recover the style of the earliest Jonsonian masques, to recover the "sage and serious" Elizabethan doctrine of Virginity, to recover an imagined "sage and serious" Spenserian harmony—it is (like the *Metamorphoses*) disabused about its nostalgias.[18] The Spenserian patronage through Sabrina is not readily available; hers is a delayed reaction, to be distinguished from an Echo now utterly naturalized. Echoic silence completes the growth of strictures on masque audiences that begins as early as Gascoigne's Kenilworth entertainments; the silence is, here, more ironic than Echo's response had ever been. That silence marks the loss of the easy and continuous responsiveness of pastoral tradition; the split of acoustic reflection from literary allusiveness prepares for a new kind of hard pastoral, displaced into a rigorous wilderness, an alien and fissured terrain—for Tityrus's Arcadia, the cool terrors of the cliffs and islands of Winander, the landscape of Childe Roland's quest.

APPENDIX
ECHO AND TYPOLOGY

We have already seen evidence of a Greco-Roman association between echo and prophecy (at Dodona, Cumae). The tradition in the southern Mediterranean, considerably better documented, had some important distinguishing features. Despite a flourishing tradition of dream interpretation during the rabbinic period, there seems to have been only a single form of specifically oracular practice—the system of *Bat kol* prophecy (see Saul Lieberman, *Hellenism in Jewish Palestine* [New York: Jewish Theological Seminary, 1950], pp. 78, 194–99). In the Mishnah, the Bat kol simply means a disembodied voice (assumed to be divine) or an utterance uncomprehended by its speaker, but in Talmudic texts the Bat kol is usually associated with the prophetic babbling of children in the synagogue. Plutarch reports that Egyptian priests ascribed prophetic powers to small children, "especially when children are playing about in holy places and crying out whatever comes into their minds" (*Isis and Osiris*, 356E).

In Palestine, the Hellenistic association of the oracular and the echoic seems to have been grafted onto this Middle Eastern prophetic tradition. I say "seems," for a noncanonical version of the Palestinian Talmud explains that a Bat kol originally denoted a simple echo. It is hard to know how much philological authority to ascribe to this assertion. It may be an extrapolation from the fact that the children's *B'not kol* (at least those that the Talmud records) are almost always repetitions of biblical texts, presumably repetitions of the liturgical texts that make up the acoustic environment of the synagogue. The text from the Palestinian Talmud is thus easy enough to explain: Bat kol prophecy takes the form of echoic utterance.

The feature that most distinguishes Bat kol prophecy from the typical Hellenistic oracular form is its hermeneutic simplicity. The biblical tag tossed off by a child at play in the synagogue is always immediately interpretable, its import unambiguous. Surely the unambiguous and undeniable status of the Bat kol is the source of the triumphal note in that most famous instance of its intervention:

> And the blind and the lame came to him in the temple; and he healed them. And when the chief priests and the scribes saw the wonderful things that he did, and the children crying in the temple, and saying, Hosanna to the Son of David; they were sore displeased. [Matthew 21:14–16]

The children join themselves to a chain of repetitions, for they repeat the cry of the crowd that has attended Jesus on his entry into Jerusalem ("Hosanna to the Son of David: Blessed is he that cometh in the name of the Lord; Hosanna in the highest"; Matthew 21:9), omitting that portion of the crowd's praise which itself echoes Psalm 118. And Jesus responds with overarching repetition: in their displeasure, the priests

> said unto him, Hearest thou what these say? And Jesus saith unto them, Yea; have ye never read, Out of the mouths of babes and sucklings thou hast perfected praise? [Matthew 21:16]

The text at issue here suggests that even before the Talmudic period, this sort of childish repetition had oracular status. Jesus thus further antagonizes the priests, who are already faced with the bitter intervention of the Bat kol, by citing a sacred text (Psalms 8:2) to reinforce the authority of the oracle.

We may take this as an inaugural moment in typological exegesis, a moment inscribed within the very plot of the gospel, for there the association of scriptural authority with echoic prophecy (an association implicit in the Greco-Roman *sorites*) imports a new oracular institution into Palestinian spiritual life; henceforth, the Old Law is not merely prescriptive, it is predictive. The divine influence informing traditional Bat kol repetition had used the repeated text as a temporary convenience and had left the original unchanged; the new, typological repetition of the Old Testament appropriates the structure of Callimachan echo as its model. Typological repetition pronounces the death of its original.

NOTES

INTRODUCTION

1 Recorded in E. K. Chambers, *The Elizabethan Stage* (Oxford: Clarendon Press, 1923), 3:424.
2 In one of the poems of the Greek Anthology (*Anth. Pal.*, IX.382), Echo is described as "either a goddess or a woman."
3 We find a similar structure of sequential induction in the opening of *Poetaster*.
4 Boccaccio, *Genealogia Deorum*, ed. V. Romano, vols. 10 and 11, *Opera*, Scrittori d'Italia, nos. 200–01 (Bari: Laterza, 1951), 10:380; van der Does [Dousa], *Echo* (Venice, 1648). Van der Does's *Echo* was first published in 1603. The front matter of the first edition consists of panegyrics on van der Does by Scaliger, Heinsius, and Grotius, poems that accomplish their praise by recalling the various classical texts that provide the raw material for a mythography of Echo: the "Lament for Bion," *Daphnis and Chloë*, Virgil's *Eclogues*, Horace's *Odes*, and Ovid's *Metamorphoses*. Dousa is praised for achievements in a verse-form that does implicit homage to an apparently heterogeneous range of models. One of the vested interests of the personified Echo is the denial of the apparent heterogeneity of such models. After 1604, abridged versions of van der Does's *Echo* were frequently bound, as was the cited edition, with Nicolaus Nomexy's (Nomessius) *Parnassus biceps*.
5 For Bacon's analysis, see below, p. 24 and n. 57.
6 I cite from Richard Lynche's translation, *The Fountaine of Ancient Fiction* (London, 1599), sigs. $Y_1v–Y_2v$; Lynche often translates freely, but this passage is uncharacteristically faithful to the original.

I choose the passage with the opening of Michel Foucault's *The Order of Things* (New York: Pantheon, 1970) in mind. Foucault begins his study with a quotation:

> A passage in Borges . . . quotes a "certain Chinese encyclopedia" in which it is written that "animals are divided into: (a) belonging to the Emperor, (b) embalmed, (c) tame, (d) sucking pigs, (e) sirens, (f) fabulous, (g) stray dogs, (h) included in the present classification, (i) frenzied, (j) innumerable, (k) drawn with a very fine camelhair brush, (l) *et cetera*, (m) having just broken the water pitcher, (n) that from a long way off look like flies."

With this account of epistemological shock, Foucault begins his invaluable history of taxonomy. It is a history based on the assumption that all such collections *should* be susceptible to rationalization and that its rationale is a proper object of critical research. I would contend that the concept of such a rationale, such an order of things, is itself heuristic and that such a concept can be abused. The positivism of this research makes small allowances for heterogeneities in cultural experience; encountering Borges's and Cartari's list, this positivism announces "the stark impossibility of thinking *that*" (Foucault, p. xv). Cultural history should perhaps learn to think such things.
7 E. H. Gombrich, *Aby Warburg* (London: Warburg Institute, 1970), pp. 260–82. Warburg had his own vocabulary for a diachronic theory of the artifact. In his early criticism, he made use of Richard Semon's term *engram* to name the symbolic concretization of psychic impulse, a crystallization which would release its potential psychic energy in the apt cultural circumstances (usually by fostering "equivalent" images). Later, he coined the term *dynamogram*—it regularly appears in the pairing,

"abgeschnurtes Dynamogramm"—to emphasize the potential in the artifact for semic slippage; the term was coined principally to describe the fallen "life" of engrams in baroque culture (see Gombrich, *Aby Warburg*, pp. 242–51). The coinage exposes Warburg's developing sense of the vagaries of iconological history—both of the potential of images for acquiring new meanings and of changes in the context and use of images.

8 For a treatment of the discomforts attendant on the Renaissance recovery of the literary and archaeological past, see Thomas M. Greene, *The Light in Troy: Imitation and Discovery in Renaissance Poetry* (New Haven: Yale University Press, 1982), particularly chapters 1, 2, and 11.

CHAPTER 1

1 Marin Mersenne, *Harmonie Universelle*, 3 vols. (Paris, 1636), 1:sig. E$_4$.
2 Paule Demats, *Fabula: Trois études de mythographie antique et médiévale*, Publications Romanes et Françaises, 122 (Paris: Droz, 1973), p. 33.
3 Bacon makes the same observation in *De Sapientia Veterum*: "Verum si quis attentius rem consideret, apparebit illas tradi et referri tanquam prius creditas et receptas, non tanquam tum primo excogitatas et oblatas," *Works*, ed. J. Spedding, R. L. Ellis, and D. D. Heath, 12 vols. (London: Longmans, 1859–74), 6:627.
4 Ovid, *Metamorphoses*, III.377–78.
5 Epigram XXXII.1.3.
6 Bacon, *Silva Silvarum*, Century III, *Works*, 2:425.
7 Wallace Stevens, "The Idea of Order at Key West," in *The Palm at the End of the Mind* (New York: Random House, 1967; reprint, Vintage, 1972), p. 97.
8 We shall not be able to escape rhetorical/acoustic doubling in such words; because of the doubling habit, echo itself became a model for certain rhetorical schemes, as well as the model for the trope of allusion. In Quintilian, one such echo-scheme represents *amplificatio* in its boldest form. This is the type of heightening "ad quem non per gradus itur et quod non est plus maximo, sed quo nihil maius est; *Matrem tuam cecidisti. Quid dicam amplius? Matrem tuam cecidisti.* Nam et hoc augendi genus est tantum aliquid efficere, ut non possit augeri" ([a height] unattainable by gradation, which is not a degree beyond the superlative, but such that nothing greater can be conceived. "You beat your mother. What more need I say? You beat your mother." For to make a thing so great as to be incapable of augmentation is in itself a kind of augmentation); *Institutio Oratoria*, VIII.iv.7.
9 Drunken Silenus, the potent singer of the sixth eclogue, equals the Tityran power over echo: "ille canit (pulsae referunt ad sidera valles)" (he sings; once more the sounding valleys hurl them to the stars); 1. 84.
10 I am indebted here to the studies of two French scholars: the dissertation of F.-X. Roiron, *L'imagination auditive de Virgile* (Paris: Leroux, 1908) and Marie Desport's *L'incantation virgilienne* (Bourdeaux: Delmas, 1952) which so handsomely develops Roiron's work.

A. J. Boyle also remarks Virgil's debt to Hesiod in the *Eclogues*, arguing that "the Hesiodic paradigm provides a clear and cardinal link between the personal poetics of the prologue and the didactic idealism of the ensuing song." His treatment of "Virgil's Pastoral Echo" (*Ramus* 6 [1977]: 121–31; preceding citation from p. 123) differs considerably from my own: Boyle conceives of Virgilian pastoral as "an exploration of the possibility of non-echoic song" (p. 122), a pastoral at odds with the resonances of its own fictive world.

11 Roiron observes (*L'imagination*, pp. 32 and 142–43) that the forest presents itself to the Virgilian imagination primarily as a locus resonans. Desport is more precise, pointing

out the special significance of the *silva* as pastoral site: resonance, she shows, is not *agrestis* or *rusticus*, but *silvestris* (*L'incantation*, p. 26).
12 Longus (*Daphnis and Chloë*, II.vii.6) identifies the phenomenon of *Eclogues* I.5 with the activity of Echo. See below, pp. 26–27.
13 I make the assertion despite J. Webster Spargo's warning that "Virgil's works . . . yield no reliable clue to the reasons underlying the metamorphosis of the poet to mage" (*Virgil the Necromancer*, Harvard Studies in Comparative Literature, no. 10 [Cambridge, Mass.: Harvard University Press, 1934], p. 303). Spargo discusses the legendary material in ancient biographies of Virgil, claiming that material as the cause of the metamorphosis, but without any meditation on the rationale governing the genesis of the legendary material itself.
  I shall discuss the crucial exceptions to Virgil's pleasure in acoustic reflection at the close of this chapter.
14 That aggressiveness elaborates an identification of Corydon with the Polyphemus of Theocritus's *Idylls*.
15 *De Rerum Natura*, IV.549–94. The phenomenon of acoustic reflection is crucial to Lucretius's "particle theory" of sound. Drawing on that theory, Virgil develops an acoustic imagery based on a vocabulary of shock—*concussus, plango, pulsus* (*pulso* is Virgil's verb for striking a lyre), *tundo*, and *frango*.
16 "Lycidas," ll. 123–25.
17 Thomas Rosenmeyer, *The Green Cabinet: Theocritus and the European Pastoral Lyric* (Berkeley: University of California Press, 1969), p. 186.
18 Desport, *L'incantation*, p. 79; emphasis hers.
19 In Plutarch's *De Defectu Oraculorum* (a text of incalculable importance for Renaissance poetics), Echo's mourning answers the announcement of Pan's death; in the fourth book of Virgil's *Georgics*, the severed head of Orpheus still wails the name of Eurydice as it floats down the Hebrus toward Lesbos: "Eurydicen toto referebant flumine ripae" (l. 527). On the relation of Echo and Orpheus, see below pp. 22 and 27–29.
20 *Metamorphoses*, XXVI. The scholiast suggests that the tale originated in book II of Nicander's lost *Heteroioumena*. See Antoninus Liberalis, *Les Metamorphoses*, ed. and trans. M. Papathomoupoulos (Paris: Les belles lettres, 1968), pp. 45 and 127–28.
21 E. R. Dodds, "From Shame-Culture to Guilt-Culture," in *The Greeks and the Irrational* (Berkeley: University of California Press, 1951), pp. 28–63.
  Perhaps here is the place to attempt a comparison between my own work and that of the master theorist of reflection. In *Beyond the Pleasure Principle*, Freud argues that the reenactment of trauma in dreams is in fact a quest for pleasure or at least for a reduction of pain. The repetition reclaims suffering under the aegis of the Will; the dreamer, omnipotent in the realm of dreams (or so the theory goes), reinstates pain in order to grow accustomed to it—mimesis as mastery. The apparently unpleasant dream is explained as a source of pleasure by an emphasis on its status as a psychological production and by implying the pleasures of production. I shall shortly argue that the threatening sound of echo is reclaimed for cultural pleasure by its transformation into Echo; whatever its malignity, the sound need no longer be imagined as hideously motiveless. The words of Echo, like the dreams of the traumatized, are recalled in the sweet kingdom of the will.
22 *Stanze . . . per la Giostra . . .* (Bologna, 1494), sig. F$_3$v; most modern editors identify Pan as the interlocutor. We might call this the first neoclassical echo-lyric. Elbridge Colby, in *The Echo-Device in Literature* (New York: New York Public Library, 1920), p. 15, cites one stanza of an echo-lyric by the thirteenth-century *trouvère*, Gilles le Vinier, giving it as the sole postclassical precedent to Poliziano's poem. Gilles, in fact, seems to have written two such lyrics, both in five stanzas of six or seven lines each with echo "tails" for all but the last lines of each stanza. Neither lyric employs the pastoral setting

so frequently associated with later echo-lyrics, nor do they project any respondent—that is, Echo never presents herself in these poems. The speaker simply continues or expands, but does not modify, his primary utterance by repeating its last syllable or syllables (generating new, but not adversative, words or phrases). In both lyrics, the lover complains that he has met with resistance, yet the beloved's hostility has been so mastered (or has been so thinly realized) that the dramatic possibilities of echoic form do not even suggest themselves within the poems. The echo never interrupts, never opposes, never reacts or reenacts, so that the device remains scheme in its merest manifestation.

23 *The Greek Bucolic Poets*, trans. A. S. F. Gow (Cambridge: Cambridge University Press, 1953), p. 134 (ll. 30–31).

24 *Allegoriae super Ovidii Metamorphosin*, III.6; text printed in Fausto Ghisalberti, "Arnolfo D'Orleans: un cultore di Ovidio nel secolo XII," in *Memorie del R. Istituto Di Scienze e Lettere* (Milan: R. Instituto di Scienze e Lettere, 1932), vol. 24, 25 della serie 3, fascicolo 4:209.

More might be said of the infernal aspect of acoustic reflection. In the *Theogony* resonance is indigenous to Hades: the infernal walls are *echeentes*. Moreover, many of the spots most famous in antiquity for their echoes seem to work as hell-mouths. In Lucian's "Peregrinus," the hero appears, resurrected after his spectacular self-immolation at Harpina, at the Echo Portico on the east side of the Altis at Olympia. Pausanius describes another Echo Portico, at Hermione, next to the temple of Demeter Chthonia, where words echoed thrice (*Descriptions*, 2). Surely an infernal site, the temple of Demeter was also flanked by a temple of Pluto, by another spot known as "the Acherusian Lake," and by a shrine to Clymenus (another name for the god of the underworld): this latter stood just next to a chasm through which Hercules was said to have rapt Cerberus out of hell.

25 *Genealogia Deorum*, Works, 10:381.

26 Virgil's vicious Fama is modeled on Hesiod's Typheous as much as on Homer's Fame and Typhoeus's resonant voice, as we have seen, preserves as it threatens. The resonances of the *Aeneid* preserve this ambivalence. Countering the voice of Fama is the voice of the sibyl, which gives the hero access to a historical frame in which to situate his own deeds and directs him toward an eternal fama.

27 *Tusculan Disputations*, III.3; and cf. the oration *Pro Archia*, 19.

To Cicero's simile, compare also Lucian's description of the nearly animate forum of "The Hall" which, he says, "should be full of praise and laudation, re-echoing softly like a cavern, following what is said, drawing out the concluding sounds of the voice and lingering on the last words; or, to put it better, committing to memory all that one says" (iii). He compares this interior phenomenon to the echoing characteristic of the locus amoenus. Debunking the fiction of Echo ("the untaught think it is a maid . . ."), Lucian displaces the mythopoeic impulse onto his own treatment of the hall itself, so that rural myth gives place to a new, urban one.

28 Cited in Robert Dernedde, *Über die den altfranzösischen Dichtern bekannten epischen Stoffe aus dem Altertum* (Erlangen: Deichert, 1887), p. 112.

29 Among other such weakened mnemonic figures might be numbered Ovid's *documentae*—mortals transformed into the immortal constituents of a landscape—and Rabelais's frozen words (*Gargantua et Pantagruel*, IV, chapters 55–56).

30 For *imago* as the term for echo or Echo, see also Varro, *De re rustica*, III.xvi.12; Virgil, *Georgics*, IV.50; Ovid, *Metamorphoses*, III.385; Ausonius, *Epistles*, XXIX.10; as well as the odes of Horace cited below.

31 Echo's memory is thus usually uncanny, manifesting a return, not of glory, but of traumatic origins. Virgil's account of the portents attendant on Caesar's death involves a nightmare revision of the founding of Rome: "pecudesque locutae / infandum! . . . et

altae / per noctem resonare lupis ululantibus urbes" (the haunted city recalls the nurture of its founders; in the city, where human voices should speak, howl wolves, while beasts take on human voice; *Georgics*, I.478–79, 485–86).

Lucan will use the phenomenon of resonance similarly in a passage on battle noise which recalls Homer but is directly indebted to Horace's ode to Clio:

Excepit resonis clamorem vallibus Haemus
Peliacisque dedit rursus geminare cavernis;
Pindus agit fremitus, Pangaeaque saxa resultant
Oetaeaque gemunt rupes, vocesque furoris
Expavere sui tota tellure relatas.   [*Pharsalia*, VII. 480–84]

[The Balkan took up the noise in its echoing valleys and gave it to the caves of Pelium to repeat; Pindus roared, the Pangaean rocks echoed, and the cliffs of Oeta bellowed, till the armies were terrified by the sound of their own madness repeated from all the earth.]

The allusion to Horace measures a mythos of purposive history against what Lucan describes as the purely random results of war; the resonance of shapeless clamor extends beyond the resonance of Maecenas's glory, beyond Pindus and Haemus, to include all of Thessaly. If resonance points to Oeta, the sites of Hercules' apotheosis, it also points to Pelion, mountain of an ancient pride which threatened all universal order with a battle more gravely chaotic than even that of Lucan's epic.

32 On the publicity of echo, see also *Satires*, I.iv.74–75, where Horace disparages poets who exploit resonant interiors to provide an artificial aura of poetic excellence (an artifice extrinsic to composition), the technological "personation" of Tityran art.
33 *Epigrams*, xxx; this construction of the poem has been disputed; see note 42 below.
34 *Scholia in Euripidem*, ed. Edward Schwartz, 2 vols. (Berlin: G. Reimer, 1887–91), *Orestes*, 1:191, no. 964.
35 *Scholia Aristophanica*, ed. W. G. Rutherford, 2 vols. (London: Macmillan, 1896), *Ranae*, 53. Much of the surviving information on the *Andromeda* is summarized in the introduction to Benjamin Rogers's edition of Arisophanes' *Thesmophoriazusae* (London: Bell, 1904), pp. xxvi–xxviii.
36 *Cluere*, the Latin cognate of *klueis*, works similarly, so that "to hear" becomes "to hear of oneself" and, finally, "to be heard of, to be famed."

The line from which the address to Echo comes, *Thes.* 1019, is notoriously corrupt, though editors agree that it begins with *klueis*. Rogers's edition renders the line, *klueis, ō, prosadousa tais eu antrois*, whereas J. van Leeuwen's more conservative edition ([2 ed.] Leyden: Sijthoff, 1968) gives *klueis, ō pros Haidou s', autas eu antrois*.

37 Cited from *Ladies' Day*, Dudley Fitts's translation of the *Thesmophoriazusae* (New York: Harcourt, Brace, and Co., 1959), ll. 996–98.

Echo's sepulchral voice wails more hideously from this mountain than it did in Olympia or Hermione; Kithaeron is surely the most infernal of Greece's high places. As the site of Oedipus's crippling exposure, of the mutilations of Actaeon and Pentheus, and as haunt of the bacchantes, we associate it with the return of all things repressed in social or individual history. Longus's Echo, discussed below, shares a mutilation story with Actaeon, Pentheus, and Oedipus: this late myth transforms her into a *sparagmos*. As in the tales of Orpheus, the rending of limbs (*melē*) makes a generation of new song possible.

38 In the opening scene of the play, Euripides' campaign for human independence from divine voice is parodied in the constant effort of the character, Euripides, to control others' speech.

Robert W. Corrigan has nicely articulated the formal consequences of Euripides' attempt to restrain the influence of the gods. Beginning with a description of Sophoclean *anagnorisis*, Corrigan writes, "It is important to see that this scene always leads to a new mode of action. Now, in a Euripidean play there is also a situation to be resolved, but the resolving of it never leads to any new recognition. (In fact, it is interesting to note that usually the hero of a Sophoclean play is in a situation where he must *do* something. Euripides' heroes, for the most part, are trying *not* to do something)"; from "The Drama of Euripides," in *The Theatre in Search of a Fix* (New York: Delacorte, 1973), p. 34. As I have already suggested, in the *Andromeda* the poet's resistance *to* action must have found expression in the heroine's incapacity *for* action.

39 "On the Morning of Christ's Nativity," ll. 173–75, 181–83.

40 Scholars have differed over whether the actor actually appeared as Echo or simply spoke the lines from offstage: lines 1086–93 have been cited to support both positions. I suspect that Echo does make an appearance and then exits just before line 1093 (*ou kairēseis*), enabling the actor doubling the role of Echo with that of Euripides (now Euripides-Perseus) to change costume and fasten himself once again into the flying machine. (He has already made an abortive pass over the stage in the machine, alluded to at line 1014).

41 J. M. Edmonds, *The Fragments of Attic Comedy*, 3 vols. (Leyden: Brill, 1957), 1:128–29, frag. 307.

42 I give the translation of P. M. Fraser in his *Ptolemaic Alexandria*, 3 vols. (Oxford: Clarendon Press, 1972), 1:591, adjusting his somewhat unsatisfactory rendering of the crucial pun (Fraser gives "'He's another's fairy'"). The editor of the Loeb edition, G. R. Mair, renders the close of the poem thus: "Lysanias, thou art, yea, fair, fair; but ere Echo has quite said the word, says someone, 'He's another's.'" The passage admits of either construction, depending on how punctuation is imposed on the text. Despite the considerable authority of the editorial tradition that Mair represents, his treatment of the lines must be rejected, for it makes nonsense of the poem by ignoring the *echoic* play on *kalos* and *allos*. Fraser, who follows Wilamowitz and Pfeiffer, brings together the evidence in the editorial dispute in his notes 298–301 (2:840). To his bibliographic references should be added Amédée Hauvette, "Les epigrammes de Callimaque," *Revue des études grecques* 20 (1907): 343.

43 The phrase comes from *Aetia*, I.25, where Callimachus uses imagery identical to that of this epigram for his description of poetic sprawl.

44 For *psyche*, see the first chapter of Erwin Rohde, *Psyche: The Cult of Souls and Belief in Immortality among the Greeks*, trans. W. B. Hillis (New York: Harcourt, Brace, and Co., 1925).

45 *Epigrams*, II.lxxxvi.3. The attack is remarkably tart, even for Martial: "Turpe est difficiles habere nugas / et stultus labor est ineptiarum" ('Tis degrading to undertake difficult trifles; and foolish is the labor spent on puerilities). Like Callimachus, he associates Echo with vulgarization: "scribat carmina circulis Palaemon; / me raris iuvat auribus placere" (Let Palaemon write poems for the general throng; my delight is to please listeners choice and few; ll. 9–12).

46 *Miscellaneorum* (Florence, 1489), sigs. e₃r–e₃v; interpreting the line, "nusquam Graecula quod recantat echo," Poliziano not only argues that Martial is not attacking all Hellenisms but goes on to describe and endorse the echo-device itself.

Poliziano saw Gauradas's poem (*Anth. Plan.*, 152) in MS., for the *editio princeps* of the *Anthologia Graeca* appeared in 1494, the year of Poliziano's death and of the first printing of his own echo-lyric, the poem appended to the *Stanze per la giostra*. The 1494 edition of the anthology, printed in Florence, includes only the collection of the thirteenth-century monk, Maximus Planudes; in 1606, the collection was greatly enlarged with the discovery of the tenth-century compilation of Constantinus Cephalas, the *Anthologia Palatina*. The Greek Anthology contains several poems about Echo, though no others are to be found there in the strict form of Gauradas's lyric; the other poems are *Anth. Pal.*, VI.79 and 87; IX.27 and 382; and *Anth. Plan.*, 153–56.

47 *Stanze*, sig. F₃r.
48 On mythos, see R. P. Hinks, *Myth and Allegory in Ancient Art* (London: Warburg Institute, 1939), pp. 1–3.
49 Volume 1 of *Ausgewählte Werke* (Darmstadt: Wissenschaftliche Buchgesellschaft, 1976–). My understanding of Schelling has been shaped by Ernst Cassirer's *Mythical Thought*, vol. 2 of *The Philosophy of Symbolic Forms*, trans. R. Mannheim, 3 vols. (New Haven: Yale University Press, 1953–57), particularly pp. 3–11.
50 Jean Seznec, *The Survival of the Pagan Gods: The Mythological Tradition and Its Place in Renaissance Humanism and Art*, trans. Barbara F. Sessions, Bollingen Series, no. 38 (New York: Pantheon, 1953), passim, but see particularly the chapter, "The Physical Tradition," pp. 37–83. Seznec never mentions Schelling: the influence is pervasive and indirect.
51 For the loves of Echo and Narcissus, see below, chapter 2.
52 A similar situation may be found in the first of Callistratus's *Descriptions*, "On a Satyr," 25, for which the Moschus fragment may provide a source. For Echo and Pan, see the Orphic *Hymn to Pan* (XI) as well.
53 *Anth. Pal.*, VI.79; attributed to Agathias Scholasticus.
   In his *Imagines* (II.11), Philostratus describes a (probably nonexistent) depiction of Pan tormented by nymphs. They threaten to persuade Echo to carry her characteristic scorn for him to the point of refusing him her answering voice.
54 Callimachus, frag. 100.
55 *Saturnalia*, I.22; Milton, "Comus," l. 241.
56 Demats, *Fabula*, pp. 21–23; Demats, though hostile to Macrobius's disregard for literary genetics, inadvertently does homage to Macrobius's remarkable achievement. In Macrobius's hands, says Demats, the myths become "detachées non seulement de leur support et de leur environnement textuels, mais de l'acte même de la création littéraire avec tout ce qu'il implique: conditions historiques et religeuses, personnalité et croyances de l'auteur (réelles ou supposées), intentions évidentes ou secretes, les fables ne forment plus qu'une masse indifférenciée" (pp. 21–22). Both critique and poem, the *Saturnalia* stands as the most violent and vigorous of mythographies.
57 I cite the editors' translation of the *De Aumentis Scientiarum* (1623), *Works*, 4:326–27; the Latin text appears in *Works*, 1:530. Bacon is continuing a revision of Macrobius begun by Giraldi, to whom he is deeply indebted for much of his mythography. This passage slightly expands an exegesis of the tale of Pan and Echo originally published in the *De Sapientia Veterum* (1609); in the later version Bacon offers his discussion as a model for scientific mythography.
58 We can trace a subversion of alien voice similar to that wrought by the mythography of Macrobius and Bacon in Augustine's philosophy of perception. In the sixth book of the *De Musica*, Augustine attempts a combination of Plotinian and Aristotelian perceptual theory in an effort to transcendentalize the theory of metrical harmony expounded in the first five books. Denying the passivity of perception, Augustine argues that the apprehension of harmony arises from the consent of motions impinging on the body, but originating outside it. The ear, for example, is the site of simultaneous impulses, itself a double resonator that responds to the motions of a vibrant air and a willing soul. Thus Augustine achieves a denial of a priority—priority being for him the proof of both superiority and agency—normally ascribed to external phenomena.
   We find a similar example of the interpenetration of Neoplatonic and Aristotelian acoustics in Bacon's *Sylva Sylvarum*: "It seemeth, both in ear and eye, the instrument of sense hath a sympathy or similitude with that which giveth the reflexion, (as hath been touched before); for as the sight of the eye is like crystal, or glass, or water; so is the ear a sinuous cave, with a hard bone to stop and reverberate the sound; which is like to the places that report echoes" (Century, III.282). Here a theory of similitude overlaps an Aristotelian discovery of the resonance of the ear. That the traditional analogy of the

transmission and apprehension of sound grows unwieldy here is telling; the mechanics of hearing are aptly described, but Bacon himself has a hard time describing the mechanics of sight. He seems to be speaking—"like a crystal, or glass, or water"—of the way the eye reflects and absorbs light, an observation that is hardly sufficient to describe the essential physiology of sight. As acoustics composed itself, the science of optics was reaching a state of theoretical crisis.
59 Lilio Gregorio Giraldi, *Historia de deis gentium* (Basel, 1548), sig. FF_2.
60 *De Anima*, trans. J. A. Smith, vol. 3 of *The Works of Aristotle Translated into English*, ed. W. D. Ross (Oxford: Clarendon Press, 1931), pp. 18–19 (420a).
61 Giraldi cited the poem in his *Historia de deis gentium* (1548) and thus established it as the single most influential classical description of Echo, with the exception of that in the *Metamorphoses*. Cartari rendered the poem in Italian in his *Le Imagini de i dei antichi* (Venice, 1571); I give George Turberville's English translation from *Epitaphs, Epigrams, Songs, and Sonnets* (London, 1567), sigs. O_2v–O_3, though Richard Lynche (*The Fountaine of Ancient Fiction*, 1599) and George Sandys (*Ovid's Metamorphoses*, 2d ed., 1632) also translated it. The text became a standard constituent of commentaries on the *Metamorphoses*, beginning with Ercole Ciofano's excellent *In P. Ovidii Nasonis Metamorphosin . . . Observationes* (Venice, 1575); Jacobus Pontanus even cites the poem in his commentary on *Georgics*, IV.50 (*Symbolarum Libri XVII Virgillii* [Augsburg, 1599], sig. Mm_3v).
62 Chloë has already been likened to Echo—implicitly, when Pan manifests his special affection for her (II.27), and explicitly, after she and Daphnis have finished singing an amorous concert in *versus alterni* (III.11).
63 Though the allusion to the opening of the *Eclogues* makes it extremely doubtful that Philetas figures, not Virgil, but the historical Philetas, Longus probably drew on the work of that poet (cf. William E. McCulloh, *Longus* [New York: Twayne, 1970], p. 96).
64 The poet of the *Georgics* describes the rural poet as "studiis florentem ignobilis oti" (IV.564); his implication is that the *Georgics*, too, are still tainted with an otium which his conclusion—both the tale of Aristaeus, Orpheus, and Eurydice, and the envoy—seeks, finally, to banish.
65 Thus Virgil provides an explicating mythos for the rule that hives not be built near echoing rocks or valleys: such places are sinister. This traditional rule of bee-keeping is recorded in Varro, *De re rustica*, III.xvi.12; Palladius, *De re rustica* (*Traité de l'agriculture*, ed. R. Martin [Paris: Belles lettres, 1976]), I.xxxvi.5; and Pliny, *Naturalis historia*, XI.65.

This passage has a more worthy explicative function, though, for it provides an elegant exegesis of the conclusion to the "Lament for Bion," where Bion himself is likened to Eurydice:

Nay, come sing to the maid [Persephone] some song of Sicily and make sweet rustic melody. She too is Sicilian and sported on the shores of Erna. She knows the Dorian strain. Not unrewarded shall thy music be, and as of old she gave back Eurydice to Orpheus' sweet harping, to thy hills she will send thee too. [ll. 121–27]

The comparison points to the sorry transience of Eurydice's reprieve and thence to Moschus's rueful sense of the inadequacy of a poet's self-consolation. Virgil indicates that Bion's mode of return to the hills is like Eurydice's, that he survives in the natural echoes to another poet's dirge. But the woeful Moschus has been replaced by the Orphic sparagmos in an image that suggests the tension Virgil perceives within literary genealogies.
66 Particularly striking is the association of virgin death with pastoral art, one of the darkest of Milton's private psychic myths, stated so plainly in Longus.

67 "Simul et circum magna sonantibus / Excita saxis suavisona echo / Crepitu clangente conchinnat"; cited in Desport, *L'incantation*, p. 64, n3. She takes these wonderfully horrific lines from Nonius Marcellus's *De compendiosa doctrina* (p. 463, ll. 13–17), but the MSS are problematic: the crucial phrase may well be "saevasona echo" or "saeva sonando," and the latter is now the preferred reading.
68 Harold Bloom, *The Anxiety of Influence: A Theory of Poetry* (New York: Oxford, 1973), p. 141.
69 We might argue that Valerius Flaccus engages in the same sort of mild *agon* with Virgil when he uses his own account of the echo of Hylas's name to engage Virgil's account—another instance of the reference to Echo as an occasion for a reflection on allusion: Echo as allusion, if not echoing as allusion. Valerius avoids repeating Virgil's text, choosing instead to internalize the phenomenon of echo within his own lines: "rursus Hylan et rursus Hylan per longa reclamat / avia; responsant silvae et vaga certat imago" (*Argonautica*, III.596–97). The crucial verb *certat* engages Virgil more than anything else in the passage, for that is Virgil's term for rivalry in pastoral song.
70 Bruno Snell, *The Discovery of Mind: The Greek Origins of European Thought*, trans. T. G. Rosenmeyer (Cambridge, Mass.: Harvard University Press, 1953), p. 237. The shift from mythology to science had received earlier, formal analyses in the works of Schelling, Müller, and Cassirer.
71 Paul Ricoeur, *The Symbolism of Evil* (Boston: Beacon Press, 1967), p. 163.
72 Ibid., p. 162.
73 *Paradise Lost*, I.746–47.
74 Again, cf. Philostratus, *Imagines*, II.11.
75 My reading here complements the extremely subtle essay of Caren Greenberg, "Reading Reading: Echo's Abduction of Language," in *Women and Language in Literature and Society*, ed. Sally McConnell-Ginet, Ruth Borker, and Nelly Furman (New York: Praeger Publishers, 1980) pp. 300–09; Greenberg also pursues the specific thematics of gender in Longus's tale. Yet she proposes an allegorical reading in which Echo figures a utopian textuality that slips the constraints of literary patriarchy. I take it that Longus's Echo is a nostalgic figure for orality, and therefore inappropriate as a utopian fantasy of textuality.

To the extent that Longus's Echo can be taken as bound to a cult of virginity, it is possible to find a purely allegorical content in the story—a rivalry between Orphic and Dionysian cults. It has been suggested that Longus himself may have been an initiate, even a priest, in one of the Dionysian cults, which, like the Orphic cults, experienced such a resurgence in the third and fourth centuries of the Christian era; certainly the studies of H. H. O. Chalk ("Eros and the Lesbian Pastorals of Longos," *Journal of Hellenic Studies* 80 [1960]:32–51) and William McCulloh (*Longus*, particularly chapter 6, pp. 79–90) reveal his familiarity with those cults and with the new literary myths of Orpheus and Dionysus that developed during the period. The tale of Echo in *Daphnis and Chloë* seems hardly to be the work of a devotee, being so very close—as Ovid's tale also is—to parody.

There is literary evidence that Echo did figure in some of these late Dionysian myths. In the *Dionysiaca* of Nonnus and in two poems from the Greek Anthology (VI.87 and XVI.156—though these may derive from Nonnus's epic itself), Echo's refusal of Pan seems to be an offense against Dionysus, since Pan is described as one of Dionysus's chief followers (and cf. the *Strategematum* of Polyaenus, in which Pan is Dionysus's *strategos*), occasionally seduced from Dionysian rites by the attractions of Echo. In one of the poems of the *Anthology*, Echo is unexpectedly reconciled to both Dionysus and Pan:

An Arcadian goddess am I, and I dwell by the portals of Dionysus, returning vocal responses. For no longer, dear Bacchus, do I hate thy companion. Come, Pan, let us talk in unison. [XVI.156]

76 "The myth is therefore not reflective contemplation, but actuality. *It is the reiterated presentation of some event replete with power*; verbal presentation, however is quite as effective as the repetition," G. Van der Leeuw, *Religion in Essence and Manifestation*, trans. J. E. Turner (London: Allen and Unwin, 1938), p. 413; emphasis his.

CHAPTER 2

1 *Imagines*, IX.433K.5–9.
2 *Descriptions*, IX.xxxi.9.
3 *Genealogia Deorum*, *Works*, 10:380. For the *Fable*, see below, chapter 3, note 31.
4 Sappho, frags. 104–05, particularly 105(c). On the relations between the Catullan and Sapphic epithalamia, see Denys Page, *Sappho and Alcaeus* (Oxford: Clarendon Press, 1955), pp. 121–22.
5 *Institutio Oratoria*, IV.i.77.
6 Most pertinent to the remarks on design that follow are Brooks Otis, *Ovid as an Epic Poet* (Cambridge: Cambridge University Press, 1966), pp. 74–90, and G. Karl Galinsky, *Ovid's "Metamorphoses": An Introduction to the Basic Aspects* (Oxford: Blackwell, 1975), pp. 79–107. But see also Gordon Williams's excellent *Change and Decline: Roman Literature in the Early Empire*, Sather Classical Lectures, no. 45 (Berkeley: University of California Press, 1978), pp. 91–101 and 246–53, and H. Frankel, *Ovid: A Poet Between Two Worlds*, Sather Classical Lectures (Berkeley: University of California Press, 1945), pp. 77–78.
7 "Preface to *Sylvae*," in *The Works of John Dryden* (Berkeley: University of California Press, 1961), 3:7. Dryden goes on to comment on Ovid's infrequent use of elision; Virgil provides the comparative standard. Statistical analyses of Ovid's prosody have been performed by A. G. Lee, for his edition of the *Metamorphoses* (Cambridge: Cambridge University Press, 1953), pp. 31–36, and by Traian Costa, "Formele Hexametrului la Ovidiu," in *Publius Ovidius Naso*, Biblioteca Antică, Studii 2 (Bucharest, 1957), pp. 211–332. Lee compares the metrics of Ovid's first book to those of Virgil's epic, using statistics on Virgil's prosody from S. E. Winbolt's *Latin Hexameter Verse* (London: Methuen, 1903), pp. 106–28. And see also Wilhelm Ott, *Metrische Analysen zu Ovid Metamorphosen Buch I* (Tubingen: Niemeyer, 1974).
8 We can also register the epic qualities of *Paradise Lost* in these terms. At the opening of book IV, a particularly resistant verse movement expresses nostalgia for primary orality, with epic voice as the unattainable aspiration of prophetic vision. The epic dialectic of performing present and envisioned past is manifest in both a deep clash of speech stress and metrical ictus and a temporal confusion comparable only to that of the first lines of the Nativity Ode.
9 A similar narrative enjambment occurs late in the poem in an episode that focuses on Ovid's place in the epic tradition. The closing lines of the poem reassure us of Ovid's grave designs on a place in literary memory, but in the great *iudicium armorum* of books twelve and thirteen, that gravity is preempted. This account of the debate between Ajax and Ulysses for the right to Achilles' arms is also nonmetamorphic, and it constitutes the poem's most extended interruption of the narrator, yet its theme of epic inheritance in the aftermath of the Trojan War would seem to be of the greatest specific concern to a poet. The seriousness of the episode is tainted with garrulousness, though, and *disertitudo* seems to mask the serious matter of desert: in response to Ajax's challenge—"Denique (quid verbis opus est?) spectemur agendo" (Finally, what need of words? Let us be seen in action; XIII.120)—comes Ovid's firm confutation—"quid

facundia posset, / re patuit, fortisque viri tulit arma disertus" (the company of chiefs was moved, and their decision proved the power of eloquence and *disertus* bore off the brave man's arms; XIII.382–83).

Richard Lanham points out that the *vir fortis* may be either Achilles or Ajax, which can only substantiate our sense of the violence Ovid does to the epic tradition (*The Motives of Eloquence: Literary Rhetoric in the Renaissance* [New Haven: Yale University Press, 1976], pp. 11–12). That is, Ulysses disrupts the rightful succession of arms from *fortis* to *fortis*: the passage of arms from Achilles to Ulysses may record the blithe succession from *Iliad* to *Odyssey*, but it also records a succession from *Aeneid* to *Metamorphoses*, a dislocation of epic progress. This break in literary continuity manifests itself in Ulysses' speech as an assault on genealogy: with Ajax having asserted a claim to the arms on the grounds of noble birth, Ulysses responds, "genus et proavos et quae non fecimus ipsi, / vix ea nostra voco" (for as to race and ancestry and the deeds that others than ourselves have done, I call these in no true sense our own; XIII.140–41). The arms must be earned—"meritis expendite causam" (judge us by our merits; XIII.150)—that is, they must be eloquently earned, which leaves the cards stacked in favor of "polytropic" Ulysses. Thus *disertitudo* (or, to adopt the more familiar Augustan term, *eloquentia*) stands at odds with simple systems of perpetuitas, and that opposition plays throughout the entire poem, *eloquentia ferente*.

10 The last of these episodes exemplifies the ultimate insufficiency of notions of imitative form to Ovidian narrative. The last of many soporific tales deployed by Mercury against Argus—the last, but the only one narrated—the story of Pan and Syrinx descends into *occultatio* as Argus's ninety-ninth and hundredth eyes wink shut: "restabat verbis referre / et precibus spretis fugisse per avia nympham" (it still remained for him to tell how the nymph, spurning his pleas, fled through the wastelands; I.700–01). The story's function (to divert) would seem to mime its form (digression from the tale of Io's fate), while it is shown to outstrip its narrative function, for it persists, as occultatio, even after its speech-act is completed. Narrative and its formal articulations here display a mutual insouciance or (to grant poetics their epic gravity) rival wills-to-power over the poem.

11 It may be noted, however, that Ovid's frequent intermingling of tales of metamorphosis with tales of mortal suffering at the hands of divine wrath has a teleological function, for it looks forward to the union of the mortal and the metamorphic in the Pythagorean allegory at the close of the poem. Metempsychosis will finally prove a natural authority for literary perpetuitas, redeeming the essentially entropic teleology of such normative metamorphic histories as Daphne's. (On Ovid's resistance to extraliterary defenses against literary deformation, see below.) Indeed, the Pythagorean teachings at the conclusion will provide a *nearly* transcendental version both of genealogy and of its synecdochic partner, chronology.

12 Galinsky, *Ovid's "Metamorphoses,"* p. 104.
13 Ibid., pp. 247–48.
14 On Ovid's biography, see Williams, *Change and Decline*, pp. 52–56.
15 Indeed, genealogy is invoked at some of the poem's key structural turns. Brooks Otis, developing suggestions in F. P. Wilkinson's unrivaled study of Ovid's poetry, analyzes the poem into four parts (*Ovid as an Epic Poet*, pp. 84–85). He finds the chronological passage broken into thematic units: books I and II organized around divine *amores*; a section from book III through to VI.400 treating of vengeance; from VI.401 through to the end of XI devoted, in Otis's phrase, to "the *Pathos* of love"; and the closing four books given over to historical metamorphoses from the time of the Trojan War. Each of these units has a contrasting "inset panel"—the Phaethon story, for example, at the center of the first thematic unit.

These are ghostly demarcations; homologous to the imperial system, the textual units are organized more by their centers than by their boundaries. In fact, genealogical relations between characters splice the first unit to the second, and the third to the fourth, as if the resistance to boundary had to take precedence over the literary bias against the biological. Certainly, the juncture in the middle of book VI—"Talibus extemplo redit ad praesentia dictis / vulgus" (straightway from such old tales to the present turns / the company)—emphasizes the persistence of narrator and audience, even as it marks the transformation of theme. The brief suspension of syntax at the line end leaves us a moment to inscribe the poet as subject of *redit*, to recognize the poet as the only true source of perpetuitas; but we may only recognize him, finally, as representative of a Roman *vulgus* willing to credit its inchoate religious and literary heritage, its cultural and imperial ideology, with intrinsic coherence.

16 Angus Fletcher sketches a theory of the literary boundary in "'Positive Negation': Threshold, Sequence, and Personification in Coleridge," in *New Perspectives on Coleridge and Wordsworth*, ed. Geoffrey H. Hartman (New York: Columbia University Press, 1972), pp. 133–64. Frank Kermode, drawing on the intriguing researches of L. Festinger, H. W. Riecken, and S. Schachter (in *When Prophecy Fails* [Minneapolis: University of Minnesota Press, 1956]), has described some of the devices we use to ease or avoid conclusions in *The Sense of an Ending* (New York: Oxford University Press, 1966). In *Structuralist Poetics* (Ithaca: Cornell University Press, 1975), Jonathan Culler articulates some of the problems in the critical discrimination of narrative units (see particularly pp. 206–12); his discussion recalls the opening of Ferdinand de Saussure's *Cours de linguistique generale*, ed. C. Bally and A. Sechehaye, with A. Riedlinger, 3d ed. (Paris: Payot, 1967), pp. 28–54, in which a careful inquiry into the constitutive boundaries of the phoneme is initiated. Writing, specifically the Greek alphabet, provides the necessary heuristic for Saussure: the phoneme is the *signifié* delimited by the alphabetic *signifiant*.

17 For Otis's schema, see note 15 above.

18 The sequence, Cadmus-Actaeon-Semele, makes perhaps the most vigorous of the poem's several feints toward genealogical structure, yet by skewing the sequence (Actaeon is Cadmus's grandson; Semele is Cadmus's daughter), Ovid introduces a chronological challenge to the genealogical (though Actaeon is Semele's nephew, he dies first). After the story of Semele—another instance of Jovial unmasking—even chronological sequence is disrupted, for the story begins with an announcement of concurrence ("dumque ea"; l. 316) which, by introducing the immortality and transcendence of divinity, does violence to the narrative primacy of the historical or the biological. At the metamorphic center of this uncanny tale, as if to flaunt the disruption of biological order, Teiresias is transformed, for striking two mating serpents, from man to woman, from woman to man.

At this point we begin to find other taxic principles shaping this section of the poem: the mating serpents hark back to the serpent slain by Cadmus, whose teeth yield that autochthonous and fratricidal race whose survivors, renouncing fratricide, aid the disowned Cadmus in building Thebes, city of the twisted affiliations. The hostility to sexual generation implicit in fictions of autochthony and necessary, Freud tells us, to the founding of cities is focused in Teiresias's violence against the serpents. Indeed, Jove and Juno, locked in a repressive competition, accept his arbitration both because of his twofold transsexual experience and because of his alliance with their efforts on behalf of denial. Just as the mutatas formas of the poem's opening has both a thematic and a structural referent, so here we find a correlation of the thematic repression of sexuality with the structural disruption of genealogical patterning.

19 When the *Cadmeans* subsides (it is difficult to speak of real conclusion) with the transformation of Cadmus into a snake, the serpentine leitmotif continues in an allusion to Perseus's slaughter of Medea:

cumque super Libycas victor penderet harenas,
Gorgonei capitis guttae cecidere cruentae;
quas humus exceptas varios animavit in angues,
unde frequens illa est infestaque terra colubris. [IV.617–20]

[As he was flying over the sandy wastes of Libya, bloody drops from the Gorgon's head fell down; and the earth received them as they fell and changed them into snakes of various kinds. And for this cause the land of Libya is full of deadly serpents.]

Far now from the archaic and tragic matter of a cursed house, the poet returns to the mock-wonder of etiology, the mythographic science that most insistently proclaims its practitioner's modernity. Book IV continues, another serpentine monster remains to threaten, but this beast is a *belua* or *monstrum*, not the *anguis* or *serpens* of the Cadmean sequence, which now appears to have passed away. Both the tale of Perseus and the Cadmean tales have tragic antecedents, but we must affiliate Perseus with the "new tragedy" perfected by Euripides.

20 Slightly equivocal evidence for Ovid's intentional allusion to Sophocles' Theban cycle might be gleaned from Ovid's assessment of Cadmus's complacency at the completion of the city's fortifications: "sed scilicet ultima semper / exspectanda dies hominis, dicique beatus / ante obitum nemo supremaque funera debet" (but surely a man's last day must ever be awaited, and none be counted happy till his death, till his last funeral rites be paid; III.135–37). The *sententia* attributed by Herodotus (I.32) and Aristotle (*Nic. Eth.*, 1100a, 10ff.) to Solon ties the *Cadmeans* securely to the tragic tradition; despite the fact that the Theban matter seems to have occupied a large place in the old epic cycles, particularly in the *Oedipoedia* and the *Theais*, Solon's dictum had a conspicuous ubiquity in tragedy. Though the tag appears four times in Euripides, as well as in Sophocles' own *Tyndaeus* and *The Women of Trachis*, surely the locus classicus is in the closing lines of *Oedipos Tyrannos* itself.

We can do little more than guess at the direct influence of the cycles on Ovid's epic. They do not seem to have been much read after the fourth century B.C., and though Greek scholars through to the fourth century A.D. occasionally seem to show familiarity with them—Athanaeus, for example, attests to Sophocles' debts to the cycles (*Deipnosophistae*, VII.277d), which attestation must have been based on the fact that the critic had some knowledge of the cycles—there is no persuasive evidence of Roman interest in these poems. Only fragments of the epic cycles now survive.

21 *Oedipus the King*, trans. Thomas Gould (Englewood Cliffs, N.J.: Prentice-Hall, 1970).
22 John Brenkman, "Narcissus in the Text," *Georgia Review* 30 (1976): 296.
23 Brenkman does not comment on the dynamic peculiar to chiasmus, the way it sets up a dialectic between the diachrony of syntax (and since we are speaking of Latin syntax, we may revise *diachrony* to *teleology*) and the synchrony of scheme. Taken teleologically, the tale of Echo and Narcissus prepares for the death of Narcissus and for the appearance of a flower where his corpse is sought. In this sense, the story is rather like a Latin sentence, the syntax and sense of which attends on a final verb that will confer semantic organization on what precedes it—the story remains suspended until the final episode which singles out Narcissus as the story's subject and his fatal enamorment as its reflexive verb. But from the more detached perspective of rhetoric, from which perspective the temporality of sequence is not perceptible, we find the episode's focus at its spatial center; taken rhetorically, the tale has a dual subject, and its central action is the verbal exchange between Echo and Narcissus.
24 The reification of dual existence remains only an ideal here (what Freud describes as narcissism is usually more resourceful, for it normally effaces itself on behalf of eroticized external objects):

"quod cupio mecum est: inopem me copia fecit.
o utinam a nostro secedere corpore possem!
votum in amante novum, vellem, quod amamus, abesset." [ll. 466–68]

["What I desire, I have; the very abundance of my riches beggars me. Oh, that I might be parted from my own body! and, strange prayer for a lover, I would that what I love were absent from me."]

25 Brenkman takes Narcissus's self-enthrallment as an allegory of reading, neglecting this curious supporting detail: the sudden exoticism of the image gives it an equally sudden access of delusive power. This phenomenology of reading is rooted in an old, uncritical lore in which the fantasist, primitivist, or impressionist deceives more fully than does the mimetic realist.

26 Actaeon's memory had been evoked only a few lines earlier: Narcissus

adspicit hunc trepidos agitantem in retia cervos
vocalis nymphe, quae nec reticere loquenti
nec prior ipsa loqui didicit, resonabilis Echo. [ll. 356–58]

[Once as he was driving the frightened deer into his nets, a certain nymph of strange speech beheld him, resounding Echo, who could neither hold her peace when others spoke, nor yet begin to speak till others had addressed her.]

Actaeon is the type of Narcissus, for both are inadvertent dupes of sight ("quod enim scelus error habebat?" for what crime is mere error?; l. 142).

27 Gaius, I.114; Gaius, II.42; Table VI.3.

For more on the legal sense of *usus*, see H. F. Jolowicz, *Historical Introduction to the Study of Roman Law*, 2d ed., reprinted with corrections (Cambridge: Cambridge University Press, 1939), p. 153, n1. The second meaning of *usus* seems to have been worked out by analogy from *usufruc[t]ion* (itself being debated during the second century B.C.); we cannot adequately date this second meaning, though by the time of the *Digest of Justinian* (530 A.D.) this meaning was firmly established; see Jolowicz, p. 282. For *usus* in Plautus, see *Amphitryon* I.375:

Mercury. quoius nunc es?
Sosia. Tuos, nam pugnis usu fecisti tuom.

Similarly "constitutional" meanings of *usus* are implicit in such Ovidian maxims as "morem fecerat usus" (*Met.*, II.345).

28 Jolowicz, *Study of Roman Law*, points out (p. 142) that relative dominion is a Germanic concept, alien to the absolute nature of Roman ownership.

29 Here, I think, Brenkman gets the tale of Echo and Narcissus subtly (and quite interestingly) wrong; by her punishment, he says,

Potentially Echo's very status as a character is undermined, and with it the coherence of the text insofar as the capacity to delimit a character is a necessary part of narrative fiction. If in the words assigned to Echo there is a radical discontinuity between her speech and her mind, then her words, though readable, could not be read as hers. ["Narcissus in the Text," pp. 299–300]

He goes on to remark that Narcissus' words in the central dialogue make possible an effacement of Echo's punishment, for those words do manage to represent her, but Brenkman then mistakes representation for identification: words and self are not absolutely congruent. Yet Brenkman renders the account of Echo's metamorphosis thus— "her voice lives in her, and she lives within her voice"—and comments, "Her sexuality has died with the body, but she has survived that death, passed through it as voice and consciousness" (p. 307). I think this binds voice and consciousness (what I have been calling "self") too closely together, so closely that it deprives the paradox of the last line of its full and scintillating play.

30 Narcissan originality is also held in check by Echo's grammatical agency: throughout the episode Narcissus' name appears only in the accusative case, whereas Echo's appears in none but the nominative.

31 Ernst Gombrich has reinforced the objection by pointing out that the pictorial arts are also "arts of time"; for his most succinct argument on the chronological scanning of pictorial and plastic art objects, see "Moment and Movement in Art," *Journal of the Warburg and Courtauld Institutes* 27 (1964): 293–306.

32 Brenkman, "Narcissus in the Text," p. 313, points out that the use of prefixes in *adrides*, *remittis*, and *refers* (ll. 459, 460, and 462) contributes to this effect.

33 *Metamorphoseon* (Antwerp, 1618), p. 147 (sig. N$_2$r), and cf. Tasso, *Aminta*, Chorus to Act I.

34 Pausanias refers to a historical Narcissus (*Descriptions* IX.xxxi.9), Narcissus the Thespian, in what appears to be an attempt to discredit the traditional story of his metamorphosis: the Hellenistic poet, Pamphos, whom Pausanias believed to have lived before Homer, gives an account of the rape of Persephone in which the beguiling last flower she plucked in the meadows of Enna is said to have been a narcissus; Pausanias argues that since the poem predates the life of Narcissus the Thespian, metamorphosis cannot explain the origins of the flower.

In his *Studi intorno alle . . . Metamorfosi di Ovidio* (Pisa, 1906; 2d ed., Rome: Bretschneider, 1964), pp. 213–21, Luigi Castiglione gives extended consideration to whether the collocation of the tales of Echo and Narcissus is an Ovidian innovation. He believes it likely that Ovid was here indebted to an Alexandrian source, but acknowledges that the evidence in the matter is slight and inconclusive; his care may stand as a valuable corrective to Wilmon Brewer's *Ovid's Metamorphoses in European Culture*, 2 vols. (vol. 1, Boston: Cornhill, 1933; vol. 2, Boston: Jones, 1941), in which, on no stated evidence, Ovid's tale is said to be derived from an Alexandrian version, "probably the work of Nicander" (1:132).

35 For Hylas transformed into Echo, a nicely compact reworking of Echo's attendance at scenes of pastoral drowning, see Antoninus Liberalis, *Metamorphoses*, XXVI, based, according to a scholiast, on a tale of Hylas in book II of Nicander's *Heteroioumena*.

36 The affirmation of that continuity that so firmly establishes itself at his death begins in the lines that describe the last stages of his life:

pectora traxerunt roseum percussa ruborem,
non aliter quam poma solent, quae candida parte,
parte rubent, aut ut variis solet uva racemis
ducere purpureum nondum matura colorem.   [ll. 482–85]

[His breast when it is struck takes on a delicate glow; just as apples sometimes, though white in part, flush red elsewhere, or as grapes hanging in clusters take on a purple hue when not yet ripe.]

The emphasis on habituation in the verb *soleo* (and cf. ll. 489 and 499), suggests the caricature of *deformation professionelle* which provides the motive for so many of Ovid's metamorphoses. The similes are similarly habitual, for both are topoi. The apples appear in Sappho (frag. 105a), Theocritus (*Id.*, VII.117), and in *Anth. Pal.*, XVI.210; the unripe grapes, in Alcaeus (frag. 119); *Anth. Pal.*, V.20, 124, and 304; and Theocritus (*Id.*, XI.21). The last is perhaps the most interesting, since it associates Narcissus with the brute pastoralism of Polyphemus.

37 Louise Vinge, *The Narcissus Theme in Western European Literature up to the Early Nineteenth Century*, trans. Robert Dewsnap, Lisbeth Gronlund, Nigel Reeves, and Ingrid Soderberg-Reeves (Lund: Gleerups, 1967), p. 41.

164 • NOTES TO PAGES 55–60

38 Eric A. Havelock, *A Preface to Plato* (Cambridge, Mass.: Harvard University Press, Belknap Press, 1963), chapt. 3, pp. 36–60. My apparently passing reference here should not obscure the pervasive influence of Havelock's study on the argument of this chapter.

39 *The Republic*, trans. Paul Shorey, in *Plato: The Complete Dialogues*, ed. Edith Hamilton and Huntington Cairns, Bollingen Series, no. 71 (New York: Random House, 1961), 10:596d–e.

CHAPTER 3

1 The plate under discussion appears in volume 2, opposite fol. Kk_4v (Iconismus XV, Fol. 264).

2 His partition of the discourse follows:

Et primo quidem novas phonocampticae artis rationes & canones proferemus; secundo Architectonicam phonocampticam sive Echometricam, ex penitissimis naturae arcanis recludemus. Tertio Echotectonicam sive Acusticorum instrumentorum fabricam. [II: sig. Gg_3]

[And first we shall offer the new theories and laws of the art of Acoustics; then we shall expound Acoustic Engineering, or Echometry, the most profound of Nature's lore; and third, Echotectonics, the art of making acoustic devices.]

3 Of course, there were efforts to free technological research from mythography. The great monument to demythologized acoustic research may be found in the work of Marin Mersenne and his circle. Echoic acoustics are of major concern to Mersenne, who tries to free Biancani's science of its antique literary trappings; only the Vitruvian lore holds his attention. A teacher and friend of Descartes, Mersenne attempts to restrict his acoustic research to geometrical principle. That effort is most pronounced in the "Traité particulier de l'Echo . . . qu'un excellent esprit feist sur Marne l'an 1625" published in his *Harmonie Universelle* (Paris, 1636), 1:sig. E_1v–E_4v. The author asks with fly disingenuousness, "Que vous semble de ce discours Poetique?" and then leaves the question unanswered; he concludes his *traité* thus:

Voila come le Createur a donné un langage aux bois, aux rivieres & aux montagnes, pour le loüer & pour le benir en son admirable disposition, don resulte l'harmonie ravissante, & la belle symmetrie qui est admirée des uns, & examinée & mise en pratique par les autres, & imitée en tous les chefs-d'oeuvres de l'artifice humain. En cette recherche de l'Echo, je n'ay eu pour toute tirasse, panneaux & filets, que les lignes geometriques; & bien qu'il y ait d'autres pieges qu'on luy peut tendre, je les laisse pour un autre Pan, c'est à dire pour une personne tres-universelle en toute sorte de science; si nous eussions eu des gens d'un mesme dessein, nous eussions mieux examiné les experiences, mais je quitte à un autre le flambeau pour courre, & pour en faire davantage. [E_4v]

The "traité" remains unattributed, though both its style and its method may well suggest the authorship of Descartes himself. He spent much of the early 1620s in northern France, though his perambulations between 1618 and 1628 are badly documented. The general subject of "echometry" was one on which Descartes and Mersenne corresponded from virtually the beginnings of their acquaintance.

4 See Frances Yates, *Theatre of the World* (London: Routledge & Kegan Paul, 1969), passim and Allardyce Nicoll, *The Development of the Theatre* (New York: Harcourt Brace Jovanovich, 1966), pp. 70–82.

5 For Jones's Vitruvian learning, perhaps the best introduction is D. J. Gordon, "Poet and Architect: The Intellectual Setting of the Quarrel between Ben Jonson and Inigo

Jones," originally published in the *Journal of the Warburg and Courtauld Institutes* 12 (1949): 152–78, but now most easily accessible in the collection of Gordon's essays edited by Stephen Orgel, *The Renaissance Imagination* (Berkeley: University of California Press, 1975), pp. 77–101. And see also Graham Parry's chapter on Jones in *The Golden Age Restor'd: The Culture of the Stuart Court, 1603–42* (New York: St. Martins Press, 1981).

6 Erasmus's colloquy, "Echo," may be found in the *Opera Omnia*, 10 vols. (Leyden, 1703), 1:817–18 (sig. Fff$_1$). The most important illustration is in Poussin's *Birth of Bacchus*; Echo also appears in illustrations of the Ovidian tale by Tintoretto and Caravaggio.

7 For the discussions of the Pythagorean motto, see Ficino, *Pythagorae aurea verba & symbola*, which occupies the last pages of his *Opera Omnia*, 2 vols. (Basel, 1576), 2:sig. PpP$_3$ and Giraldi, *Pythagorae Symbolorum Interpretatio*, in his *Opera Omnia*, 2 vols. (Basel, 1580), 2:sigs. TT$_2$v–TT$_3$.

8 Guarini's echo-scene is IV.viii of *Il Pastor Fido*; see the discussion below.

   Barbaro's Vitruvius was published in Venice in 1567; I give the text of his poem as reprinted in Cartari's *Imagini*:

Echo figlia de i boschi, e delle valli
Ignudo spirto, e voce errante, e sciolta,
Eterno essempio d'amorosi falli,
Che tanto altrui ridice, quanto ascolta,
S'amor ti torne à suoi allegri balli,
E che ti renda la tua forma tolta,
Fuor d'este valli abbandonate, e sole
Sciogli i miei dubbi in semplici parole.
Echo, che cosa è il fin d'amore?   amore.
Chi fa sua strada men sicura?   cura.
Vive ella sempre, o pur sen more?   more.
Debbo fuggir la forte dura?   dura.
Chi darà fine al gran dolore?   l'hore.
Com'ho da vincer chi è spergiura?   giura
Dunque l'inganno ad amor piace?   piace.
Che fin'è d'esso, guerra, o pace?   pace.   [sigs. R$_1$r-v]

[Echo, daughter of the woods and valleys
Simple breath and nimble, wandering voice
Eternal example to thwarted lovers,
Who reports to others everything that she hears:
If Love again takes you up into his pleasant dances
And restores to you the form he took from you,
And removes you from these lonely and abandoned valleys,
Then dissolve my doubts with simple words.
Echo, what is the end of love?   Love.
Why are the paths of love so insecure?   Misgivings.
Will misgivings endure or die within my breast?   Die.
Must I flee this unyielding strength?   Endure
Who will end this mammoth pain?   Time.
How can I win her who is forsworn?   Swear.
So such a trick will please Love?   It will.
And to what end—War, or Peace?   Peace.]

9 Michel Foucault, "What Is an Author?" in *Textual Strategies*, ed. Josué V. Harari (Ithaca: Cornell University Press, 1979), pp. 158–59.

10 She arrived on Saturday the ninth and left on the twenty-seventh, a Wednesday.
11 Nearly all the early Elizabethan progresses share this emphasis on locale; see Alice S. Miskimin, "Ben Jonson and Captain Cox: Elizabethan Gothic Reconsidered," *Renaissance Drama* 8 (1977): 179. Miskimin's analyses of the Kenilworth entertainments, treating mainly of the performances by the local troupe, are extremely valuable.

   I cite *The Princely Pleasures* from the text in *The Complete Works of George Gascoigne*, ed. John W. Cunliffe, 2 vols. (Cambridge: Cambridge University Press, 1910), 2:91–131; the quoted passage is from p. 93.
12 That there were more macaronics to come before the entertainments were over and that Jonson would find them an *especially* choice target for satire is the central argument of Miskimin's essay, referred to above; see pp. 197–200 in particular. My purpose here and in the following chapter is to extend Miskimin's thesis by showing how fully Jonson had reflected on the Kenilworth shows, adopting the drama of echoic locale as model.
13 Stephen Orgel, *The Jonsonian Masque* (Cambridge, Mass.: Harvard University Press, 1965), pp. 37–42. Orgel never *quite* explains the pertinence of this suggestive phrase to the Kenilworth festivities; I hope to articulate *a* meaning in the following pages. This is certainly the moment to remark my indebtedness throughout this study to Orgel's research on English masquing.
14 Richard Laneham, *Letter . . .* (London, 1575), sigs. B_6r-v.
15 Prudence could hardly have been misplaced. For all the administrative sophistication we find in the development of the Office of the Revels, English festivity was still executed with an almost mystifying ham-handedness. In 1524 King Henry was nearly killed at tilt by the duke of Suffolk, who was apparently blinded momentarily by his own visor (it may be recalled that France's Henry died of wounds suffered in a tournament in 1559). More recently—indeed, only three years before the Kenilworth entertainments during a previous royal progress through Warwickshire—squibs from a dragon set fire to a fort, contrary to plan, in the midst of a mock siege, then ignited two or three homes in the immediate vicinity (one of which burned to the ground), and finally tossed forth fireballs "as farre as almost to Saint Mary Churche, to the great perill, or else great feare of the inhabitants of this Borough: so as, by what meanes is not yet knowen, foure houses in the Towne and Suburbes were on fyre at once" (cited in John Nichols, *The Progresses and Public Processions of Queen Elizabeth*, 2d ed., 3 vols. [London: Nichols, 1823], 1:320). All of which may explain why, in 1575, all the Kenilworth fireworks displays were executed in aquatic settings.

   On the development of conventions to safeguard courtly revelers, see Howard C. Cole, *A Quest of Inquirie: Some Contexts of Tudor Literature* (New York: Pegasus, 1973), pp. 359–60 and 372–73.
16 A revision of Moschus or, perhaps more immediately, of the *Aminta*. The *Aminta* was performed in Ferrara in 1573, though it was not published until the end of 1580 (with a date of 1581 on the title page). Albert Feuillerat suggests that the *Aminta* may have been one of the plays performed for the queen by Italian players in July of 1574 when they entertained her at Windsor and afterwards at Reading; see his *Documents Relating to the Office of the Revels in the Time of Queen Elizabeth* (Louvain: Uystpruyst, 1908), pp. 227–28 and 458.
17 That the "games" do not refer to Hunnis's device is clear: the freeing of the Lady of the Lake is entirely a male exploit. It has been argued that Gascoigne *may* have been referring to the Hock-Tuesday play performed by the Coventry guildsmen on the following Sunday. No text of the play survives, yet Laneham's *Letter* provides an enthusiastic summary of

   their olld storiall sheaw: Of argument how the Danez whylom heere in a troublous seazon wear for quitenesse born withall & suffeard in peas, that anon by outrage & importabl insolency . . . wear all dispatcht and the Ream rid. And for becauz the matter mencioneth how valiantly our English women for loove of their cuntree behaved themselvez: expressed in actionz & rymez after their maner, they thought it moought moove sum myrth to her Majestie the rather. [sigs. C_1v–C_2]

At any rate, the Savage Man almost certainly predicted a Thursday performance of *Zabeta* (postponed permanently, perhaps because of rain) or the Hock-Tuesday play (postponed until Sunday, but without provoking a remark on the postponement from either Gascoigne or Laneham).

18 This impersonal *I* appears in the 1587 *Works* text throughout, yet it never quite dissociates Gascoigne from the narrator. The text concludes with the final device (and not with any editorial peroration)—a device written and performed by Gascoigne— and a subscripted motto, "Tam Marti, Quam Mercurio," one of several that work as Gascoigne's particular literary signatures; he has the last word.

19 The measure, printed in this format, might also be called ballad stanza, but the absence of enjambment at the end of the second and fourth lines, the presence of enjambment at the end of many of the odd lines, and the fact that only the even lines are rhymed clearly indicate that the short line is not the unit of composition. Poulter's measure, the more "literary" form of this rhythmic configuration, prevails.

20 This difficulty with the censorious court may well have contributed to the somewhat furtive nature of Gascoigne's participation in the narrative voice of the text; see note 18 above.

21 At this moment, Leicester may well have been the most powerful *man* in England, despite a multitude of enemies. Earlier in the decade he had begun stockpiling weapons at Kenilworth, making it, in the words of Lawrence Stone, "a fortress that could compare in strength to the royal castles of the Tower and Berwick" (*The Crisis of the Aristocracy*, abridged ed. [London: Oxford, 1967], p. 107). Armaments seem to account for a fair portion of the astonishing sum of 60,000 pounds which he spent on improvements to Kenilworth, an estate originally obtained, by grant in fee, for 24 pounds. He had leases of duty on the import of nearly all important Mediterranean trade goods, clear evidence of the queen's particular favor or respect.

C. T. Prouty, Gascoigne's most assiduous biographer, suggests that one reason for suppressing *The Adventures of Master F. J.* may be that it contains an episode that could be taken as alluding to the Sheffield affair; see Prouty's *George Gascoigne: Elizabethan Courtier, Soldier, and Poet* (New York: Columbia University Press, 1942), p. 193. If Prouty is correct, then the choice of Gascoigne to be one of the masterminds of the queen's reception must seem slightly peculiar, though it is not unaccountable; the choice may well have been Leicester's flamboyant assertion that he stood above scandal.

22 We find a similar metalepsis in Gascoigne's *The Steele Glas*, where the conventions governing the trope of reflection shift constantly. On metalepsis in general, see Quintilian, VIII.vi.37–38, and Gérard Genette, *Figures III* (Paris: Seuil, 1972), pp. 243–45, both of whom use the term to imply considerably more than the circumlocution-by-etiological-narrative that is the definition applied to the figure in Puttenham's occasionally reductive rhetoric.

23 See Orgel, *The Jonsonian Masque*, p. 38, and Cole, *A Quest of Inquirie*, pp. 330–36.

24 After the transcript of a long portion of Sylvanus's speech, *The Princely Pleasures* includes a report on the action:

Here her majestie stayed her horse to favor *Sylvanus*, fearing least he should be driven out of breath by following her horse so fast. But *Sylvanus* humbly besought her Highnesse to goe on, declaring that if hys rude speech did not offend her, he coulde continue this tale to be twenty miles long. [p. 123]

Like Iris, Sylvanus barely catches the train of the departing queen's attention. This pursuit seems almost to anticipate the suppression of *Zabeta* even as it dramatizes the effort of securing a royal hearing.

Apparently, the queen keeps moving, and her motion is *scripted*. A few pages later in Gascoigne's text, the narrator's voice interrupts Sylvanus to point out that motion: "At these wordes her Majestie came by a close Arbor, made all of Hollie, and while Sylvanus pointed to the same, the principall bush shaked" (p. 127).

25 Part of the coherence of these entertainments lies in an easy distributability of attributes of plot and character: Sylvanus has the *appearance* of a woodwose; Zabeta affects men as does Elizabeth.

26 The printed text, it may be observed, is self-sufficient, not *requiring* prior familiarity with the tale of *Zabeta*.

27 There are few such published accounts of royal progresses (from which category I exclude those accounts that form parts of larger works of historiography, accounts of fundamentally antiquarian appeal) from before this date. Only Tottel's record of *The Passage of our most drad Soveraigne Lady Quene Elyzabeth through the Citie of London, etc.* (1558–59) and "The Whole Order howe our Soveraigne Ladye Queene Elizabeth, was receyved into the Citie of BRISTOWE, etc.," included in *Churchyardes Chippes* (1575) have even remotely comparable literary and iconographic detail.

28 The source is Edward Hall's *Chronicle*, as cited by Enid Welsford, in *The Court Masque* (Cambridge: Cambridge University Press, 1927), p. 130, who gives the passage an extensive and valuable exegesis.

29 These echo-lyrics are the technical derivatives of the poem by Gauradas from the Planudean anthology (cited by Poliziano and imitated by him), which was first widely available in a Latin translation by Alciati in 1529 (*Selecta Epigrammata*, ed. Janus Cornarius [Basel], Z_3v); later in the century, we find translations by Sabeo into Latin and Tamisier into French. Grotius's Latin version appeared early in the next century.

In the *De deis gentium* (Basel, 1548), Giraldi observes of Echo's popularity—"& deam poetae dixere, de qua non solum veteres graeci & latini plerique luserunt, sed nostri etiam temporis poetae" (and the poets call her a goddess, with whom not only the ancient Greek and Latin writers have played but those of our own day as well; FF_2). Besides those echo-lyrics alluded to above, there is evidence for others from early in the century. G. M. Crescimbeni refers to an echo-lyric by Amalteo in his *Dell'Istoria Della Volgar Poesia*, 6 vols. (Venice, 1730–31), 1:386, as does Francesco Quadro, in his *Della Storia e della Ragione D'Ogni Poesia Volumi Quattro*, rev. 3d ed. (Bologna, 1739), 1:229, who also refers to an echo-lyric by Pollastrino; neither Crescimbeni nor Quadrio give texts of these poems, and I have been unable to locate such texts elsewhere. (Quadrio may be inheriting a ghost from Crescimbeni, to whom he is elsewhere much indebted, though Amalteo certainly had a fondness for echo-effects, which he handily exploits in epyllia on Hylas and on Orpheus.) Besides the more eminent poets noted in my text, the following also wrote Gauradan echo-lyrics, the texts of which are still available: Du Pont, Mocenigo, Sabino, San Martino, Johannes Secundus, and, of course, van der Does.

The immediate literary influence of Gauradas begins to fade late in the sixteenth century, when Gaurini's bravura echo-scene eclipses its Gauradan precursor. Subsequent echo-lyrics by Pasquier, Tasso (though the canonicity of this text is in doubt), Cieco d'Adria, Panigarola, Friselin, Melissus, and others show obvious signs of Guarini's influence, as do the many echo-scenes in French and Italian baroque drama.

30 Madeleine Doran, "Some Renaissance Ovids," in *Literature and Society*, ed. Bernice Slote (Lincoln: University of Nebraska Press, 1964), pp. 44–62; and cf. Demats, *Fabula*, pp. 140–41. On the Renaissance edition and annotation of Ovid, there is perhaps no more useful reference text than D. C. Allen's *Mysteriously Meant: The Rediscovery of Pagan Symbolism and Allegorical Interpretation in the Renaissance* (Bal-

timore: Johns Hopkins University Press, 1970); my debt to his researches in Renaissance mythography is enormous.
31 See also *The Fable of Ovid treting of Narcissus* (London, 1560), a translation of the relevant lines from the *Metamorphoses* followed by twice as many interpretive verses in which the allegorizations of Bersuire and Agostino are conjoined with those of Boccaccio and Ficino. The author, T[homas] H[owell], even provides a long allegorical reading of his own, in which the oracular and demystifying powers of Echoic response are made more homely: Echo is identified as a figure for "good advice." This is, incidentally, the only Renaissance translation of Ovid in which *no* effort is made to reproduce the aphaeresis and antanaclasis which are the rhetorical signature of Echoic response.
32 Bersuirre's moralizations had a wide influence, with a special prestige in England, a prestige deriving from misattributions of the *Ovidius moralizatus* to such Englishmen as Thomas Walleys, Nicholas Trivet, and Robert Holkot; see Richard Hamilton Green, "Classical Fable and English Poetry in the Fourteenth Century," in *Critical Approaches to Medieval Literature*, ed. Dorothy Bethurum (New York: Columbia University Press, 1960), p. 115.
33 Jonson may be drawing on a euhemerist tradition, available in Comes and originating in Pausanias, in which the imago is said to represent Narcissus' twin sister, of whom he grew enamored and whose death left him so grieved that he drowned himself.
34 This formalism is not maintained throughout the play. Instead it prepares for a plot that descends into moral satire, a plot in which narrative and character collapse into a static system of moral counters; this mimetic collapse is a dramaturgic device already worked out in the humours plays. In a plot that reverses the history of Tudor dramaturgy, personality is slowly effaced by a Vice-trait; see, in particular, IV.iii.
35 As will be argued below, the marginal pathos of Echo's position in *Cynthia's Revels* is extreme within baroque drama, for Jonson, unlike most baroque dramatists and lyricists, makes much of the antique narrative etiologies of Echo. Another important exception may be noted in Thomas Watson's very elaborate echo-lyric in *Hekatompathia* (1582), no. 25, in which "the Author walking in the woods and bewayling his inward passion of *Love*, is contraried by the replies of *Echo*: whose meaning yet is not so much to gainsay him, as to express her owne miserable estate in daily consuming away for the love of her beloved Narcissus: whose unkindnes *Ovid* describeth at large" (D_1). Excepting the translations of Ovid's fable, Golding's (1567) and Howell's (1560), and the two Renaissance epyllia on Narcissus, Thomas Edwarde's obscurantist poem of 1595 and Shirley's more insouciant text of 1648, very few English echo-dialogues restore attention to any of the narrative etiologies of Echo, narratives in which she is invariably a victim, hence Jonson's claim to be *reviving* Echo in *Cynthia's Revels*. The conclusion of William Percy's echo-lyric in *Coelia* (1594) is a rare and unemphatic recollection of Ovid:

Then will she yeeld at length to Love? To love.
Ev'n so? Ev'n so. By Narcisse is it true? True
Of thine honestie? I. Adieu. Adieu. [C_2]

36 This was Jonson's second imprisonment at Marshalsea, though for the previous year's crime he would have been sent to the felon's prison at Newgate; his earlier confinement at Marshalsea was in July of 1597, for participating in the composition and performance of *The Isle of Dogs*. Henslowe lent him money on this occasion as well, apparently securing Jonson's continued services as a collaborating playwright.
37 Thus *Eastward Ho*, the 1605 collaboration with Chapman and Marston, is excluded from the folio *Works*. Jonson apparently did complete at least one play for Henslowe single-handedly—we have a record of Henslowe's rather lavish ten-pound payment for a *Richard Crookback*—though this is exceptional; aside from *Eastward Ho*, none of his

Henslowe scripts was ever published. It is remotely possible that Henslowe refused to grant copy for printing these scripts, though if he had wanted them published, Jonson could probably have pirated the scripts with little difficulty and one feels certain that he would have given such a refusal some appropriately vituperative commemoration.

38 See Philip J. Finkelpearl, "John Marston's *Histrio-Mastix* as an Inns of Court Play: A Hypothesis," *Huntington Library Quarterly* 29 (1966): 223–34.

39 The *Conversations* are transcribed in volume I of Herford and Simpson's edition of Jonson's *Works*; the citation is from ll. 284–86.

This is perhaps the place to acknowledge the considerable body of literature that has sprung up around the so-called War of the Theaters, although an exhaustive account of this material is impossible. The nineteenth-century tradition of scholarship in the field culminates with Josiah H. Penniman, *The War of the Theatres* (Boston: Ginn, 1897), and the somewhat more persuasive work of Roscoe A. Small, *The Stage-Quarrel Between Ben Jonson and the So-Called Poetasters* (Breslau: Marcus, 1899). The most enlightening work of this century may be found in O. J. Campbell, *Comicall Satyre and Shakespeare's Troilus and Cressida* (San Marino: Huntington Library, 1938); E. W. Talbert, "The Purpose and Technique of Jonson's *Poetaster*," *Studies in Philology* 42 (1945): 225–52; Alfred Harbage, *Shakespeare and the Rival Traditions* (New York: Macmillan, 1952), pp. 90–119; and Stuart Omans, "The War of the Theaters: An Approach to Its Origins, Development, and Meaning," Ph.D. diss., Northwestern University, 1969.

40 *The Plays of John Marston*, ed. H. Harvey Wood, 3 vols. (Edinburgh: Oliver and Boyd, 1934–39), 3:273–74; I reassign the first speech to Belch, where Wood preserves "Bell." which is the usual abbreviation in the text for Bellula.

41 Marchette Chute, *Ben Jonson of Westminster* (New York: Dutton, 1953), pp. 81–82. There were, of course, other good reasons for entering the Guild, not the least of which is that it gave him rights of citizenship in the City of London.

42 Jonson's theory of imitation has been the object of much useful scrutiny, most recently in Richard S. Peterson's *Imitation and Praise in the Poems of Ben Jonson* (New Haven: Yale University Press, 1981) and in the final chapter of Thomas Greene's *The Light in Troy*, cited above. The best available summary of the intellectual history of Renaissance imitative theory may be found in G. W. Pigman III, "Versions of Imitation in the Renaissance," *Renaissance Quarterly* 33 (1980): 1–32.

43 Algernon Charles Swinburne, *A Study of Ben Jonson* (London: Chatto & Windus, 1889), 20–21.

44 The master of the company, Nathaniel Giles, received his commission in July of 1597, a month after the death of William Hunnis, the former master of the Chapel Boys, but the impressments of actors did not begin until 1600.

45 Critics have agreed on the particular debt of Jonson to *Endimion*. And surely A. C. Judson's suggestion that the Cupid of *Cynthia's Revels* owes something to the Cupid of Lyly's *Gallathea* is correct; see the introduction to Judson's edition of *Cynthia's Revels*, Yale Studies in English, no. 45, ed. A. S. Cook (New York: Holt, 1912), pp. lxi–lxii, as well his note to line 50 (line 47 in the Herford and Simpson edition) of Jonson's own introduction. (For more on the influence of *Gallathea*, see note 51 below.) These specific debts serve only to point up the generalized influence of Lyly's epiphanic dramas on Jonson's conception of *Cynthia's Revels*.

For Saccio's description of "situational dramaturgy," see his *The Court Comedies of John Lyly: A Study in Allegorical Dramaturgy* (Princeton: Princeton University Press, 1969), p. 2.

46 See *Satiromastix*, IV.i.187–91, where "the humorous poet," Master Horace, is tempted with assurances of the revels mastership. Jonson finally did receive the reversion in 1621, but at that time he stood third in line for the office.

47 Jonas Barish's brilliant treatment of *Ben Jonson and the Language of Prose Comedy* (Cambridge, Mass.: Harvard University Press, 1960) suggests the structural grounding of this dramaturgy in the syntax of Jonson's prose.
48 To some extent, this structural strategy is exploited by the passage cited earlier in which Cupid describes the resort of "all sorts of ingenuous persons" to court; these persons are both the dramatis personae of *Cynthia's Revels* and the entertainers who gather before Elizabeth, and thus the parataxis of *Cynthia's Revels* serves to point the diversity of purpose of the various plays. (The folio version of Act V could well be taken as a capping contribution, an apotheosis of this structural fragmentation; on the structural significance of Act V, see below.)
49 G. K. Hunter, *John Lyly: The Humanist as Courtier* (Cambridge, Mass.: Harvard University Press, 1962), p. 294.
50 For Echo's indictment of Cynthia, see I.ii.82–92.
51 It should be noted that Lyly violated his own normal pattern of potent and pure divinity. Jonson could have found a model for the parodic theophanies of *Cynthia's Revels* in Lyly's own *Gallathea*. Both Lyly's Cupid and his Neptune act with a remarkable frivolity until Venus reclaims the former, and the necessity of settling a quarrel between Venus and Diana effects Neptune's sudden return to regal sobriety.
52 II.iii.8–10. Cupid proposes this *askesis* as a means to new power: "in . . . disguise . . . I will get to follow some one of DIANAES maidens, where (if my bow hold, and my shafts flie but with halfe the willingnesse, and aim they are directed) I doubt not, but I shall really redeeme the minutes I have lost, by their so long and over-nice proscription of my *deitie*, from their court" (I.i.106–12). Cupid defers his assault on maidenly virtue until the fifth act.

This inquiry into the "benefit" of descent provides a pattern for later Jonsonian dramaturgy. For an interesting examination of such "slumming" in *Bartholomew Fair*, see Jonathan Haynes, "Festivity and the Dramatic Economy of Jonson's *Bartholomew Fair*," forthcoming in *English Literary History* (1984?).
53 We may compare the openings of III.i and III.ii, in which significant court events, placed offstage, are alluded to. Again, enactment is displaced to make way for more critical commentary.
54 The special *theatricality* of courtly behavior is evident throughout the play; it receives most explicit statement at III.iv.55–74.
55 This alludes perhaps to the magic wishing hat of *Old Fortunatus*, capable of transporting the wearer anywhere, and thus motivating Dekker's picaresque plot. Andelocia describes his magic hat as one of an array of "trickes, devises, and mad Hieroglyphickes, mirth, mirth, and melody"; cited from vol. 1 of *The Dramatic Works of Thomas Dekker*, ed. Fredson Bowers, 4 vols. (Cambridge: Cambridge University Press, 1953–58), V.ii.32–33. To this moment in I.iv of *Cynthia's Revels*, compare the similarly mistaken estimation of "devices" at II.ii, where Anaides receives the epithet, "my deare invention" (l. 45), and Hedon's devices are personified (ll. 68–75).

Jonson's tense ambivalence to the pictorial (on which, see note 71 below) is turned to comic purpose elsewhere, when, in III.i, Amorphus suggests reasons for Asotus's first failure in the "presence":

I doe now partly aime at the cause of your repulse—(which was omenous indeed) for as you enter at the doore, there is oppos'd to you the frame of a woolfe in the hangings, which (surprizing your eye sodainely) gave a false alarme to the heart. [ll. 75–79]

The topos—to be seen by a wolf—is from Theocritus (*Idyllia*, XIV) and Virgil (*Eclogues*, IX); here the topos is hypostasized as objet d'art, so that Asotus is cowed by the presence of the very artifice to which court life is so dedicated and which he so foolishly literalizes.

56 Compare a passage from *Discoveries*: "When too much desire, and greedinesse of vice, hath made the body unfit, or unprofitable; it is yet gladded with the sight, and spectacle of it in others: and for want of ability to be an Actor; is content to be a Witnesse" (1470–74). Earlier in the *Discoveries* (1093–1109), a distinction is made between vicious and virtuous spectatorship: the former gains its freedom from blame by observing from a great distance.

Jonas Barish was the first, to my knowledge, to isolate the profound antitheatricality that keens through so much of Jonson's work. His essay, "Jonson and the Loathèd Stage," in *A Celebration of Ben Jonson*, ed. W. Blissett, J. Patrick, and R. Van Fossen (Toronto: University of Toronto Press, 1973), pp. 27–53, also examines the satire of self-display in *Cynthia's Revels* (he is one of the few critics to have remarked how central are the play's concerns to the Jonsonian oeuvre). The essay does not take up Jonson's rather more troubled treatment of *viewing*.

57 *Satiromastix*, I.ii.379–80. Dekker does treat these characters as if they spoke for Jonson—a misreading perhaps, but one widespread among Jonson's contemporaries and one which he never undertook to correct.

58 This is not quite play-within-play, for containment is neither complete nor even purposed. The incidence of observation and the vantage of the observers are both irregular, providing for a sense of uncontrollable and heterogeneous critical response. In V.i, Mercury makes the fact of a heterogeneous audience explicit when he assures Crites that though some will take the masque as an attack on courtly behavior, "the better race in court / That have the true nobilitie, call'd vertue, / Will apprehend it, as a gratefull right" (ll. 30–32). Of all Elizabethans, Jonson most emphatically insists on the work of art as quite literally analytic of its audience. Pavy, for example, begins his betrayal of the play's plot (for which, see below) by administering a literacy test; see Induction, ll. 40–42.

59 V.xi.25–29. Here it is particularly important to distinguish between the revels as part of a masque (a slightly more technical meaning of the term), that is, as that interim of figured-dancing which dissolves the proscenium convention within a masque (the moment of masquing "after the maner of Italie"), and the interim of Misrule which was the calendrical occasion of the masquing itself. The revels of *Cynthia's Revels* involve a figurative extension of the latter meaning.

60 *Plays of John Marston*, 2:233 (Induction).

61 The chief additions to the play in folio are: III.i.32–75; III.iv.22–42; IV.i.132–214; IV.v.76–100; and, most important, IV.v.142–V.v.1. The folio revisions also sharpen the idiosyncratic texture of the dialogue—thus discriminating slightly more clearly between the character groupings—and render the play structurally more coherent, but at considerable cost. The paratactic pageantry of the play becomes nearly overwhelming and further saps the play of its already imperiled stageworthiness.

62 The folio makes this clearer, adding a warning to Cupid to this effect at the end of IV.v; lines 77–83 of V.x imply the same nonetheless. The additions to the folio which close the fourth act contribute to that program in the revisions which gives new (and somewhat detached) coherence to the fifth act, for they prepare a special plot for the final act: "Cupid's Arrows Enchanted." This device would seem to be another manifestation of Jonson's dislike for romantic plotting, for what he called "cross-wooing." He had already wrought a send-up of romantic comedy in *Every Man In*; here he rationalizes the exclusion of romantic plotting as the result of Echo's curse on the fountain: she has rendered such plotting impossible.

63 The alternative titles appear thus in the 1616 folio: *Cynthias Revels, or The Fountayne of Selfe-Love*, reversing the order in which they appear in the 1601 quarto. The later version quietly claims a triumph: the title need no longer make its first appeal to the popular appetite for satire.

64 As in Hobbes's *Leviathan*, theatrical representation is analogous to political representation (surprising as it may seem to find such representational political thought so early in the century); for theatrical representation in Hobbes, see Angus Fletcher, *The Transcendental Masque: An Essay on Milton's "Comus"* (Ithaca: Cornell University Press, 1971), pp. 14–16.

65 This summarizes the plot of the Jonsonian masque, and though it overtly asserts the evanescence of comedy and a transfiguration of the stage, it covertly suggests a connection between the masque of Cupid and the comic shows that precede it. The answer to Cupid's query, "What have serious repetitions / To doe with revels, and the sports of court?" lies here in Cupid's answer: it may be divined from his description of the interim of Morian revels as a "licentious time."

Although the appearance of Cynthia will bring about the end of license, the period of revelry must not be taken as unrelated to the Cynthian moment. That is, we need to recognize that the concept of license depends on institutional indulgence. Through the provisions of such institutions as the Office of the Revels comedy has its sway; the office exists to place the royal stamp on a pagan tradition of revelry, a tradition that could be made Christian precisely because the abrogation of normal behavior could be made to figure the abrogation of Old Law by New. But the work of mapping a linear program of ethical transcendence upon a fundamentally seasonal cycle in which quotidian and festival behavior alternate results in some ethical scrambling, for the pagan license of Misrule is both momentary and recurrent, bound in opposition to the normative (the license of secular law is similarly dependent on coexistent norms), whereas on the other hand the license of the New Law is itself normative. Thus the license of Misrule in the Christian court appears duplicitous: insofar as it represents the freedom of the Last Things, it may function as a model; insofar as it represents an assault on normative behavior, it is unfortunate, a cautionary mirror.

66 The song embeds Cynthia's masque in cyclical time: it is an interim, hardly the image of an *eschaton*. As Cupid sulks over the loss of his arrows' force, Mercury twits him with a final observation: "I pray thee, light hony-bee, remember thou art not now in ADONIS garden, but in Cynthia's presence, where thorns lie in garrison about the roses. Soft, CYNTHIA speakes" (V.x.111–14). This slightly wistful Mercury distinguishes a necessitous masque-world from the pure potency at the visionary center of Spenserian art, a center that transcends (or claims to transcend) the ethical sphere. The anagogic transformations of Spenser and Lyly are here displaced and Cupid's mischievousness remains. Though vice is inhibited, it is inhibited by a range of factors, for Jonson cannot dismiss his doubts about the power of vision to effect reform.

Jonson later insists on Cynthia's consciousness of the circumscription of her power over the scene of vice, in deference to the masque-device. For the masque that closes the play, Crites contrives the revelation of an ensphered figure (a favorite transformation device, even before the ascendancy of Jones's stagecraft), at which Cynthia exclaims,

What shape? what substance? or what unknowne power
In virgins habite, crown'd with lawrell leaves
And olive branches woven in betweene,
On sea-girt rockes, like to a Goddesse shines?
O front! Ô face! Ô all cælestiall sure,
And more then mortall! ARETE, behold
Another CYNTHIA, and another Queene,
Whose glorie (like a lasting *plenilune*)
Seemes ignorant of what it is to wane!   [V.viii.4–12]

The device seems to figure Elizabeth, suggesting traits both Venereal ("on sea-girt rockes") and Cynthian. Most important, the apparition implies not a trope of mimetic reflection but one of mutual subordination; the vision is both derivative ("another CYNTHIA") and superior ("a lasting *plenilune*," in which I should want to emphasize *lasting*).

67 To this compare the antic echo-scene with which Dekker's *Old Fortunatus* commences.

68 Jonson preserves the Ovidian language of property law, perhaps inadvertently, when Mercury tells Echo to "forgoe thy use and libertie of tongue" (I.ii.80)—a dark phrase, since the *libertie* here is a term both of property law (like *usus*) and also of personal law (see the discussion of *license* in note 65, above). The entire phrase, "libertie of tongue," has another, more specific sense: a liberty of tongue was a special arch in the bit of a bridle, contrived to minimize a horse's discomfort when carrying the bit. Echo's freedom is partial, a concession within a larger system of constraint.

69 Estienne can help us explain further mythographic oddity in the scene—the association of Niobe with the Boeotian vale of Gargaphie and, more important, with a tradition of Theban transgression. In his entry on Niobe (sig. Rr_6v), Estienne describes her as "uxor . . . Amphionis, regis Thebanorum. . . . [Latona] Niobemque ipsam sibi conviciantem turbine venti in Asiam rapuit, & iuxta Sypilum urbem (quae illi patria erit) in saxum transformavit" (the wife of Amphion, king of Thebes. . . . Because Niobe put herself in competition with Latona, the goddess swept her off to Asia in a whirlwind & there, near the city of Sypilus (which was her homeland), transformed her into a stone). Estienne neglects to indicate that Sypilus is in Phrygia and that Niobe had also been born in Phrygia; an inattentive Jonson *might* have overlooked the phrase, *in Asiam*, and casually determined that Niobe was rapt to her homeland, *near Thebes*.

That Jonson may have followed Estienne into confusion ought to make something obvious that has been often neglected. Jonson's antiquarian scholarship does not begin in its full humanist glory until he began writing masques. There is little evidence that he ever consulted such mythographic handbooks as Cartari or Comes until the accession of James began to bring him steady work as a court poet. He seems then to have quickly expanded his library and intensified his researches.

70 *Pleasure Reconcil'd to Vertue*, l. 264.

71 But see chapter 4.

72 *Discoveries*, ll. 39–40 (and cf. ll. 2031–32). The passage suggests that Jonson had begun developing some doubts about his own acoustic favoritism (he also registers some embarrassment over his hostility to the temporal present, but that is another matter). Still, his apprehensions about the power of the spectacular persist elsewhere in the *Discoveries*, for example: "[Picture] doth so enter, and penetrate the inmost affection (being done by an excellent Artificer) as sometimes it orecomes the power of speech, and oratory" (ll. 1526–28). Thus the ambivalence about sight continues: the long meditation on painting in *Discoveries* (ll. 1509–85) is prefaced by a statement of the preeminence of poetry; the meditation on the power of visual mimesis leads immediately to a discussion of flattery. Thus the *Discoveries* gives evidence of Jonson's persistent sense of sight and sound as *competitors*. The early masques constitute an attempt to evade that opposition, but it obtrudes again as the quarrel with Jones gains momentum.

73 "The third requisite [after "Nature" and "Exercise"] in our *Poet*, or Maker, is *Imitation*, to bee able to convert the substance, or Riches of another *Poet*, to his own use" (*Discoveries*, ll. 2466–69).

74 Just after Crites' speech, Arete appears and they regale each other with descriptions of the subtle Proteuses of Cynthia's outer court—slight prototypes to the Proteus-figures of the masques; the descriptions of this "strangest pageant, fashion'd like a court" (III.iv.4) proceed in a serial fashion which provides public fragmentation as contrast to the private integration of Crites.

75 Jonson apparently had painful memories of acting "mad Hieronimoes part" in Kid's *Spanish Tragedy*; Dekker's reference to this performance is clearly intended to tread on a sore spot. Jonson occasionally received small commissions from Henslowe to write additions to the play. Surely there is considerable animus in "Jack's" description of the fop who protests *"That the old Hieronimo* (as it was first acted) *was the onely best, and judiciously pend play of Europe"* (*Cynthia's Revels*, Induction, 209–11).

76 Note the use, in *way-lay,* of the same metaphor of travel for the adumbration of plot as is to be found in the prologue, where Jonson promises to prove "new wayes to come to learned eares."

77 "You shall sweare not to bumbast out a new Play, with the old lynings of Jestes, stolne from the Temples Revels" (*Satiromastix*, V.ii.295–96).

78 By 1605, Marston and Jonson were again collaborating, which suggests that the quarrel did not remain bitter. Perhaps he felt his position had been vindicated by his employment at court or, if not vindicated, at least sufficiently distinguished that the charges of a Marston could no longer sting.

CHAPTER 4

1 D. J. Gordon, the most considerable authority on the quarrel, takes Epigram CXV (c. 1612) as an attack on Jones; I am not persuaded. But see Gordon's "Poet and Architect," in *The Renaissance Imagination*, p. 77.

2 Actually the text of *Cynthia's Revels* is similarly fetishized. In the textual introduction to the Oxford edition, Herford and Simpson comment, "The five copies of the quarto that have been collated supply a copious amount of variants, which show Jonson's scrupulous care in ensuring the correctness of his text. He must have harried the printer beyond measure" (4:5).

3 See *Blacknesse*, 82–89. This is the first time in which Jonson used the term *prospective* to mean anything more than "scenery." His admiration for the idea of so endowing the picture plane with depth is obvious throughout his career; perspective provides a pictorial correlative of the Jonsonian ethical ideal of human plenitude, the enrichment of the behavioral surface. On the intransigence of the English eye, see Stephen Orgel and Roy Strong, *Inigo Jones: The Theatre of the Stuart Court*, 2 vols. (Berkeley: University of California Press, 1973), 1:11–12.

4 I refer to the revels's songs in defense of the chaste Loves (340–74) which, as Gordon has shown, derive from Pico's commentary on Benivieni's *Canzona de Amore*; see Gordon, "The Imagery of Ben Jonson's *Masques of Blacknesse and Beautie*," in *The Renaissance Imagination*, p. 144.

5 I am drawing here on the very suggestive chapter, "*Platea* and *Locus*: Flexible Dramaturgy" in Robert Weimann's *Shakespeare and the Popular Tradition in the Theater: Studies in the Social Dimension of Dramatic Form and Function*, ed. Robert Schwartz (Baltimore: Johns Hopkins University Press, 1978), pp. 73–85.

6 Stephen Orgel, *The Illusion of Power: Political Theater in the English Renaissance* (Berkeley: University of California Press, 1975), p. 50.

7 For all its power, Gordon's work on masque symbolism is most defective here. Because Gordon gives no attention to the dynamic structure in which that symbolism unfolds, he does not give sufficient weight to the moment in which a figurative world is physically enmeshed with its "real" complement. More particularly, he neglects the songs that attend on the revels: the persistence of echo-song goes unremarked, and rather more surprising, the allusion to "orphic cosmology" in the revels of *Beautie* receives no comment.

8 There seems to be a further debt, to Spenser's echoic *Epithalamion*.

9 *The Works of Thomas Campion*, ed. Walter R. Davis (Garden City, N.Y.: Doubleday, 1967), p. 216.
10 Ibid., pp. 223–24.
11 The importance of naming in Jonson's oeuvre can hardly be underestimated. In *The Masque of Queenes*, fame depends on "renowme," a continued propagation of names. The *Epigrams* are full of poems whose major work is the inspection, protection, and reification of the names of the worthy. The two great epitaphs on his children, for example, both involve a reenactment of christening, in which the adequacy of a name is rediscovered and the name thus reconsecrated.
    For Britain as "a world divided from the world," see also Jonson's contribution to James's coronation festivities, *Part of the King's entertainment, etc.*, ll. 41–50.
12 Cf. the echoes of Browne's *Inner Temple Masque*, siren voices enlisted on behalf of Circe. The Elizabethan masque of *Proteus and the Adamantine Rock* is an important source for this use of siren's song. On the Odyssean paradigm behind this masque plot, see chapter 5.
13 The voice of the sea continues, "if not," meaning, should the waters retire and the land not press its suit, then

> impute it to each others matter;
> They are but earth   And what you vow'd was water
> 1. Ecch. But earth,   1. Ecch. And what you vow'd was water.
> 2. Ecch. Earth.   2. Ecch. You vow'd was water. [ll. 320–23]

The premise is preposterous, of course; Jonson uses the stanzas to reinforce the victory of "intertaynment," and he does so by pointing to the mutability of the sublunary earth and water, the elements that had previously been the constituents of bounded unity.
14 *Blacknesse*, note to l. 118.
15 The first sign of charity toward hieroglyphics may be found in the coronation entertainment of 1604. Jonson wrote of the ornamentation of his painstakingly researched Fenchurch Arch "that the *Symboles* used, are not, neither ought to be, simply *Hieroglyphickes*, Emblemes, or Impreses, but a mixed character, partaking somewhat of all" (ll. 253–56). Despite the researches of D. C. Allen ("Ben Jonson and the Hieroglyphics," *Philological Quarterly* 18 [1939]: 290–300), little can be securely asserted about Jonson's notion of the distinction between these symbolic types. (Allen cites the remarkably unenlightening *De Symbolica* of Nicholas Caussin [1618], which Jonson seems to have read—he owned the 1623 edition, but may well have seen the first edition. I suspect that he could have learned very little from Caussin's forms.) Jonson uses *symbol* indifferently, both as a generic label and as a specific one. He tends to rank *imprese* as the lowest form (cf. *Cynthia's Revels*, V.ix.15–18), for he treats them as a rather elaborate form of gift—but cf. Amorphus's gift of the hieroglyphic hat: nearly all these forms seem to take on an exchange value, as if they were a special currency within the court.
16 Cf. Davison's (and Campion's?) *Proteus and the Adamantine Rock*. For the aquatic tenor of the hieroglyphics, see Gordon, "The Imagery of *Blacknesse and Beautie*," in *The Renaissance Imagination*.
17 From *For the Unfallen* (1959), reprinted in *Somewhere Is Such a Kingdom* (Boston: Houghton Mifflin, 1975), p. 22.
18 *Il Pastor Fido, The Faithfull Shepherd* translated (1647) by Richard Fanshawe, ed. J. H. Whitfield, Edinburgh Bilingual Library, no. 11 (Austin: University of Texas Press, 1976), Prologue; all subsequent citations are from this edition.
19 The other paradigmatic myth is also invoked: "Uccidono i cignali i tuoi devoti; / ma i devoti di lei miseramente / son dai cignali uccisi" (Wilde Boars are killed by thy Worshippers: / By wilde Boars miserably kild are hers; IV.viii).

20 *Il Pastor Fido*, IV.viii; the first translation departs from Fanshawe's.
21 In baroque drama, though, the conversion to hope is considerably more common than Silvio's conversion to love: we find such a conversion to hope preserved in Thomas Lodge's *The Wounds of Civil War* (1588?), despite the loss of the amatory associations usually exploited in the echo-dialogue. This is probably the first such dialogue on the public stage, and its content is political, though otherwise similar to Guarini's. It restores the fugitive Marius to hopes of rejoining a social world:

Six hundred suns with solitary walks
I still have sought for to delude my pain,
And friendly Echo answering to my talks
Rebounds the accent of my ruth again.

Yet where he expects "reporting of my sorrow," Echo challenges the sorrow itself:

Thus Marrius lives disdain'd of all the gods	O ods.
With deep despair late overtaken wholly	O ly.
And will the heavens be never well appeased?	appeased
Is any fortune then at hand?	at hand.
Then farewell, Echo, gentle nymph farewell;	farewell.

[Thomas Lodge, *The Wounds of Civil War*, ed. Joseph W. Houppert [Lincoln: University of Nebraska Press, 1969], III.iv. 27–30, 43–45, and 49–50]

His outburst is a noble self-indulgence—"O pleasing folly to a pensive man" (l. 51)—a Roman dalliance with the apolitical, even frivolous rural scene, yet his condescension is not allowed to vitiate the serious and prophetic force of the dialogue. (Condescension to the echo-dialogue, its use even as a nonsensical device, is common enough: see Wilson's *The Cobbler's Prophecy*, Dekker's *Old Fortunatus*, Middleton's *Anything for a Quiet Life*, or the anonymous *The Maid's Metamorphosis*. Burlesques of echo-scenes are also common in Continental parodies of *Il Pastor Fido*.) Young Marius enters immediately—it is probably the first moment at which the two Mariuses both hold the stage—and his speech extends the idea of replication:

My countrymen and favorites of Rome,
This melancholy desert where we meet
Resembleth well young Marius restless thought. [ll. 54–56]

Echo objectifies speech, scene externalizes thought, child reduplicates father: Lodge teases out the possible forms of replication as he prepares for the recovery of Marius from political isolation, a political correlative of Silvio's recovery from erotic isolation.
22 It is hardly surprising that this conversion corresponds to categories developing in the contemporary poetics of Jacopo Mazzoni, whose analysis of literary production into *dramatica phantastica*, *dramatica icastica*, *raccontativa phantastica*, and *raccontativa icastica*, though by no means a complete taxonomy of literary forms, had begun a neo-Aristotelian theory of genre based on mode of presentation as well as on object of imitation. This analysis is hierarchical, with *dramatica phantastica* preferred as the *most* imitative of the *most* ideal objects available to mimesis; lyric has no determinate place in Mazzoni's taxonomy, though its subordination to drama is certain and, for my purposes, crucial. It establishes the generic preeminence of dramatic presence.

Mazzoni is perhaps the most perspicacious of several contemporary theoreticians who aim at extending the range of canonical genres; see, for example, Tasso's *Delle differenze poetiche*. For an invaluable introduction to problems of generic theory in the Italian Renaissance, see Bernard Weinberg, *A History of Literary Criticism in the Italian Renaissance*, 2 vols. (Chicago: University of Chicago Press, 1961).
23 The following discussion owes much to W. W. Greg, *Pastoral Poetry and Pastoral Drama*

(London: Sidgwick and Jackson, 1905; reprint, New York: Russell, 1959), Appendix I, "On the Origin and Development of the Italian Pastoral Drama," pp. 423–43; see also Vittorio Rossi, *Battista Guarini ed Il pastor fido* (Torino: Loescher, 1886), pp. 161–79. A caveat must be entered here: Greg (and through him, Rossi) have had perhaps too much influence on recent historiography of pastoral, for they both overestimate the *novelty* of Tasso's and Guarini's tragicomedies; its novelty may be a theme of Guarini's play, but his claim will not sustain historical scrutiny. Louise Clubb and, before her, Violet Jeffery have engaged in that scrutiny: see Jeffery's series of articles on "Italian and English Pastoral Drama of the Renaissance," published in various numbers of the *Modern Language Review* for 1924 and Clubb's "The Making of the Pastoral Play: Some Italian Experiments between 1573 and 1590," in *Petrarch to Pirandello: Studies in Italian Literature in Honor of Beatrice Corrigan*, ed. J. A. Molinaro (Toronto: University of Toronto Press, 1973), pp. 45–72.

24 Giason Denores, *Discorso* (1586), cited in Weinberg, *History of Literary Criticism*, 2:1075.

25 A. S. F. Gow has described this curious feature of Theocritan pastoral when he submits that no amount of source study "explains how such subjects came to be treated in dramatic form yet in the verse not of drama but of epic"; Introduction to *The Greek Bucolic Poets* (Cambridge: Cambridge University Press, 1953), p. xv.

26 The dialogic would seem to have become a distinctive aspect of the Virgil received by the early Middle Ages. James Holly Hanford has made it possible to trace the connection described in the text in his "Classical Eclogue and Medieval Debat," *Romanic Review* 2 (1911): 17–31 and 129–43.

27 For a more extensive summary of the features of this genre, see E. Faral, "La Pastourelle," *Romania* 49 (1923):209–36. We can fairly say that the eclogue provided a source for the formal features of the pastourelle—not the only source, of course, since less institutionalized flyting also contributed to such patterns. The debate on the origins of the pastourelle is an old one. In *Les origines de la poésie lyrique en France au moyen-age* (Paris: Hachette, 1889), pp. 13–16, Alfred Jeanroy links the pastourelle to the Theocritan idyll, but without any particular documentary authority; Jeanroy is, finally, less interested in the classical antecedents than in the native origins of the form, in its emergence as a courtly modification of the popular *chansons de danse* (for which, see also his reviewer, Gaston Paris, who argues, in *Les origines de la poésie lyrique en France au Moyen Âge* [Paris: Imprimerie Nationale, 1892], pp. 26–34, that the form should be traced to the *fêtes de mai*).

It should be noted that no *Italian* exemplars of the form survive. The importance of the genre, however, lies in the way its existence forced French theorists of pastoral to conceive of the pastoral mode as rather elastic, at least in its formal manifestations; such conceptualizations seem to have had somewhat cosmopolitan influence.

Whether the form is of folk origins or is scholastic—derived directly from Virgil or mediately from the débat—remains mysterious. As early as the thirteenth century, one of the most important Christian allegorists of pastoral, John of Garland, brings eclogue and pastourelle into accord: "Est autem materia versuum quomodo iuvenis oppresit nimpham, cuius amicus erat Coridon. Per nimpham significatur caro; per iuvenum corruptorem, mundus vel diabolus; per proprium amicum, ratio. Dicitur ergo sub persona mundi sic" (The subject matter of these verses is how a youth ruined a nymph whose beloved had been Corydon. The nymph signifies the Flesh, the young Seducer the World or the Devil, the beloved Reason. The speaker of the poem is the World; *The "Parisiana Poetria" of John of Garland*, ed. Traugott Lawler [New Haven: Yale University Press, 1974], pp. 24–25). The narrative density of pastourelle here displaces the specified texture and arch decor of classical pastoral, opening the pastoral milieu up to narrative.

28 Cited from the second edition (Paris, 1535; facs., Geneva: Slatkine Reprints, 1972), sig. H$_4$v.

   The "common ground" described here is shadowy, for the category of the dramatic was still badly discriminated—though the broader professionalization of the theater was focusing the category. Sebillet observes that, within the tradition of vernacular poetry "tu verras aussi le Dialogue estendu jusques aux Epigrammes"; such a spectrum remained possible precisely because of the *maintes especes* of dialogue actually being performed in the flexible theatrical environment of the early sixteenth-century court. Later in his discussion (H$_6$v), Sebillet will provide a native term, *la Bergerie*, as a substitute for the Greek *eclogue*, thus rendering his triad of subgenres culturally homogeneous.

   For further evidence of the perceptual blurring of the distinction between eclogue and drama, see Scaliger's use of the terms *boukoliastai* and *ludiastai* as synonymous means of denoting the itinerant players of classical Italy; see his *Poetices libri septem* (Venice, 1561), sig. b$_2$v.

29 *Compendio della poesia tragicomica*, edited together with the text of *Il Pastor Fido* by Gioachino Brognoligo (Bari: Laterza, 1914), pp. 271–72. The *Compendio* incorporates and revises his two early defenses of the play, the *Verato* of 1588 and the *Verato secondo* of 1593.

30 Guarini uses figures of vegetable growth—sometimes somewhat unnatural vegetable growth—for generic developments. In the *Verato* of 1588, he describes the evolution of pastoral as involving a sequence of *graftings*; see Greg, *Pastoral Poetry and Pastoral Drama*, pp. 426–27.

31 The implication of fortunate transgression finds its thematic correlative in that persistent and distinctive erotic motif which is Guarini's chief contribution to the genre. *Il Pastor Fido* gives particular attention to the piquancy that violence adds to courtship (this, presumably, is the source of a continuing tradition of censorious response to Guarini). Even the embrace of Mirtillo and Amarilli, a triumph of mutuality, is figured as a delicate sadism, "un atto mista / di rapina e d'acquisto" (an Act mixt of conquest and compact; V.viii). Indeed, wherever the play celebrates union or restoration, we always find a countervailing attention to violence or dislocation.

32 On the bodily presence of theatrical character, see Stanley Cavell, "The Avoidance of Love," in *Must We Mean What We Say?* (New York: Scribners, 1969), particularly pp. 317–34. And see also Kenneth Burke's "Antony in Behalf of the Play," in *The Philosophy of Literary Forms* (Berkeley: University of California Press, 1973), pp. 329–43.

33 The voice of the pleasance remains an authority on Mirtillo's sorrow until the concluding act; thus his plaint to Amarilli:

Ch'i't'ami e t'ami più de la mia vita,
se tu nol sai, crudele,
chiedilo a queste selve,
che tel diranno. [III.iii]

[That I do love thee more then I do love
My life (if thou doubt'st Cruel) ask this Grove,
And that will tell thee.]

34 This repetition of ancient signs is finally alleviated when "l'alta pieta del pastor fido, / degna di cancellar l'antico errore" (the high piety of the faithful shepherd stoops to expiate the ancient crime [my translation]). Both the repetition of the laws and the sepulchral resonance end:

non stilla più dal simulacro eterno
sudor di sangue, è piu non trema il suolo,

né strepitosa più, né più putente
è la caverna sacra; anzi da lei
vien sì dolce armonia, sì grato odore
che non l'avrebbe più soave il cielo. [V.vi]

[No longer stood
Th'eternall Image in a sweat of blood,
The earth no longer shook, the holy Cave
No longer stank, and shrikes no longer gave:
But such sweet harmony and redolence
As Heav'n affords.]

The repetitive structures of tragic law, structures associated with unwavering cultural tradition, are here simply negated.

35 When Guarini shifted from his authorial to his editorial role, he managed to maintain his focus on echoic liminality. His notes to the scene (sigs. $X_1v–X_2$ in the 1605 edition) include a debate on the proper format for echo-poetry—whether Echo's replies should be integrated into the metrical structure of a line or whether they should properly be hypermetrical, marginal. He defends the latter practice, but attends to the echoic threat to textual integrity.

36 Commentary to Ascensius's 1501 *Metamorphoses* (Leyden), sig. g_3.

37 The glosses on Echo in the mythographies that Jonson most frequently consulted all appear in articles on Pan, articles that Jonson had already studied with considerable care as he prepared the Highgate entertainment of 1604, the so-called *Penates*, the device of which so influenced his later Panic fictions—*Oberon*, *Pleasure Reconcil'd to Vertue*, and *Pan's Anniversary*.

    The Macrobian gloss may touch on a buried allegory in the masque. The appropriation of echoic response to serve the glory of Amor may be a triumphal monument to that favorite Renaissance mystery of the wrestling match between Cupid and Pan, in which the victory of the former proves that *Amor vincit omnia*. The transfer of power over the earth would thus correspond to the shift from the delicate lasciviousness of the voice of the land in *Blacknesse* to the forthright divinity of Eros in *Beautie*.

38 On allusiveness as prophecy, see the appendix.

39 Indeed, when the device of *Beautie* makes room for the assistance of a benign Proteus, it becomes clear that Jonson is reflecting not only the Cynthian *Blacknesse*, but also the first great Elizabethan masque at Kenilworth: the Proteus of the 1580s and 1590s had been a vicious agent of mutability; Jonson could only have found a benignly prophetic Proteus where he found the first English Echo.

40 A Christmastide masque in conception, *Queenes* was postponed a month because of difficulties having to do with invitations to the rivalrous French and Spanish ambassadors. The performance took place on 2 February 1609.

41 Pp. 73–74.

42 I adopt the quarto and folio reading of line 429 (the quarto has considerable claim to authority). The holograph reading, "To make her, once more, visible to light," might stand, for we could take it as a reference to the magnanimity of Anne's continued participation in these masques and to the special *kind* of visibility the masque confers on its participants, so that James sees Anne anew. The first song of the revels enacts the allegorical genealogy on the grammatical level, for there the imperative, "Sing then good Fame," is addressed both to Fame and to the assembled masquers ("good Fame" as the tenor of their song); thus Fame celebrates and is celebrated. In masque, the object of reference frequently rises to agency and subjectivity.

43 Title of chapter 1, Angus Fletcher, *The Transcendental Masque: An Essay on Milton's "Comus"* (Ithaca: Cornell University Press, 1971).

44 Lines 425–27. James should certainly follow her example, reverencing the God who gave him his worth. Anne's love for God, like Eve's, is mediated by her love for her husband: the "he" who gave her her virtues is dual.
45 The research for *Queenes* opened the area of occult lore to Jonson, no doubt stimulating the conception of *The Alchemist*.
46 See chapter 1.
47 Recorded in the notes to the Oxford edition, 10:498. The comments of foreign visitors have a peculiar authority. More familiar with the sorts of visual spectacle that Jones devised, they offer informed opinion, yet the English response provides an index of the *difficulty* the form presented to novice viewers; the devisers were proffering an avant-garde art, yet such viewers as the French ambassador, La Boderie, were inured to many of its shocks. James Carleton's response to the Daughters of Niger shows the risks that Jones and Jonson took, even exploited: "theyr apparel rich, but too light and curtisan-like; Theyr black faces, and hands which were painted and bare up to the elbowes, was a very lothsome sight, and I am sorry that strangers should see owr court so strangely disguised" (10:449).
48 I wish to note here my debt to the valuable work of Leah Sinanoglou Marcus on the historical occasions of the Jacobean masque. I intend the argument that follows, on the Jonsonian resistance to occasion, as a supplement to her explorations in "'Present Occasions' and the Shaping of Ben Jonson's Masques," *English Literary History* 45 (1978): 201–25. The strategies of topicality and extraoccasional closure eventually become complementary in Jonson's work. Marcus's analyses of the late masques as political critiques suggest that Jonson's closural techniques (to be outlined in the balance of this chapter) eventually gave him the power to adopt a more adversarial political attitude to his audience. For Marcus's brief reflections on the occasional and extraoccasional "doubleness of the masques," see her "Masquing Occasions and Masque Structures," *Research Opportunities in Renaissance Drama* 24 (1981): 7–16.
49 Letter to Queen Anne, in an autograph dedication to a presentation copy of *Queenes*, ll. 5–7.
50 The table of contents that follows the title page of William Stansby's 1616 folio lists not only the nine plays and the various groups of poems and entertainments included, but also the dedicatees: Camden, Richard Martin, Lord Aubigny, Francis Stuart, Lady Wroth, Pembroke, the Inns of Court, the Universities, and (for *Cynthia's Revels*) the Court.
51 *Queenes*, ll. 32–36. The idea of an authoritative fullness receives slant representation in the antimasque figures of Silenus (*Oberon*), Christmas (*Christmas his Masque*), and Comus (*Pleasure Reconcil'd to Vertue*), whose Jonsonian fat carries the significance of the Socratic Silenus-box, the antic exterior of which mysteriously guards the internal plenitude. These characters are the embodied correlatives of Jones's machines; for the machine as plentiful body, see *Hymenaei*, 109–34.
52 Two years later, Jonson dedicated *Catiline* to Pembroke, claiming that "it is the first (of this race) that ever I dedicated to any person" (ll. 10–11). This is *not* conclusive evidence that the *Queenes* dedication is a dedication of the annotation, since a masque could justly be claimed as of a different "race." Yet it certainly is evidence of Jonson's circumspection about dedication, not only as a socially constrained act, but also as a gesture of consequence in the creation of a cursus.
53 It is possible that Jonson provided the copy text for those plays published before 1616 that had been dedicated in quarto (*Volpone*, *Catiline*, and *The Alchemist*) and that he had already begun to exercise some authority over his published texts. For there is a curiously neat progression in the publication history. *Sejanus*, which was not dedicated, but which was accompanied by eight commendatory verses in the poet's honor (an altogether unusual procedure), gives no reference to the acting company (i.e., no "as

performed by the Admiral's Men" or some such customary advertisement). It is true that the play failed miserably in performance, which could itself explain why reference to theatrical details are scanted on the title page, but then there are no references to the companies that performed *Volpone, Catiline,* and *The Alchemist* on their quarto title pages either. The title pages themselves withdraw the texts from their status as scripts. That is, publication would seem to be a means of subverting the proprietary claims of the theater on work that Jonson was coming to see more and more as his own continuing property. The increasing confidence surely stems from his experiences as a court entertainer and as a publisher of court entertainments.

I take comfort that these bibliographic details support an argument complementary to that of Richard C. Newton, "Jonson and the (Re-)Invention of the Book," in *Classic and Cavalier: Essays on Jonson and the Sons of Ben*, ed. Claude J. Summers and Ted-Larry Pebworth (Pittsburgh: University of Pittsburgh Press, 1982), pp. 31–55.

54 Roughly analogous is the bipartite publication of such texts as the *Faerie Queene*, yet the second portion of Spenser's work effaces the closure of the first. On the relation of such bitestamentary fictions to traditions of echo, see the appendix.

55 The title page to *The New Inn* works just such a denial of the theater: the text is described as "A COMOEDY. As it was never acted, but most negligently play'd, by some, the Kings Servants. And more squeamishly beheld, and censured by others, the Kings Subjects. 1629. Now, at last, set at liberty to the Readers, his Majesties Servants, and Subjects, to be judg'd. 1631."

56 I have already mentioned the subversive presence of Virgilian and Ovidian values in Jonson's presentation of Fame. But the song that describes Jonson's Fame is alive with more intimate, less debilitating debts. The final maxim of the song, "For, who doth fame neglect, doth vertue scorn" (l. 730), is from Tacitus, but it is more immediately from Jonson's *Sejanus*; similarly, the citation from Virgil has a mediate source in *Poetaster*, from the long scene in which the character Virgil reads to Augustus from the *Aeneid* and in which the playwright displays his skills as a translator of Virgil. The mediate sources give witness to the internal coherence of Jonson's literary activity, making him a major source of his own fullness.

57 The performance of *Hymenaei* took place on two separate nights, the second part of which was not a masque but a tournament. Jonson takes care to mark their distinction: the first was "the night of the *Masques*" (l. 36), while "on the next *Night* . . . [the] *solemnitie* was of *Barriers* (all mention of the former being utterly removed and taken away)" (ll. 679–81). I refer above to the first portion of the masque. The second does have elements of masque in it: the tournament is crowned by a sudden and spectacular apparition, yet only an angel descends and not a group of courtiers in costumed array, the courtiers having already entered and performed.

58 *The Works of Thomas Campion*, p. 227.

59 The most significant alterations involve the antimasques: the antimasque of *Neptune's Triumph* is the celebrated dialogue between a Cook and a Poet, a comparison of their two crafts with inevitable ancillary analyses of taste; the antimasque of *The Fortunate Isles* is a more chaotic but equally vigorous lampoon of contemporary occult sciences, as well as an homage to the native poetic tradition.

60 On Jonson's "dismay," see *Beautie*, 270–74: "The order of this *Scene* was carefully, and ingeniously dispos'd . . . by the *Kings* Master Carpenter. The Painters, I must needs say, (not to belie them), lent small colour to any, to attribute much of the spirit of these things to their own pen'cills."

61 That is, instead of a final speech or stage direction marking the closing of the machine, we have the closing direction, "*Galliards and Coranto's*," which signals open-ended revelry.

62 The revels usually followed this pattern: an entrance dance by the masquers, bringing

them onto the main dancing floor; a main dance, elaborately figured (sometimes spelling out words, often performing a ritual action intrinsic to the plot of the masque), also performed by the masquers; a dance in which the masquers took members of the audience out onto the dance floor, uniting audience and spectacle in a measured social dance; and, finally, more vigorous social dancing, offering special opportunities for display outside the masque device—these were the galliards and corantoes.

63 Lines 200–05. I follow the Oxford editors' bibliographic account, despite Greg's strictures on their assessment in "Jonson's Masques—Points of Editorial Principle and Practice," *Review of English Studies* 18 (1942): 152.

64 Orgel cites a letter of the chaplain of the Venetian embassy in London, Orazio Busino, which treats at length of *Pleasure Reconcil'd to Virtue* and which records a number of scenic details unmentioned in Jonson's text. Orgel then summarizes: "Indeed, far from being the record of a particular production on a particular evening in 1618, the text seems almost to testify to the irrelevance of the spectator's experience" (*The Jonsonian Masque*, p. 150). Jonson was engaged in a radical approach to publication; the extent of scenic detail and the amount of annotation in these texts make the discovery of comparable texts impossible. The spectator's experience would indeed seem an artificial standard against which to measure the adequacy of the text: Jonson is trying to represent the soul of the masque, and that representation is governed by intentions different from those governing the chaplain's correspondence.

65 Orgel, *The Illusion of Power*, p. 52.

66 For richly persuasive treatments of the politics of pastoral, see the work of Louis Adrian Montrose, particularly his "'Eliza, Queene of shepheardes,' and the Pastoral of Power," *English Literary Renaissance* 10 (1980): 153–82, and Richard Halpern's discussion of *Il Penseroso*, "Usury and Melancholy," in "The Divided God: Bacchic and Ascetic Strains in Milton's Early Poetry, 1629–34," Ph. D. diss., Yale University, 1983.

See also Clifford Geertz, *Negara: The Theatre State in Nineteenth-Century Bali* (Princeton: Princeton University Press, 1980), pp. 123–36, for a useful, if not absolutely rigorous critique of what Geertz calls the "great fraud" view of political ceremony.

67 The second entry thus gives a form in pageantry to the bumbling pastoral parodies in Theocritus's eleventh idyll—the complaint of Polyphemus—and Virgil's second eclogue—the *incondita studio inani* of Daphnis.

68 Whereas in *Pleasure Reconcil'd* the vocabulary of an ethics and an aesthetics of *mensura* figures the dancing of the revels, in *Pan's Anniversary* the language of pastoral absorbs the measures: pastoral itself replaces a more *obtrusively* ideological discourse.

69 Notice that, in the entrance song, visualization persists as an abstracted, impersonal event. The masquers are exhorted to take partners from the audience on the grounds that "it will be good / To see some wave it like a wood": the events will be visible, but the construction elides personal spectatorship.

70 The problem is complicated by the uncertain allegorical significance of Spenser's Pan. In his glosses on the April eclogue, E. K. writes, "that by Pan is here meant the most famous and victorious King, her highnesse Father, late of Worthy memorye K. Henry the eyght. And by that name, oftymes (as hereafter appeareth) be noted kings and mighty Potentates: And in some place Christ himselfe, who is the verye Pan and god of Shepheardes" (*Spenser's Minor Poems*, ed. Ernest DeSelincourt, vol. 1 of *The Poetical Works of Edmund Spenser*, 3 vols. [Oxford: Oxford University Press, 1909–10], ll. 232–36). Pan is God in the next eclogue, the pope in the July eclogue, and Christ in the September eclogue.

71 Certainly the special recourse to the *Epithalamion* suggests other means by which Jonson claimed his preeminence as author of *Pan's Anniversary* against his rivals, the architect and the king. Despite the speaker's pathos in the *Epithalamion*, his unsettlingly alien-

ated vantage throughout the poem and the frightened passion of his response to that which he invokes, he does have extraordinary powers of invocation. It is his own show, for Spenser motivates both the occasion and the poetic response to the occasion—it is a control to which Jonson must have aspired.
72 See note 70 above.
73 Orgel, *The Jonsonian Masque*, p. 89.

CHAPTER 5

1 *Grand dictionnaire universel du dix-neuvième siècle*, 17 vols. (Paris: Larousse, 1866–90).
2 Virgil contrives a gravely facetious touch when he introduces the sixth eclogue as "agrestem tenui meditabor harundine Musam" (l. 8), for the poem is anything but slight. On the union of Bacchic and Apollonian potencies in Silenus's song, see C. P. Segal, "Virgil's Sixth Eclogue and the Problem of Evil," *Transactions of the American Philological Association* 100 (1969): 420.
3 *The Life and Works of George Peele*, ed. Charles Tyler Prouty, vol. 3, *The Old Wive's Tale*, ed. Frank S. Hook (New Haven: Yale University Press, 1970), ll. 119–25.
4 Ibid., ll. 400–08.
5 John Hollander, *The Untuning of the Sky: Ideas of Music in English Poetry, 1500–1700* (Princeton: Princeton University Press, 1961), pp. 322–23.
6 This muted critique of the audience—Milton at his most Jonsonian—is supported by the Lady's deftly equivocal praise of her two brothers. Appealing to Echo, she asks, "Canst thou not tell me of a gentle Pair / That likest thy Narcissus are?" and so both describes their beauty and figures them as likenesses of Narcissus—*imagines* before an arguably Narcissistic audience.
7 Note the analogy between resonance and infection, acoustic and psychological influenza. For the fullest Renaissance exploration of this analogy, see Girolamo Fracastoro, *De sympathia et antipathia* (Venice, 1546).
8 Cited and briefly discussed in Leo Spitzer, *Classical and Christian Ideas of the World's Harmony* (Baltimore: Johns Hopkins University Press, 1963), pp. 104–05.
9 Barthélemy Aneau, note to III. 377 of Ovid, *Trois premiers livres de la Metamorphoses*, trans. C. Marot and B. Aneau (Lyons, 1556), Sig. Q$_3$v.
10 *Settenario* (Venice, 1571), sigs. Ee$_8$.
11 Ibid., sigs. Ee$_8$–Ff$_1$.
12 Romans 10:17.
13 Her error is, of course, registered otherwise. There is, for example, the charmingly indecorous compliment to her brothers—"that likest thy Narcissus are"—which could function as an emblem of the self-delusions risked in such aristocratic revelry.
14 See Barbara Breasted, "Comus and the Castlehaven Scandal," in *Milton Studies III*, ed. James D. Simmonds (Pittsburgh: University of Pittsburgh Press, 1971), pp. 201–24.
15 Fletcher, *The Transcendental Masque*, p. 200.
16 John Carey draws attention to the alexandrine in his annotations to Comus in *The Poems of John Milton*, ed. John Carey and Alastair Fowler (London: Longmans, 1968), p. 188. Fletcher cites the observation in *The Transcendental Masque* (p. 199), but neither Carey nor Fletcher remarks the Spenserian allusion in this prosodic touch.
17 As John Guillory points out in his *Poetic Authority: Spenser, Milton, and Literary History* (New York: Columbia University Press, 1983), the volitional genetics of Comus do not involve a simple suppression of the classical, for Spenser is "chosen" over Shakespeare as well; Shakespeare, however, cannot be so easily suppressed and so reasserts himself in the parting words of the Attendant Spirit. See his chapter on Comus, "'Some Superior Power,'" pp. 68–93.
18 "The Sage / And serious doctrine of Virginity" (*Comus*, ll. 786–87); "our sage and serious poet Spenser" (*Areopagitica*).

INDEX

Accius, 28, 157
acoustics, 9, 11, 13, 25, 59–60, 155, 164. *See also* echo and Echo
Aeschylus, 19
Alcaeus, 163
Alpheus, 96, 100, 103, 107–08, 110–11
anachronism and anachrony, 102, 113, 117, 127
anagnorisis, 18–19, 154
Aneau, Barthélemy, 143
Anne, Queen of England, 95, 96, 101, 114–15, 117, 120, 180, 181
Anthologia Graeca. *See* Greek Anthology
Antoninus Liberalis, 14
Aristophanes, 19–23, 90, 153, 154
Aristotle, 24–25, 106, 155, 161
Arnulph of Orleans, 16, 74, 115–16
Athanaeus, 161
Augustus, 41
Ausonius, 10–11, 15, 25–26, 90, 104, 135

Bacon, Francis, 6, 11, 24, 112, 150, 155–56
Barbaro, Daniel, 61, 73, 165
Barish, Jonas, 171, 172
Bat kol, 57, 143, 144, 145, 147–48
Beccari, Agostino, 106–07
Bersuire, Pierre, 74, 169
Biancani, Giuseppe, 59, 164
Bion, 13, 15, 52, 141, 156
Bloom, Harold, 29
Boccaccio, Giovanni, 5, 8, 16, 33, 106, 169
Bolzani, Piero Valeriano, 74
Borges, Jorge Luis, 149
Boyle, A. J., 150
Brenkman, John, 45, 50, 161, 162–63
Bridgewater, Earl of. *See* Egerton family
Browne, Anthony (Viscount Montague), 66
Browne, Thomas, 176
Browning, Robert, 146
Busino, Orazio, 183

Cadmus, 161. *See also* Ovid—*Metamorphoses*, individual narrative units: *Cadmeans*
Callimachus, 20, 23, 112, 142, 148; his echo-lyric, 18–19, 21–22, 25, 32, 54, 154
Callistratus, 33, 155
Campion, 96, 97, 120, 125
Caravaggio, 165
Carey, John, 184
Carleton, James, 181
Cartari, Vincenzio, 7–9, 60, 73, 112, 149, 156, 165, 174
Cassirer, Ernst, 29, 157
Castiglione, Luigi, 163
Castlehaven scandal, 145
Catullus, 34, 158
Caussin, Nicholas, 176
Chamberlain's Men, 75–76
Chapman, George, 169
Charles I (King of England), 59–60
Chaucer, 116–17, 146
Chettle, Henry, 76
Children of the Chapel, 78–79
Chute, Marchette, 77
Cicero, 16, 146
Clubb, Louise, 178
Colby, Elbridge, 151
Comes, Natalis, 8, 112, 169, 174
Conon, 53
Corrigan, R. W., 153–54
Culler, Jonathan, 160
cursus. *See* generic career

daemons and the daemonic. *See* Jonson—individual works: *Cynthia's Revels*: daemonic in; mythography, Renaissance; theatrical presence
Davison, Francis, 176
Dekker, Thomas, 76; *Satiromastix*, 79, 82, 92, 172, 175; *Old Fortunatus*, 135, 171, 174
Demats, Paule, 10, 32, 155
Denores, Giason, 104, 105, 106, 111

185

Descartes, René, 164
Desport, Maries, 14, 150–51
dialogic form, 26, 105–06, 108, 110, 178, 179. See also pastoral, dramatization of; Virgil—individual works: Eclogues and pastoral: and dramatization
Dodds, E. R., 14
Döes, Johann van der, 5, 149, 168
Doran, Madeleine, 73–74
Drummond of Hawthorndon, William, 76
Dryden, 36, 158
DuBellay, Joachim, 73

E. K., 130, 131, 183
echo and Echo, 2, 9, 15, 18–19, 50, 152, 154; personification of, 2, 11, 14, 15, 22–23, 26, 54–55, 77; and historiography, 5, 17; and liminality, 5, 19, 41, 75, 77, 110; and imitative poetics, 6, 77–78, 90, 129–30; as figure of mythological narrative, 10–11, 29, 31–32; resonance and repetition, 11–15, 22, 109, 144; and mourning, 14, 52, 90, 151; and *fama*, 16–22, 31, 56, 60; and orality, 17, 55–56; and narrative myths, 23, 157–59; etiology of, 26–27, 30–31, 33, 46–47, 48, 79–80; and marginality, 35, 80–81, 88, 144, 169. See also acoustics; echo-scenes; etiology; imitation and imitative poetics; Jonson—individual works: *Cynthia's Revels, The Masque of Beautie, The Masque of Blacknesse, The Masque of Queenes, Pan's Anniversary*
echo-lyric, 5, 6, 9, 22, 72–73, 102, 112, 154, 168, 169; post-classical continental versions, 15–22, 60–61, 72–73, 75, 151–52, 154, 168; Callimachus', 18–19, 21; adapted to stage, 72–73, 102, 112, 120, 122, 168, 175. See also echo and Echo; echo-scenes; Guarini, Giambattista; Jonson—individual works: *Cynthia's Revels, The Masque of Beautie, The Masque of Blacknesse, Pan's Anniversary*; Milton: *A Mask Presented at Ludlowe Castle (Comus)*
echometry. See acoustics
echo-scenes, 6, 60, 61, 88, 97, 168, 174, 177; Jonson's, 5, 6, 61, 90, 92, 96–97; antique, 19–21; Guarini's, 61, 72, 90, 104, 108–10, 122, 168, 177; Gascoigne's, 64–65, 72–73. See also echo and Echo; echo-lyric; Jonson—individual works: *Cynthia's Revels, The Masque of Beautie, The Masque of Blacknesse, Pan's Anniversary*; Milton: *A Mask Presented at Ludlowe Castle (Comus)*
Edwarde, Thomas, 169
Egerton family, 134–41, 145
Elizabeth I (Queen of England), 78, 101, 139, 166–67, 167–68, 171, 173; at Kenilworth, 61, 62–69, 70–73
Elvetham entertainment, 97
Erasmus, Desiderius, 2, 60, 89, 134
Essex, Second Earl of (Robert Devereux), 78, 96
Estienne, Charles, 88–89, 174
etiology, 26–27, 45, 46–48, 29–31, 161, 167. See also echo and Echo: etiology; Ovid—*Metamorphoses*, individual narrative units: Echo and Narcissus
Euripides, 6, 19–21, 146, 153, 161

fama and Fame, 16–18, 56, 116–17, 123–24, 152, 180, 182; in *The Masque of Queenes*, 111, 114–18, 120. See also House of Fame
Farra, Alessandro, 143
Feuillerat, Albert, 166
Ficino, Marsillo, 60, 98, 112, 115, 143, 165, 169
Fitts, Dudley, 21
Fletcher, 114, 132, 145–46, 160, 173, 184
formalism: in Renaissance mythological imagination, 74–75, 113
Foucault, Michel, 61, 119–20, 149
Fracastoro, Girolamo, 184
Fraser, P. M., 154
Freud, Sigmund, 53, 151, 160, 161
Frye, Northrop, 86

Galinsky, G. Karl, 36, 39, 40
Gascoigne, George, 6, 61–74, 89, 111, 118, 119, 146, 166–68
Gauradas, 22, 60, 61, 154, 168
generic career, 13, 28, 83–84
Genette, Gérard, 167
Gerbier, Balthazar, 59–60

Gilles le Vinier, 151–52
Giraldi, Lilio Gregorio, 8, 24, 60–61, 112, 155, 156, 168
Golding, Arthur, 2, 74, 169
Gombrich, E. H., 8–9, 163
Gordon, D. J., 112, 175
Gow, A. S. F., 178
Greek Anthology, 22, 23, 60, 149, 154, 157, 163, 168
Greenberg, Caren, 157
Greene, Thomas M., 150, 170
Greg, W. W., 106, 177–78
Guarini, Giambattista, 6, 61, 106–07, 121, 134, 168, 178, 179; *Il Pastor Fido*, 61, 72, 74, 103–11, 122, 126, 177, 179–180
Guillory, John, 184

Havelock, Eric, 55
Haynes, Jonathan, 171
Henrietta Maria (Queen of England), 124
Henry, Prince of Wales, 119, 120
Henslowe, Philip, 75–77, 169–70, 175
Herford, C. H., Simpson, Evelyn, and Simpson, Percy, 123
Hesiod, 8, 11–12, 14–15, 29, 38, 41, 150, 152
hieroglyphics, 9, 81, 100–01, 176
Hobbes, Thomas, 173
Hollander, John, 136
Homer, 29, 139, 152, 153, 159, 176
Horace, 17–18, 90, 130, 153
House of Fame, 93, 114, 116–17
Howell, Thomas ("T. H."), 169
Hunnis, William, 170
Hunter, G. K., 80
Hylas, 53, 157, 163
Hymn to Pan, 11, 14, 20, 23

imago and image, 16, 17, 49–50, 55, 75, 143, 169
imitation and imitative poetics, 5–6, 51–53, 55, 116–18, 129–30, 170; and plagiarism, 77–78, 90–92

James I (King of England), 98, 125, 126, 131, 132, 174, 176; as audience and witness of Jonson's masques, 114–15, 129, 131, 132, 133, 139, 180, 181
Jeffery, Violet, 178

John of Garland, 178
Jolowicz, H. F., 162
Jones, Inigo, 97, 103, 114, 121, 122, 123, 124, 164–65; Jonson's rivalry with, 6, 93–95, 128–29, 133, 174, 175; his designs for the Whitehall Banqueting House, 59–60, 61; his designs for *The Masque of Queenes*, 93, 116, 118, 181; and perspective, 94–95
Jones, Richard, 61, 71
Jonson, Ben, 5, 60–61, 66, 73, 171, 172, 174, 175; acoustic sublime, 6, 90, 94, 174; and Milton, 19; and the Kenilworth entertainments, 69, 71, 166; and formalism, 74–75, 77, 169; biography, 75–78, 169–70, 174–75; and marginality, 77, 80; imitation and plagiarism, 77–78
—masque form, 6, 74, 93–136, 139, 146, 175, 181; antimasque and main masque, 84, 86–87, 113, 126–27, 130–31, 173; revels, 96, 172; transformation scene, 135, 136, 173. *See also* masque
—printed works, 76, 84, 89, 122–23, 140, 169–70, 181; revisions of *Cynthia's Revels* for print, 84, 171, 172; printing and authority, 119–20, 123, 125
—spectacle and vision, 143, 172; in *Cynthia's Revels*, 80–83, 87–88, 89–90, 93–94, 100, 171, 172, 173–74; in the masques, 93–95, 97, 100, 113, 115, 128–29, 183
—individual works:
The Alchemist, 181–82
Catiline, 181–82
Chloridia, 124
Christmas His Masque, 117, 127, 181
Cynthia's Revels, 6, 14, 74–75, 77–95, 100, 101, 118, 127, 169, 170, 171, 172, 173, 174, 175, 181; anticipations of masque in, 78, 83–88, 93–95, 100, 127, 172, 173, 174; daemonic in 1–5, 20, 61; Lyly's influence on, 78–79
Discoveries, 89, 91, 172, 174
Eastward Ho, 109
The Entertainment at Althrope, 69–70, 120, 126
Epigrams, 176

Jonson, Ben—individual works (cont.)
  Every Man In His Humour, 76, 119, 172
  Every Man Out of His Humour, 75–77, 80
  The Fortunate Isles, 121, 126, 139, 182
  The Golden Age Restored, 122–23, 182
  Hymenaei, 94, 96, 113, 120, 125, 128, 181, 182
  The Isle of Dogs, 169
  King James His Royal . . . Entertainment, 176
  The Lord Haddington's Masque (The Hue and Cry After Cupid), 113, 120
  Love's Triumph Through Callipolis, 139
  The Masque of Beautie, 96–102, 112–13, 115, 120–23, 125, 127, 135, 139, 175, 180, 182; theoretical preface to, 93–94
  The Masque of Blacknesse, 93–103, 112–13, 120, 122, 125, 135, 139, 175, 176, 180, 181; theoretical preface to, 93–94
  The Masque of Queenes, 102, 113–18, 119–20, 123–24, 176, 180, 181, 182; House of Fame in, 93, 111, 114, 116–17, 120
  Neptune's Triumph for the Return of Albion, 113, 121, 125–26, 139, 182
  The New Inn, 182
  Oberon, 132, 180, 181
  Pan's Anniversary, 126–34, 180, 183
  Penates (the Highgate entertainment), 180
  Pleasure Reconcil'd to Vertue, 89, 113, 126, 180, 181, 183; alignment of ethics and aesthetics in, 124, 130–31, 132, 183
  Poetaster, 76, 149, 182
  Prince Henries Barriers, 118
  Richard Crookback, 169
  The Sad Shepherd, 126
  Sejanus, 181–82
  The Vision of Delight, 113, 118
  Volpone, 119, 134, 181–82
Judson, A. C., 170
Juvenal, 90

Kenilworth entertainments, 61–75, 77, 89, 126, 166, 167–68; influence of, 67, 69, 71, 97, 146, 166, 180
Kermode, Frank, 160
Kircher, Athanasius, 57–59, 61, 164

Kratinos, 21
Kyd, Thomas, 91, 174–75

Lactantius (pseudo-), 33, 35, 60, 74
Laneham, Richard, 62–63, 166–67
Lanham, Richard, 159
Lawes, Henry, 138, 145–46
Leicester, Earl of (Robert Dudley), 61, 65, 66, 69, 71, 72, 167
liminality. See echo and Echo
Lodge, Thomas, 177
Longus, 26–32, 90, 105, 146, 151, 153, 156, 157; his tale of Echo compared to Ovid's, 33, 35, 55, 56; influence in the Renaissance, 60, 111
Lucan, 153
Lucian, 2, 89, 152
Lucretius, 13, 29, 151
Lyly, John, 78–80, 82, 84, 89, 90, 170, 171, 173
Lynche, Richard, 7–8, 149, 156

Macrobius, 7–8, 23–24, 24–25, 112, 116, 155, 180
Mantuan, 125, 130
Marcus, Leah Sinanoglou, 181
marginality, 80–81, 83, 88. See also echo and Echo: and marginality
Marlowe, Christopher, 1, 4
Marot, 73
Marston, John, 76–77, 82, 84, 92, 169, 170, 175
Martial, 22, 89, 130, 154
Marvell, Andrew, 125
masque, 61, 62, 69, 72, 135, 139, 180; Tudor, 71–72, 95; revels, 71–72, 96–97, 133, 172, 182–83; Jacobean, 95, 121, 139; transformation scene in, 135, 136, 173. See also Jonson—masque form
Mazzoni, Jacopo, 177
Mersenne, 10
Milton, 28, 71, 113, 125, 156; A Mask Presented at Ludlowe Castle (Comus), 6, 19, 24, 67, 73, 134–46, 184; "Lycidas," 13, 83, 140, 145; "On the Morning of Christ's Nativity," 20, 138, 141, 158; Paradise Lost, 114, 142, 143–45, 158; spectacle and vision in, 136, 143; "L'Allegro," 138; "Il Penseroso," 138, 146; "On the Passion," 141; "At a Solemn Music," 142
Miskimin, Alice, 166

Moschus, 23, 64, 127–28, 155, 166; "Lament for Bion," 13–14, 15, 141, 156
Munday, Anthony, 77
mythography, Renaissance, 2, 4–5, 7–8, 57–61, 73–74
mythos and antique mythology, 22, 23, 25, 29–33, 158

narcissism, 45, 109, 114–15, 161, 184. See also Ovid—*Metamorphoses*, individual narrative units: Echo and Narcissus
Narcissus: accounts other than Ovid's, 55, 74–75, 115; traditions deriving from Ovid's *Metamorphoses*, 60, 88, 93, 115, 129, 143–44, 163, 169, 184. See also Ovid—*Metamorphoses*, individual narrative units: Echo and Narcissus
Narcissus the Thespian, 163

Oedipus, 42–43, 45, 46, 53, 60, 153
Orgel, Stephen, 62, 95, 125, 131, 132, 166, 183
Orpheus, 22, 27–29, 30, 97, 134, 151, 153, 156, 168
Otis, Brooks, 36, 41, 158, 159
Ovid, 28, 79, 89, 158; and Virgil, 12, 35, 38–39, 45
—*Metamorphoses*, 8, 35–36, 152, 158–60; and Virgil's *Eclogues*, 12, 38–39; and Virgil's *Aeneid*, 16, 36, 40, 42, 47, 51–52, 53, 158–59; rhetorical schema, 33–34, 36, 45–46, 48, 161; *taxis*, 36, 41, 42, 160; *perpetuitas*, 36–41, 56, 158–60; genealogy in, 38, 40–41, 42, 159–60; represented in the mythographic tradition, 60, 73–74, 143, 156
—*Metamorphoses*, individual narrative units:
Actaeon, 43, 47, 153, 160, 162
Aesculapius, 38–39, 40
Cadmeans, 35, 41–47, 53, 55, 105, 160–61; and Oedipus, 42–43, 45–46; defined, 43
Callisto, 37–38
Coronis, 38
Daphne and Apollo, 37, 38
Echo and Narcissus, 10, 12, 15, 30, 35–36, 43–52, 53–56, 161–63; and rhetorical schema, 33–34, 45–46, 49, 169; and tale of Oedipus, 43–46, 53, 60; *usus* in, 47–48, 51, 162, 174; and *imitatio*, 51–53, 56, 90; and Renaissance mythography, 59, 60, 74–75, 77, 111, 143, 169; influence of episode on *Cynthia's Revels*, 75, 77–78, 79–80, 89, 92, 93; influence on Jonson's masques, 93, 99, 111–12, 115–16, 129; and *Il Pastor Fido*, 104; influence on Milton, 144, 146; and Actaeon, 162; illustrations, 165
Europa, 41
Fame, House of Fame, 16, 116, 182
Four Ages, The, 42
Io and Jove, 37, 38
Iudicium armorum, 158–59
Minyeides, 43, 56
Pan and Syrinx, 159
Phaethon, 36–37, 38, 39, 159
Pygmalion, 55
Pythagoras, 39–40, 159
Semele, 43, 160
Teiresias, 42–43, 44, 46, 47, 160
Ovide Moralisée, 74

Pamphos, 163
Pan, 14, 61, 112, 128–30, 142, 159; in Longus, 23–24, 26; Echo beloved of, 23–24, 26, 30–31, 57, 88, 128, 156, 157–58; in Renaissance mythography, 24, 89, 155, 180; Spenser's ambivalence toward, 131–32, 183. See also Jonson—individual works: *Pan's Anniversary*
pastoral, dramatization of, 103, 105–09, 125–32, 179
pastourelle, 105–06, 178
Pausanias, 33, 53, 152, 163, 169
Pavy, Salomon, 88, 92, 172
Peele, George, 89, 134–36
Percy, William, 169
perspective scenery, 94–95, 117, 175. See also Jonson—spectacle and vision: in the masques
Petrarch, Francesco, 146
Philostratus, 155
Pico della Mirandola, 175
Pindar, 16
Plato, 26, 50, 55–56
Plautus, 48, 162
Plotinus, 143, 155
Plutarch, 20, 142, 151

Poliziano, Angelo, 15, 22, 60, 106, 151–52, 154
Pontanus, Jacobus, 51–52, 156
Portington, William, 121
Poussin, Nicolas, 165
The Princelye Pleasures . . . at Kenelwoorth, 61, 62, 70, 71, 167. *See also* Gascoigne, George; Kenilworth entertainments
printing, 62, 70, 71, 140, 168; Jonson and, 93–94, 111–12, 118–20, 123, 140, 183. *See also* Jonson—printed works
Propertius, 52–53
proscenium, 98–99, 122, 128, 172
Proteus and the Adamantine Rock, 97
Prouty, C. T., 167
Pythagoras, 60, 165. *See also* Ovid—*Metamorphoses*, individual narrative units: Pythagoras

Quintilian, 35, 150, 167

Rabelais, François, 113, 124, 152
Regio, Raphael, 111
Ricoeur, Paul, 29, 30
Ripa, Cesare, 73
Roiron, F.-X., 150
Rosenmeyer, Thomas, 13
Rubens, Peter Paul, 59

Saccio, Peter, 78, 87
St. Augustine, 155
St. Paul, 143
Sandys, George, 74
Sappho, 34, 158, 163
Saussure, Ferdinand de, 160
Scaliger, J. C., 179
Schelling, F. W. J. von, 23, 29, 155, 157
Sebillet, Thomas, 106, 179
Seneca, Lucius Annaeus, 11, 89, 91, 94, 98, 103
Serafino de' Ciminelli dall' Aquilla, 73
Servius the grammarian, 10
Seznec, Jean, 8, 23, 155
Shakespeare, William, 1, 4, 19, 81, 83, 87, 134, 184
Shelley, P. B., 14
Sidney, Philip, 102, 113
Silenus. *See* Virgil—*Eclogues* and pastoral: *Eclogue VI* and transcendental pastoral
slip of the tongue (*lapsus linguae*), 18, 104
Snell, Bruno, 29
Socrates, 181
Solon, 26, 161
Sophocles, 4, 42, 153–54, 161
Spargo, J. Webster, 151
Spenser, Edmund, 90, 125, 129–32, 134, 146, 173, 184; *Faerie Queene*, 36, 67, 146, 182; *Shepheardes Calender*, 62, 83, 130–32, 183; "Epithalamion," 129–30, 175, 183–84
Stansby, William, 119, 181
Stevens, Wallace, 11, 145
Stone, Lawrence, 167
Swinburne, Algernon, 78

Tacitus, 182
Tasso, 126, 166, 178
Tebaldeo, 73
Thales, 29
theatrical presence, 6, 179; daemonic, 1–4, 74, 103; in Jonson, 1–4, 90, 112, 118, 121, 128, 133; Echo's, 6, 90, 105, 110–12, 128, 133; in Guarini, 103, 105, 107, 110–11, 177, 179
Theocritus, 27, 29, 105, 163, 171, 178, 183; and Virgil, 13, 27, 151
Thibaut de Champagne, 17
Tintoretto (Jacopo Robusti), 165
Turberville, George, 25, 156

usus, 47–48, 51, 75, 162, 174

Valerius Flaccus, 14, 157
Vinge, Louise, 55

Virgil, 34, 58, 111; and Ovid, 12, 35, 38–39, 45; and Milton, 28, 146; and Propertius, 52–53; Renaissance annotation of, 59, 60, 111; *cursus Virgiliani*, 83
—individual works:
  Eclogues and pastoral, 12–14, 22, 51, 125, 131, 150–51, 153, 157; and Ovid's *Metamorphoses*, 12, 38–39; and Longus, 27–29, 156; Renaissance annotation of, 60; and drama-

tization, 73, 105–06, 178; and Jonson, 97, 100, 103, 112, 130, 134, 171, 183; *Eclogue VI* and transcendental pastoral, 133–34, 184; and Milton, 136, 141, 142
Aeneid, 13, 16, 28, 42, 152; and Ovid's *Metamorphoses*, 16, 36, 40, 42, 47, 51–52, 53, 158–59; and Jonson, 113, 116–17, 124, 125, 182
Georgics, 16, 28–29, 130, 151, 152–53, 156, 157

Vitruvius, 57, 59–60, 61, 73, 111, 164, 165

War of the Theaters, The, 77, 78, 92, 170
Warburg, Aby, 8, 149–50
Warburg Institute, The, 8
Watson, Thomas, 169
Wilkinson, F. P., 159
Williams, Gordon, 36
Wordsworth, William, 146

OHIO UNIVERSITY LIBRARY

Please return this book as soon as you have finished with it. In order to avoid a fine it must be returned by the latest date stamped below.

MAR 27 1994

Quarter Loan

QUARTER LOAN

APR 0 6 1999

JUN 0 6 1999

CF